FIDEL CASTRO'S
PERSONAL REVOLUTION
IN CUBA:

1959–1973

BORZOI BOOKS ON LATIN AMERICA

Consulting Editor

LEWIS HANKE

University of Massachusetts, Amherst

FIDEL CASTRO'S PERSONAL REVOLUTION IN CUBA: 1959–1973

Edited with an Introduction by

James Nelson Goodsell

The Christian Science Monitor

ALFRED A. KNOPF   New York

THIS IS A BORZOI BOOK
PUBLISHED BY ALFRED A. KNOPF, INC.

First Edition
9 8 7 6 5 4 3 2 1

Library of Congress Cataloging in Publication Data
Goodsell, James Nelson, comp.
Fidel Castro's personal revolution in Cuba:
1959–1973.

(Borzoi books on Latin America)
Bibliography: p.
1. Cuba—History—1959–   —Addresses, essays, lectures.   I. Title.
F1788.G63   972.91'064   74–17216
ISBN 0–394–48891–1
ISBN 0–394–31502–2 (pbk.)

Manufactured in the United States of America

Dedicated

to

Alice Goodsell

In appreciation of her unflagging

support through the years

Acknowledgments

The preparation of this volume has been aided immeasurably by the wise counsel and patient understanding of Lewis Hanke. His ever-eager alertness, for example, spotted numerous references to Cuba in obscure journals that otherwise might have escaped detection. But even more important was his steady encouragement over the three years that the book was in formation. Others might have despaired of the editor's frequent travels, which upset one target date after another for completion of the book. Lewis Hanke, however, took these delays with a calm that helped make the task of bringing this material together all the more rewarding.

And rewarding it was! The richness of published research and comment on the history of the Castro years came as something of a surprise. The hundreds upon hundreds of articles on Cuba in journals, reviews, magazines, and newspapers, as well as several hundred books, provide a treasure trove of material on dozens of subjects to tantalize historians for years to come. Obviously it is not all of the same quality. But surprisingly much of the material, which I eventually rejected for inclusion in these pages, was worthy of reprinting. Indeed, the more I worked with the material, the more I wished that the number of pages permitted in this Borzoi title could be doubled or tripled.

I would be remiss if I did not express some word of appreciation to numerous friends, in addition to Lewis Hanke, who assisted in the preparation of these materials. At the same time, I think it fitting to express some personal gratitude to each of the authors of the books, articles, and materials surveyed for possible inclusion in these pages. Their writings have expanded my own understanding of Cuba and the Cubans and of Fidel Castro himself.

It would be well to note also that invaluable help has come my way from both Cubans on the island loyal to Castro and Cuban opponents of Castro who have fled. Among the former, I should cite Roberto Fernández Retamar of the Casa de las Américas in Havana, for special assistance over the years during numerous visits to Cuba.

Responsibility for interpretation, comment, and choice of selections, as well as condensation of many of the selections, however, rests fully with the editor. I can only hope that these pages make something of a contribution to the understanding of what has taken place in Cuba in the years since Fidel Castro came to power in 1959.

JAMES NELSON GOODSELL

Dover, Massachusetts
March 1974

Contents

FIDEL CASTRO'S
PERSONAL REVOLUTION
IN CUBA:
1959–1973

Introduction

Fifteen years into the Castro era, it is still not possible to write definitively about the Cuban revolution and the role of Fidel Castro himself. The revolution has steadily evolved, twisting and turning as it went, and it is still doing so. Castro similarly is evolving and the forty-seven-year-old revolutionary, who today rules Cuba, has changed a great deal from the man who marched triumphantly out of the Sierra Maestra in 1959.

But there is no doubt that Castro's successful overthrow of the hated Batista dictatorship in 1959 launched a new era for Cuba and also for the Western Hemisphere.[1] Things have not been the same since.

Few observers at the time of Castro's victory, however, were prepared for what was to come during the 1960s. Indeed, few Cubans (and perhaps Castro himself) were aware of the vast changes that lay in store for the island and for the Americas. Yet the fifteen years since have brought with them major upheaval and vigorous political, economic, social, and cultural change in Cuba. The effect of the upheaval and the change accompanying it have been felt even beyond the Western Hemisphere.

[1] The best single account of the events that led to Fidel Castro's overthrow of Fulgencio Batista is Hugh Thomas, *Cuba: The Pursuit of Freedom* (New York: Harper & Row, 1971). Writing with the advantage of sober reflection more than ten years after the events took place, he is obviously more reflective in his judgments than many of the writers who chronicled those events in the early 1960s. Still, some of these earlier works are worth consulting. See for examples, Herbert L. Matthews, *The Cuban Story* (New York: George Braziller, 1961) and Rufo López-Fresquet, *My 14 Months with Castro* (Cleveland: World Publishing Company, 1966).

It is clearly too early to assess fully the Castro years and their impact on Cuba. The Cuban revolution, unlike the traditional Latin American revolution, is an ongoing affair. It has yet to come to full fruition. One suspects this is the way Castro wants it. For nothing characterizes the Cuban revolution more than Castro's own personal commitment to vigorous change and ongoing reform in Cuba. He is as much involved in such change now, some fifteen years after coming to power, as he was in 1959. Moreover, he personally seems most at home in a revolutionary setting.

This should not seem strange, for Fidel Castro is basically a revolutionary. In both words and actions, he has been demonstrating this for a generation. Even a brief perusal of his speeches over the past twenty-five years gives evidence of how determined Castro has been to bring about extensive and meaningful change in Cuba. His goal has been a total reorganization of Cuban society at all levels—political, economic, social, and cultural. He was talking of such basic and dramatic change long before he came to power. His speeches today regularly include comment about creating a new man, a new society, a new politics, a new economy. In short, he is talking of revolution.

But it is not talk alone. It is more importantly action. Cuba is clearly changing, perhaps not as fast as Castro wants, but his goal of a new society, if not necessarily a new man, is emerging. No one who knew Cuba before Castro came to power and sees it now can doubt that this is exactly what is taking place on the island.

In recent years, however, Castro appears to have become somewhat dissatisfied with the progress of the changes. With due regularity, as he approached the fifteenth anniversary of his overthrow of Batista, he kept indicating that the revolutionary tasks were far from complete. "The revolution must continue and must become even more a factor in our society," he said in a 1971 speech, and he has echoed this refrain in other speeches since. In Castro's thinking, the Cuban revolution is obviously far from over and the revolutionary changes he desires in Cuba are still in the making.

This ongoing sense of revolution suggests the need for particular care in making assessments of the Cuban revolution and the important changes going on as a result of the revolution. Still, some sort of assessment is desirable and also possible. The selections in this volume, although far from a complete compendium of comment on the Cuban revolution, indicate some of the conclusions, tentative though they may be, that can be drawn from what has transpired in Cuba during the past fifteen years.

In the first place, the Cuban revolution is in considerable measure a personal revolution, so much so that it is difficult to disassociate Castro and the revolution. Lee Lockwood, the photojournalist who has frequently visited Cuba in recent years, titled his 1967 book *Castro's Cuba, Cuba's Fidel* to suggest his view of "the interrelationship between the man and the society," which he added is "so close as to border upon identity." [2] Almost all decisions of consequence in Cuba today depend on Castro personally. At the same time, his continuing popularity with large portions of the Cuban people has permitted him to change course or action with an ease that is the envy of most national leaders.

There can be no mistaking Castro's qualities of charisma. Together with his radical style of leadership, this charisma has given the revolution its essential animus. It is argued sometimes that Castro's role is little more than that of the traditional Latin American *caudillo* or strongman, with perhaps certain Cuban overtones tempering the term. But this view is a limited one, mistaking the deep-seated revolutionary ethic that is so much a part of Castro and the Cuban revolution. To be sure, like some historic *caudillos,* Castro has virtually run Cuba as a personal fiefdom. At

---

[2] Lee Lockwood, *Castro's Cuba, Cuba's Fidel* (New York: Vintage Books, 1969), p. xix.

one time, he talked of institutionalization of the revolution, but now in the 1970s there is little evidence that much has been done in this direction. Moreover, he shows no particular concern that such a process has not occurred. In fact, he seems to shun it. This, of course, gives him the *caudillo* cast, but it overlooks the whole fabric of revolutionary society, the constant sense of change, even improvisation, that is so evident in Cuba today. The traditional *caudillo* in Latin American history never embarked on such an ambitious program of broad-ranging reform.

A number of commentators, as well as some associates of the Cuban leader, suggest that his relationship with the Cuban masses has a populist tone to it. The ability he has so frequently and easily displayed to stir a generation or more of Cubans with revolutionary ardor and to continue kindling revolutionary ferment is evidence of Castro's unique appeal—an appeal that does indeed have a populist touch.

There are, however, limits to Castro's personal leadership, as some of the following selections suggest. These limits have appeared more in the late 1960s than they did in the heady days of the revolution in the early 1960s. Castro's difficulties in keeping the Cuban economy moving are part of the problem.[3] Since 1967, it is clear that the Cuban economy has steadily worsened. This worsening has had its effect on Castro's popularity. How serious an effect is hard to tell at this stage, but it is clear that a growing number of Cubans, nominally Castro supporting, are beginning to question why the economic picture is not brighter. This is bound to have an effect on Castro's image. Many of the selections in this volume discuss the economic problems facing the Cuban government, and some are quite specific in noting areas of the economy where the revolution has been spectacularly unsuccessful in reaching its goals.

[3] See K. S. Karol, *Guerrillas in Power: The Course of the Cuban Revolution* (New York: Hill & Wang, 1970), pp. 405–426.

Those goals of a better life for all Cubans and of Cuban control over its natural resources, production, and agriculture have only been partially met, as Castro himself agrees. With fifteen years of struggle, the revolution is far from the success that its supporters claim, but it is also far from the failure that its enemies argue. It is a mixed picture.

On the positive side, the Castro revolution has provided more educational opportunities, free health services, milk for children, a sense of community, and the encouragement of the arts and literature. In short, there has been considerable cultural and social improvement. Simultaneously, the Castro revolution has argued that physical labor and hard manual pursuits are of major importance.

On the negative side of the ledger, there would necessarily be the absence of personal liberty, a continuing atmosphere of crisis and tension, the tragedies of lives and families that are deeply divided by politics, and a strident propaganda machine permeating life and leisure in a way that dulls individuality.[4]

An accounting of this sort, however, does not get at the heart of the Castro revolution. One of the problems in making any assessment of the revolution is the fact that this particular revolution does not fit into neat categories nor does it fit the pattern of traditional Latin American revolutions and change. This point needs emphasis. The Castro revolution is unique. In some measure, this uniqueness stems from the closeness of Cuba geographically to the United States and the tight hold on the Cuban economy that United States business interests held in pre-Castro times. Castro virtually destroyed this economic link and rid Cuba also of the overt North American influence in Cuban political life. Cuba once was little more than an island colony of the United States, even though it was nominally independent.

---

[4] One interesting look at this issue is contained in Richard Fagen's article "Mass Mobilization in Cuba: The Symbolism of Struggle," *Journal of International Affairs*, XX, 2 (1966), 254–271.

That colonial link no longer exists. The revolution has cast aside not only the political and economic links with the United States, but it has severed many of the cultural links as well. One has to make an exception here, particularly in the issue of baseball, which proved too deeply rooted to be altered. Anyway, Castro discovered he liked the game! [5] In the process of getting rid of United States economic control, Castro has also largely done away with private ownership of property. He has been so effective that there is little likelihood that such ownership will ever again play a role in Cuban society, even if Castro were at some point overthrown and a less radical government installed.

In all of this, Castro emerges as the prime mover. His touch in all the changes going on in Cuba is unmistakable. It could not be otherwise. Combining prodigious energy, a restless ambition, and a questioning intellect, Castro has clearly created the Cuban revolution and shaped its tone and approach. [6]

Only two others have shared in the process to a degree that they sometimes expressed themselves and influenced Castro to considerable extent on particular issues. These two were Raúl Castro, Fidel's younger brother, and Ernesto Che Guevara, the Argentine-born close associate of Castro who died in Bolivia in 1967, while trying to create a new Cuba in the South American heartland.

Raúl Castro has been extremely close and loyal to his brother both in the days before they came to power in 1959 and in the years since. In times of great stress and serious crisis, it is to Raúl that Fidel Castro most frequently turns in a manner similar to John Kennedy's heavy reliance on his brother, Robert, in times of great crisis.

6 There are numerous studies of Castro's charismatic leadership. Many of these are mentioned in the bibliography. An early look at the subject is contained in Theodore Draper, *Castro's Revolution* (New York: Frederick A. Praeger, 1962), pp. 115–172.

Raúl has served as one who frequently advances solutions, but also one who acts often as a sounding board.[7]

Che Guevara played a different role. In the first six years of the revolution, there is little doubt that Guevara offered Castro a viewpoint that put a degree of realistic idealism into some of the revolution's concepts. Guevara had a keen mind, one that often got to the heart of an issue more quickly than even Fidel Castro himself. If anyone influenced Castro in the early years of the revolution, it was Guevara. His departure from Cuba in 1966 left a vacuum that has yet to be filled. It may well be that some of Cuba's economic problems in recent years have arisen precisely because Guevara is no longer around to give Castro his counsel.[8]

Still, having given deserving credit to Raúl Castro and Guevara, one is struck with the personal quality of the Cuban revolution and how much it is the embodiment of Fidel Castro himself. In the long run, the revolution's ultimate success or failure depends very much on Fidel Castro personally.

The question before Cuba at this time, fifteen years into the revolution, is whether the island can somehow lift itself out of the economic morass it is now in and move ahead with economic development that brings about the goals of a better life for all Cubans. There is also a related question of whether the revolution ought not to have some sort of institutionalization.[9] These pages appear at the moment these issues are uppermost in the thinking of those who analyze the twists and turns of Cuba's revolution.

[7] Raúl Castro generally stays out of the limelight. But he occasionally substitutes for his brother on important occasions and his speeches are reprinted in full in newspapers and magazines. Moreover, he is generally on the platform when Fidel Castro speaks.

[8] See Karol, *op. cit.,* pp. 297–298.

[9] Also of interest is the related issue of bureaucracy that the central committee of the Cuban Communist party tackled in an editorial entitled "The Struggle Against Bureaucracy: A Decisive Task," in *Granma Weekly Review,* Year 2, 10 (March 5, 1967), 2–3 and Year 2, 11 (March 12, 1967), 2–3. It sounded a clarion call to take the offensive in the "war against bureaucracy."

In speeches of 1970—in May and again in July—Castro seemed to recognize this dilemma. He acknowledged personal, as well as collective, "responsibility" for himself and his government in connection with the setback in the 1970 sugar harvest. The target had been 10 million tons, but the *zafra* (sugar harvest) reached only 8.5 million tons after a Herculean and in some respects disastrous effort, which disrupted almost every other area of the economy.[10] In his speech of July 26, 1970, he admitted a number of reversals and gave an unhappy forecast of continued hardship ahead. He talked vaguely of administrative reforms, a strengthening of the Communist party apparatus, and control over dissenting elements in the nation. Since that speech, there is some evidence that Castro has moved in the directions he indicated. More such movement may be forthcoming. To date, however, the economy is still in a slump. Sugar harvests, a key factor because of the island's traditional heavy dependence on sugar, have failed to measure up to goals. Each year, Castro admits the difficulties and talks of needed changes in the economic leadership and in economic planning. Pressure from the Soviet Union, which is supplying considerable aid and credit to the Castro government may, at least in part, be responsible for some of the changes that seem to be taking place. But Castro is something of a pragmatist and recognizes the need for some change in his approach if he is to continue to have the support of the majority of Cubans.

Does this all imply movement toward a less personalized leadership in the future? The answer may become apparent later in the 1970s.

While the future of the Cuban revolution is clearly uncertain, the revolution's impact to date is increasingly evident. Some of the readings in this book suggest what the impact has been in certain areas. It is clear, for example, that Cuba under Castro has undergone a basic transforma-

---

[10] See Fidel Castro's speech of May 20, 1970, *Ediciones COR* (May 20, 1970), pp. 23–45 (official Cuban government translation).

tion in its political, economic, social, and cultural structures and that the revolutionary rhetoric about such change
is more than mere words. These changes are fundamental
and suggest that no matter whatever else happens in the
future, the changes to date will influence and shape future
events.

Perhaps the most lasting testament to Castro's pervasive
influence is one that most Cubanologists would accept—
namely that the basic changes that have been accomplished
so far are such that Cuba will never return to being even
a semblance of what it was before 1959. The future may
be hard to forecast, but the basic structural changes in
Cuban society and life appear lasting and permanent. Both
society and life will undoubtedly change more in the years
ahead, but the way life is ordered today in Cuba is bound
to have a major effect on whatever else Fidel Castro orders
for his nation.

Getting rid of Batista and his corrupt legions, turning on
the United States and eliminating the American economic
influence, linking up with the Soviet Union in economic
and political matters, embracing socialism and destroying
most vestiges of private ownership, and spurring new advances in arts and literature have all had their mark not
only on Cuba, but also on the Western Hemisphere. For a
long time Castro endeavored to export his revolution. The
results were the economic blockade of the island by the
United States and the Castro government's ostracism from
the councils of the Western Hemisphere.

But times are changing and at the very moment that
Castro is wrestling with the means of solving his economic
dilemma, there is a growing call throughout the Americas
to reestablish ties with Cuba. Even in the United States,
where a strong lobby of Cuban exiles (approximately
600,000) keeps up a steady barrage of anti-Castro invec-
tive, a move is growing to find ways of accommodation
with Cuba. It seems likely that some sort of rapprochement
is in the offing between Washington and Havana.

As the Castro government and the Cuban revolution entered their fifteenth year in power, it seemed reasonable to suggest that the Cuban revolution and Fidel Castro were gaining a respectability that eluded them throughout much of the 1960s.[11] Perhaps this is the best time possible for an assessment of where the Cuban revolution has been and where it is going. Castro has lost none of his idealism, and he certainly has not basically altered course. But tactics and approaches to change can vary from time to time, and it appears that Castro himself is considering new tactics and new approaches to carrying on a revolution that he admits has only been "successful in parts."

Whatever happens, however, the Cuban revolution is bound to continue owing a great deal to Castro. There is every evidence that, although he has moments of despair about conditions on his island, Castro is basically as optimistic about his eventual success as he ever was. One of the strong characteristics of the Cuban revolution has been Castro's own personal faith in himself and his determination to fight on "to the death" if necessary. It is not lost on observers that he and his associates end every speech with the comment "Patria o muerte; ¡venceremos!" (Fatherland or death; we will win!) This is more than mere rhetoric. It is deeply engrained in the philosophy and the folklore of the revolution. It is a concept to which Castro is committed and which he has used with meaningful results to spur his supporters. There is no doubt that without Castro and his commitment the revolution would have long since faltered or fallen apart.

Fidel Castro is remarkable in the way that, with his charisma and leadership style, he has dominated events in

11 Throughout Latin America, there is growing clamor for the return of Cuba to the inter-American community. Argentina, Panama, and Peru have resumed relations with the Castro government in recent years and other nations, notably Colombia, Ecuador, and Venezuela, are moving in the same direction. Castro, for his part, seems to welcome this new trend, although he pointedly exempts the United States from the list of nations he accepts as diplomatic partners.

Cuba since 1959. No other factor emerges so strongly from an assessment of the Cuban revolution than this personal leadership and this complete domination of a nation's course by one man.

The readings which follow were not necessarily selected to support this point. The majority touch on the specific impact of the revolution on a variety of activities in Cuba and upon the impact of the changes in Cuba on the rest of the hemisphere. A few of the readings mention Castro only indirectly. Some of the readings are obviously very much pro-Castro in tone; others are equally anti-Castro. There is no unanimity of opinion on the bearded revolutionary who has had so much impact on Cuba and the Americas.

The selections were chosen not to support a point of view, but rather to show the variety of research and comment on Fidel Castro's revolution from 1959 to the present. Obviously more will be written—some of which may well change the assessments in this collection. But as the revolution moves toward the conclusion of its second decade, these selections appear representative.

In sorting out the materials and comments available on the Cuban revolution, it early became clear that much of the information fell within five broad topics: the political thrust of the revolution; the economic and social side; the cultural sphere; the international implications, particularly in the Americas; and finally a broad area of opinion and comment about the revolution.

The final section of the book, dealing with recent assessments, touches largely upon material published after Castro had been in power for ten years. Except for this bit of chronology, there is no effort in these pages to choose selections based on any sort of chronology.

I

The Political Thrust

*

1

HUGH THOMAS

THE ORIGINS
OF THE CUBAN REVOLUTION

*Hugh Thomas has been one of the most devoted
students of the Cuban revolution. From the time of
his visit to Cuba, which was shortly after Castro came
to power, until he published his monumental history
of Cuba in 1971,[1] Thomas has written a steady flow
of articles and commentary on Cuba for English
newspapers and magazines.*

*In the following article, he puts forward his own
concept of how the Cuban revolution came about.
Although United States control of many aspects of
the Cuban economy obviously contributed to the climate for change, Thomas argues that a stagnant
economy, based heavily on sugar and coupled with
ineffective institutions, such as the army, the church,
and the civil service, was behind Castro's rise to
power. Although this article was written fairly early
in the Castro era, it has stood the test of time.*

The Cuban revolution happened quite quickly; the transformation of society occurred between 1 January 1959 and

Reprinted from Hugh Thomas, "The Origins of the Cuban Revolution," *The World Today*, 19, 10 (October 1963), 448–460, by
permission of the author and the Royal Institute of International
Affairs, London.

[1] Hugh Thomas, *Cuba: The Pursuit of Freedom* (New York:
Harper & Row, 1971).

the end of 1960. The revolution was also comparatively bloodless; though a figure of 20,000 often appears for the number killed by Batista between 1956 and 1958, the dead on both sides in the civil war may have been as few as 2,000.

Various explanations are current for what happened. There are those who maintain that the course of the revolution was dictated by the U.S. Government; had it not been for the mistakes of the State Department and the selfishness of U.S. business interests in Cuba, this theory goes, the Cuban revolution would have remained "humanist," as Castro proclaimed it in May 1959. . . .

The present Cuban explanation of events is that Cuba, previously a semi-colonialist society, was so severely exploited by U.S. and Cuban capitalists that the condition of the working class eventually became intolerable, the tension being especially sharpened under the tyrant Batista (1952–8); Castro's 26th of July Movement and the Communist Party therefore formed the *élite* which led the masses towards a coherent realization of their misery and the country towards the "objective conditions" for revolution. Yet this explanation is also inadequate. Cuba, although a poor country in many respects, was certainly among the richer countries of Latin America. *Per capita* income reached a figure of $341 at its highest level in 1947. The average daily salary about the same time for the best-paid sugar worker was $3.25, which probably would have given him an annual wage (with a six-day week for the five-month sugar harvest) of nearly $500. This is a small wage, but in many countries in Latin America it would be considered high. Wages apart, however, the general availability of consumer goods, the social services per head, the labor laws, the communications system, literacy rates, all normal criteria indicate that Cuba was among the leading nations of Latin America—to be ranked in terms of development below only Argentina and Uruguay, and perhaps on a level with Chile. Certainly, Cuba had had for two generations before the revolution the highest standard of living of any tropical area in the world. It does not therefore seem to be poverty, any more than North American foolishness, that caused the revolution to take the turn it did.

The difficulty of explaining what happened in Cuba in Marxist terms has led some people to another extreme: they have seen the whole series of events as dictated by the whims of one man. The trouble with this argument is that it really credits Castro with greater powers than any man can singly possess. Instead of describing a monster, this argument creates a god.

The origins of the revolution seem more likely to be found in the fact that Cuban society was not so much under-developed as stagnant: semi-developed perhaps, with some of the characteristics of advanced countries when they enter decline. Cuba was not a country in the depths of poverty, but one extraordinarily frustrated, where opportunities existed for economic and social progress but where these were wasted—and the fact of the waste was evident. The undoubted advances whetted the imagination of the working class, but did not satisfy it. The case of the well-paid sugar worker symbolizes the situation; getting $3.25 a day for the five months of the harvest, afterwards he could expect to earn nothing. Unused to saving, and perhaps incapable of doing so since he had to pay off debts incurred during the previous dead season, his life collapsed. For half the year he was comparatively well off, able to choose between a quite wide selection of consumer goods; for the rest of the year he lived in resentment, possibly more extreme than if he had been unemployed all the time, as a large fraction (around one-fifth) of his colleagues in the trade were. About 500,000 persons were in this frustrating position, nearly one-third of the total labor force of about 1.7 million. Nearly all of them were in debt throughout their lives—being disposed for that reason alone to hope for a violent upturn in society, which might declare a moratorium on, or even an annulment of, debts.

The key to Cuban society before the revolution is, in fact, the sugar industry. Sugar-cane is grown quite easily and is therefore an obviously economical source of income for landowners. The cane is cut, hauled, in Cuba's case, to the 160 or so mills—a sort of rural factory—and grinding begins about 1 January every year. The period of activity lasts for about five to six months. From about the start of the first World War up to 1959, Cuba was the world's largest sugar producer, and she is still far the largest exporter of sugar. However, she was, as a producer, overtaken by the Soviet Union in 1959, and sugar production elsewhere has been rapidly catching up. . . .

In addition to being the world's largest producer of sugar, Cuba was, for about a century, the major single source of sugar for the United States, and for a time after the Civil War her sole source of sugar. For most of this century up to 1960, Cuba supplied between 40 and 60 per cent of U.S. sugar, with a drop towards 30 per cent and for a time 25 per cent during the 1930s depression. After this unstable period, Cuba secured a part of the U.S. market by a specific quota, allocated annually according to the U.S. Secretary for Agriculture's estimate of U.S. sugar needs. . . . The quota was a great advantage but also a great bondage, and therefore there is a certain logic in the Cuban Revolutionary Government's criticism of its existence in early 1960 and denunciation of its disappearance in August of the same year. The tragedy of the Cuban sugar industry in the years before the revolution is that it was hard to see how, even with the most effective methods of production, it could expand its share of the world market, or its own production. Both U.S. and world markets were quota-controlled and tariff-protected to the point where expansion was almost forbidden.

One should note, however, that a large percentage of Cuban sugar mills were in fact U.S.-owned. . . . In 1958 there were thirty-six U.S.-owned mills against 121 Cuban, with the U.S. mills producing only 37 per cent of the total. This increasing Cubanization of mill-owning was hardly to be regarded as a victory for nationalism, however, but rather as a recognition that Cuban sugar was no longer such a good investment. U.S. total investment in Cuba in 1958 was about $900 m., considerably less in real terms than the figure for 1930. Of course, it was natural for Cubans to denounce the high percentage of foreign ownership, throughout this long period, of the staple product of the country, especially when other sections of the commanding heights of industry were also U.S.-owned; these included almost all public utilities in Havana, railways, and banks, which had been largely U.S.- and Canadian-owned since the bank crash in the 1920s. However, there were some advantages in this: foreign ownership could help to keep the door open to new ideas in technology and research; some of the best schools in Cuba seem to have been run by Americans, some being financed as a public obligation, others privately; American firms were also probably less given to tax evasion than Cuban. The overall effect of U.S. ownership of such prosperity as there was in Cuba was that the Americans could not avoid being blamed when things went wrong with the economy; and the economy had been in crisis for as long as anyone could remember.

In fact, Cuban sugar before the revolution was going through the classic experience of a great industry in decline. Cuban sugar-growers never sought to make the best use of their ground, the yield per acre, for instance, being far below that of Puerto Rico or Hawaii. Irrigation was not only rare but not apparently even planned, though it was obvious that it gave a higher yield. There was very little research as to the type of cane best suited for Cuban conditions: the agricultural research center at Sagua la Grande was hardly able to carry on, since even the meagre ear-marked funds often "disappeared" before they got there.

Further, the industry was hamstrung by bureaucratic control. The opening of grinding each year was announced by presidential decree. The Sugar Stabilization Institute estimated the crop to be harvested and divided it among the different markets—the U.S. quota, the world market, domestic consumption, the special reserve. The sugar output of each mill, according to grinding capacity, was also divided among these four markets. On top of this, there were governmental regulations for freight rates, size of bags, port of shipment, official average price for settling with non-mill growers of cane, and so on. An elaborate pattern of control which almost anticipated nationalization had thus been set up. . . .

The country was also at the mercy of world sugar demand. Changes of a percentage of a cent in the world market price of sugar not only meant the creation of ruin of fortunes in Cuba, but also indicated whether ordinary life was intolerable or acceptable. Assuming exports of 3 million tons, a one cent variation up or down in the price of sugar could make a difference of $60 m. in Cuban receipts; and world market prices of sugar have varied extraordinarily. Between 1920 and 1958, Cuban production reached an approximate total of 4 million tons eight times: the value got for this amount varied between $1,000 m. and $200 m. Cuba was in fact a kind of litmus paper on which every world depression, war, or crisis would inevitably be marked. . . .

Credit was almost impossible to obtain unless the proposed project was in some way connected with sugar, yet investment in new industries (perhaps making use of sugar by-products) and diversification of agriculture were the only way forward. This blockage could be observed throughout the economy. Education, health, social services of all kinds, public services, commerce, departments of agriculture other than sugar, trade unions, all gave the impression of being not only incapable of development, but also afraid of it. The Cuban educational system had deteriorated between 1925 and 1959. A smaller proportion of school-age children were enrolled in Cuban schools in 1950 than in 1925, and the loss of pupils between the first and eighth grades, during the course of education, was considerably higher in 1950 than in 1925. The number of hours' instruction had even been cut. There was a disproportionate increase of private-school enrolment—which inevitably intensified social class differences. The illiteracy rate actually rose between 1931 and 1953. . . .

There were, however, other factors which caused the Cuban neurosis to be articulated eventually in the most extreme way: these were political and institutional. The institutions of Cuba in 1958–9 were amazingly weak. The large middle and upper class had failed to create any effective defense against the demands of what may be taken to be the majority, when those demands came at last to be clearly expressed, as they did in January 1959, by a group self-confessedly middle class in origin.

Perhaps the first and strongest factor working in favor of the revolution was the absence of any regionally based obstacles. Cuba is a small country with a traditionally centralized administration. There is no problem of an Indian population and though the Negro and mulatto minority (perhaps 30 per cent) is most numerous in Oriente there are large Negro and mulatto minorities elsewhere. In the early years of the Republic there did seem a possibility that the local bosses found elsewhere in Latin America would emerge to withstand the carrying out of legislation: President Gómez was, for instance, undoubtedly the political boss of Santa Clara. But these bosses did not develop as politically important after the 1920s. A possible reason for this was the survival, even among the violent disputes of the early days of the Republic, of a general sense of Cuban identity forged during the generations of struggle against Spain—after all, no Spanish colony took so long to become

independent as Cuba. Possibly the central highway, constructed in the late 1920s, played a part in making it easy
for potential local chiefs to get fast to Havana, where so
much patronage and cash could be got so easily—and
thence on to Miami and the Florida real estate agencies.
The proximity to America, the degree of U.S. interest and
investment in Cuba, was perhaps another factor limiting
regional feeling. And, in January 1959, the 26th of July
Movement was the effective boss of the most likely rebellious area, Oriente.

To the absence of a regional restraining force was added
the weakness of two other traditional conservative forces
—the Church and the regular army. The Cuban Church
has never really found an identity. Churches are few in
Cuba. The Church played no part in the development of
the Cuban spirit of independence, which instead was nur-
tured by freemasonry and rationalism. Few priests before
1898 were Cuban born, and even after 1900 the majority
continued to come from Spain. Church and State had been
separated in the Constitution of 1901, State subsidies also
disappearing. Later on, the Church made something of a
comeback, a large number of Catholic schools being
founded in the 1930s; in 1946 a Catholic university was
also founded. In the 1950s this educational emphasis led
to the appearance of a number of almost radical Catholic
groups which opposed Batista. In Oriente there was, in the
early stages, some degree of relationship between the 26th
of July Movement and the Church—chiefly since it was
widely known that the intervention of the Archbishop of
Santiago had helped to save Castro's life after the Moncada attack in 1953. The leading Catholic and conservative
newspaper the *Diario de la Marina* was, on the other hand,
among the first to suggest that the 26th of July Movement
was communist.

After Castro got to power, the Church made no serious
move to gather middle-class opposition, and it was only in
1960, when it was too late, that a series of sporadic pas-

toral letters appeared denouncing communism. All church schools and convents were closed by the end of 1961, and most foreign priests and secular clergy (i.e. the majority) were expelled. Since then there has been a surprising calm in the relations between Church and State, presumably by mutual consent; the Church in Cuba has, in short, never been a serious factor in the situation.

The regular army, the second traditional opponent of revolutionary regimes, was even less of an obstacle. By early 1959 it had in fact ceased to exist—not simply due to its demoralization in 1957 and 1958, when fighting Castro in the Sierra, but also to the repeated divisions which had weakened its *esprit de corps* during preceding years. . . .

The trade unions also could offer no serious opposition to the revolution; yet the revolution destroyed them, or anyway converted them into departments of the Ministry of Labor. Cuban labor began to be effectively organized under the shadow of the depression and the Machado dictatorship. Batista enabled the communists to form and dominate a congress of unions in the late 1930s—in return for communist electoral support for himself. Between 1938 and 1947 the unions were, if not structurally, at least in effect a section of the Ministry of Labor. The rather cynical alliance of Batista and the communists (till 1944) was responsible for some enlightened labor legislation: a minimum wage; minimum vacation of one month; forty-four-hour week and forty-eight-hour-week pay; nine days of annual sick leave; security of tenure except on proof of one of fourteen specific causes for dismissal, and so on—all admirable measures in themselves, enshrined in the 1940 Constitution, and all in effect till 1959. These measures were in fact so favorable to labor in the late 1940s and early 1950s as undeniably to hinder the economic development of Cuba; labor opposition to mechanization, for example, seems to have been a serious handicap. The general impression to be gained from the labor scene just before Batista's second *coup* was less that of solid benefits won by a progressive working class than of a number of isolated redoubts, held with great difficulty and with continuous casualties, in a predominantly hostile territory. . . .

It was equally hopeless to expect the civil service to be a restraining factor in the revolution, although, with nearly 200,000 employees, it was the second largest source of employment, ranking after the sugar workers. Despite the passage of numerous laws, starting in 1908 under the Magoon administration, no Government was able to depend on a reliable civil service. With the exception of the National Bank, during the short period from its inception in 1949 to the Batista *coup,* all departments of state were regarded as the legitimate spoils of political victors. Of course, in this Cuba was no different from other countries. But in few countries of a comparable degree of wealth was the absence of an administrative career in government so conspicuous. In some Ministries, employees never seem to have appeared except to collect pay; the absence of responsibility was possibly most marked in the Ministry of Education. Also, since the salary scale was low, there was every incentive for employees of all grades to dip their hands in the government till, as their political masters did. Since governmental and non-governmental pension funds, which were lodged with the Treasury, had been used by the Grau Government to help pay other lavish but unspecified government expenses, it was very difficult after 1947 to allow any employee to retire. Many people thought that in fact 30,000–40,000 government employees were really pensioners. Thus government employment was a kind of social assistance.

The scandal of the old bureaucracy is certainly a reason why, after the victory of the 26th of July Movement in 1959, the idea of a total break with the past seemed so attractive. The word government had been debased for so long: not only the old bureaucracy but the old political parties were widely and with justice regarded as organizations for the private distribution of public funds. Who in 1959, even after seven years of Batista, had really forgotten the scandal of Grau's schoolteachers; or of Grau's Minister of Education, Alemán, who had arrived suddenly one day in Miami with was it $10 m. or was it $20 m. in cash in a suitcase? In what way was Batista's cheating in the State lottery worse than Prío's? It was all very well to return to the Constitution of 1940: but how far had it worked between 1940 and 1952? It had in many instances merely laid down general principles; the subsequent legislation had never been carried out to implement it. . . .

Although Castro did not come to power with a real party organization, or even a real political plan, he nevertheless did have behind him a real revolutionary tradition, a tradition which was firmly rooted in the previous sixty years of Cuban politics, almost the whole of which had been passed in perpetual crisis. This tradition had been most recently expressed among the *Ortodoxo* Party founded by Eddy Chibas and to which Castro himself had belonged until about 1955. . . .

All the time between 1902 and 1959, Cubans were trying to prove themselves worthy of the heroic figures of the War of Independence—Martí, Gómez, or Maceo. Efforts were made, understandably, necessarily perhaps, by Castro to make himself, Camilo Cienfuegos, and others the equals of the heroes of the past. The men of 1959 were undoubtedly in many cases the real sòns of the men who made the revolution in 1933. Castro was to do the things that many people had been talking about before. Many moderately middle-class Cubans suspected, without much economic knowledge, that the only way out of the chronic sugar crisis, the only way to diversify agriculture, was to embark on very radical measures: to nationalize American property and to force a break in commercial relations with the United States.

Amateur Marxism was a strong force on the left wing of the *Ortodoxo* Party in the early 1950s, though it is now proving an illusion to suppose that even Marxist-Leninism can bring a swift diversification of agriculture. One can see how the illusion nevertheless became widespread, how anyone who seemed likely to realize it was certain of backing, regardless of whether he trampled on formal democracy. There can be only one reason why the moderates in the Cuban Cabinet of 1959—the admirable professional and liberal persons who now perhaps back Manuel Ray and argue that Castro has betrayed the revolution—failed to unite and resist Castro, backed by the considerable strength of the Cuban middle class: the reason is surely that they half felt all the time that, given the betrayal of so many previous revolutions, Castro was right. Many moderates after all did stay in Cuba, and many are still there.

What of the communists? They have never dictated events, but merely profited from opportunities offered to them. Founded in 1925, their greatest figure was undoubtedly their first leader Mella, the glittering student of the generation of 1922. He was murdered in 1929 in Mexico by either Machado or his own communist friends. Thereafter the Communist Party progressed from internal splits to collaboration with Batista and Grau San Martín, with various changes of name and also of policy, though rarely of leadership after 1933. It was overcome with surprising ease by Prío and Mujal in 1947. The communists got 117,-000 votes in the presidential elections of 1944, but they were by that time in a curious position, being less a party of revolution than one which had a great deal to lose, almost conservative in their reactions in fact. Thereafter their influence waned, throughout the intermediate period between then and the Castro civil war, until mid-1958 when, after some difficulty, they established a working alliance with Castro, whom they had previously dismissed as a "putschista." Since then, they have, of course, come into their own in many respects, if not quite absolutely; but their role in the origins of the Cuban revolution seems to have been small.

To sum up: the origins of the Cuban revolution must be sought in the state of the Cuban sugar industry. Similar conditions may exist in other countries of Latin America, in respect of other crops; these have hitherto been less pronounced. Even although other revolutions in the area may in fact be equally due, they have been hindered by the strength of institutions or regional habits, which in Cuba, for historical reasons, were especially weak. Finally, the Cuban revolution of 1959, far from being an isolated event, was the culmination of a long series of thwarted revolutions.

2

FIDEL CASTRO

THE PROBLEM OF CUBA

Fidel Castro addressed the United Nations General Assembly on September 26, 1960, outlining Cuba's position on a variety of international issues and dwelling at some length on the goals of the Cuban revolution. In the course of his long speech, Castro also explained something of the background of his revolution.

The problem.　　꺗ba? Some representatives are perhaps well-informed; some of them not so well—it depends on your sources of information—but there is no doubt that for the world as a whole the Cuban problem is one that has arisen in the last two years; it is a new problem. Formerly the world had little reason to know that Cuba existed. To many people it was rather like an appendix to the United States. Even for many citizens of this country, Cuba was a colony of the United States. It was not so on the map. On the map we were shown in a different color from the United States; in reality, we were a colony. . . .

The government of Fulgencio Batista was a typical government of force, a government that suited the United States monopolies in Cuba. But it was not, of course, the type of government that suited the Cuban people. With great loss of life and much sacrifice the Cuban people overthrew that government.

What did the revolution find after it succeeded in Cuba? What wonders did it find? It found, first of all, that 600,000 Cubans fit for work were permanently unemployed—a figure that is, in proportion, equal to the number of unemployed in the United States at the time of the Great Depression which shook this country and almost led to disaster. Three million people, out of a total population of a little over 6 million, had no electric light and enjoyed none of the benefits and comforts of electricity. Three and a half million people, out of a total population of a little over 6 million, were living in hovels and huts unfit for human habitation. In the towns rents accounted for as much as one third of family incomes. Electricity rates and rents were among the highest in the world.

Thirty-seven and a half percent of our population were illiterate, unable to read or write. Seventy percent of the children in the rural areas were without teachers. Two percent of our population were suffering from tuberculosis, that is to say, 100,000 people out of a total of a little over 6 million. Ninety-five percent of the children in rural areas were suffering from diseases caused by parasites. Infant mortality was consequently very high. The average life span was very short. In addition, 85 percent of small farmers were paying rent for their lands amounting to as much as 30 percent of their gross incomes, while 1½ percent of all the landowners controlled 46 percent of the total area of the country. The proportion of hospital beds to the number of inhabitants of the country was ludicrous when compared with countries with average medical services. Public utilities, electricity and telephone companies were owned by United States monopolies. A large part of the banking and import business, the oil refineries, the greater part of the sugar production, the best land, and the chief industries of all types in Cuba belonged to United States companies. In the last ten years, the balance of payments between Cuba and the United States has been in the latter's favor to the extent of $1,000 million, and that does not take into account the millions and hundreds of millions of dollars removed from the public treasury by corrupt and tyrannical rulers and deposited in United States or European banks—one thousand million dollars in ten years! The poor and underdeveloped country of the Caribbean, with 600,000 unemployed, contributing to the economic development of the most highly industrialized country in the world!

3

THEODORE DRAPER

CASTRO AND CASTROISM

*One of the major problems posed by Castroism and
the Cuban revolution is the obstinacy with which they
refuse to fit into any neat ideological and philo-
sophical category. In 1965 Theodore Draper, one of
the most responsible observers of the revolution and
of Fidel Castro himself, wrote that Castroism by its
very nature as "a living political phenomenon . . .
does not yet lend itself to easy definition." But Draper
in the following selection attempts to interpret just
what Castroism is.*

*During the 1960s Draper became a leading com-
mentator on the Castro revolution through a series
of books and lengthy articles in such publications as
Encounter, The New Leader, and The Reporter. The
following selection is from a book published in 1965.*

Historically, Castroism is a leader in search of a movement, a movement in search of power, and power in search
of an ideology. From its origins to today, it has had the
same leader and the same "road to power," but it has
changed its ideology.

If Castroism were merely an extension of its leader, it
would belong to the traditional *caudillo*-type movements
of Latin America in which power is its own justification.

But Castro is not a traditional *caudillo;* he is a new type of *caudillo* with a need to justify his power ideologically.

Yet Castro's ideology has never come out of himself. He has only produced a "road to power," which has attached itself to different ideologies. He won power with one ideology and has held it with another. This is perhaps the most peculiar aspect of the Castroite phenomenon.

[There are] three schools of thought . . . [that] explain this phenomenon in different ways. The first contends that there was no change in ideology, at least in Castro; that he was always a Communist, but a secret one. The second maintains that there was a natural, consistent development from his pre-Communist to his post-Communist ideology. The third—at least as I understand it—believes that Castro did not have an ideological core of his own and filled the vacuum in himself with different ideologies to serve his power in different ways at different stages of his political career.

Castro himself seems increasingly to have adopted the third view. For example, on January 2, 1964, he stressed the unpreparedness of both the Cuban leadership and the Cuban people for building socialism, and their lack of "organization, tradition, habits, customs, ideas, and mental attitude" for the new task. In a similar vein, Guevara had previously remarked that the revolutionary leaders had been "only a group of fighters with high ideals and little preparation."

The old-time Communist leaders have agreed on a revealing formula to define Fidel Castro's "great historical merit." As one of the oldest and most authoritative of them has written, it has consisted essentially in his ability "to find the right road for achieving victory, that of the armed struggle of the people, the only possible road in the conditions of Cuba of 1952–58." As late as January, 1964, the former Communist General Secretary, Blas Roca, paid tribute to Castro's "great historical merit" in virtually the same terms, always with emphasis on the fact that he had found the right road to power rather than what he had done with it.

In effect, Castroism gave Communism total power in Cuba, and Communism gave Castroism an ideology of total power. In a previous period, Castroism might well have adopted a different ideology of total power. In this sense, Castroism has never been self-sufficient or homogeneous; it has been made up of elements from different traditions and movements; it has mainly contributed means and sought elsewhere for ends.

Thus, the reason for Castroism's coalescence with Communism can be explained less by what it was than by what it was not. It was not a movement with a serious political thought or a serious political thinker. It has had a leader with great gifts of popularization, demagogy, and dissimulation, with a contagious sense of mission and *jefatura,* with the physical attributes of a warrior-hero. But he has also had a deep, persistent feeling of intellectual inadequacy and inferiority, a tendency to depend on others for fundamental values or systematic theorizing, an inherent political superficiality and instability. Before taking power, he could put his name to fine democratic aims and principles, admittedly without believing in them, not because he was profoundly committed to other beliefs but because he did not believe in anything very profoundly.

But it is only in Cuba that Castroism has gone through enough stages to make its relationship with Communism clearly visible and openly avowed. In other countries, one may detect Castroite tendencies which reflect earlier stages of Cuban Castroism and which still maintain a seemingly tenuous or ambiguous relationship with existing Communist movements. Thus, non-Cuban Castroite groups may resemble the Cuban Castroism of 1955 or 1957 much more than the Cuban Castroism of 1961 or 1965. The former may seem to be a revolutionary mood rather than a movement; it may be distinguished by its "pure" adherence to "armed struggle" or "direct action" without the (temporary) encumbrance of an ideology; it may even, like its progenitor, claim to be an alternative rather than a road to Communism. But it is much more difficult for any non-Cuban Castroism to pretend to be "democratic" and non-Communist, as Cuban Castroism once pretended to be, precisely because the latter has demonstrated what such professions were worth. The success of Cuban Castroism in turning itself into a Cuban form of Communism has, ironically, hindered Castroite groups elsewhere from achieving success in quite the same way. The hopes and illusions on which Cuban Castroism once fed can hardly be made to order for any other Castroite group, and we may even get a Castroite tendency somewhere which promises to avoid the mistakes and excesses of Fidel Castro.

There are, it seems to me, two main dangers to be avoided in any analysis of Castroism today. One is to separate it from the world Communist movement, and the other is to equate it with everything else in the world Communist movement. It is just as logical to say that Fidel Castro cannot be a Communist because he is a Castroite as to say that Mao Tse-tung cannot be a Communist because he is a Maoist or that Tito cannot be a Communist because he is a Titoist. On the other hand, it is just as illogical to deny the peculiar characteristics of Castro's Communism as to deny the peculiar characteristics of Mao's or Tito's or, for that matter, Khrushchev's or Khrushchev's successors'.

In short, Castroism today represents a tendency within the world Communist movement. There is no such thing as Castroism per se. Indeed, the term Castroism is not used in Cuba today, and Castro himself seems very coy about acknowledging the existence of Castroism. It is necessary to distinguish between the "ism" of the genus "Communism" and the "ism" of a species, such as Castroism. But, for better or worse, the different Communist tendencies are also called "isms," and this practice is not likely to be given up.

In this sense, Castroism may be distinguished from other Communist tendencies by its leadership, its history, its geographical sphere of influence, its language, and its "road to power."

1. The inspiration and source of authority of the Castroite tendency is Fidel Castro, not the Soviet leadership, Mao, or anyone else. Castro has his own personal cadre and independent following in Cuba, and to a lesser extent elsewhere, which have given him an increasing margin of maneuverability vis-à-vis the old-time Communists in Cuba and the other Communist states and Parties.

2. Castroism is the only tendency within world Communism which came into the movement from the outside and did not develop organically from within, as did Maoism or Titoism. In Cuba it has needed world Communism to give it a doctrine, a social and economic pattern, and material assistance, but it feels that world Communism needs it externally for expansion in Latin America.

Castro and his closest associates have repeatedly spoken of Cuba as the "example" which most of Latin America must follow to make the revolution. Many of the Communist Parties of Latin America date from the early 1920s (one, the Mexican, from 1919), and the old leaderships were brought up on the proposition that the "example" to follow with some modifications and adaptations was the Russian revolution and the Russian Party leadership. The "example" of the Chinese revolution was the first great challenge to the Russian prototype, but Castro hopes that the Cuban "example" will supersede both of them. The ultimate authority, of course, on who is and who is not correctly following the "Cuban example" will be found in Havana, not in Moscow or in Peking.

3. In effect, Castro has staked out for himself a Communist sphere of influence. He has, on occasion, made nothing less than a bid to be recognized as the Communist leader of Latin America, to be treated eventually on a par with the Soviet leadership and Mao Tse-tung. This may

smack of delusions of grandeur for the leader of a country as small and weak as Cuba, but it is precisely Castro's point that numbers are not important. If a dozen men could start a revolution in Cuba, why should not little Cuba be able to set off the revolution in Latin America, or at least claim credit for it?

4. Guevara has pointed out that Cuba has "something" for Latin Americans which no other Communist power can match. "That something," he said, "which speaks to them in Spanish, in their own language, and which explains in a clear form what they have to do to achieve happiness, is called the Cuban revolution." The same idea, less obtrusively, but no less unmistakably, has been publicly voiced by Blas Roca: "The Cuban revolution established the first socialist country in America and has made the first Marxist-Leninist revolution in the Spanish language. And that is for all time." Language, in fact, reinforces and perhaps even outweighs geography as a factor in the Castroite sphere of influence. The language factor indefinably exacerbates and nationalizes whatever other differences may exist between the various Communist tendencies.

5. Finally, the Castroite "road to power" is not the traditional Communist one. In the orthodox Communist view of the past, revolutionary force or violence has been considered the last, not the first, stage of the revolutionary struggle. Objective conditions created the basis for armed struggle; armed struggle did not create objective conditions. As the veteran Argentine Communist Victorio Codovilla has said of the Chinese Communists, but which he might just as well have aimed at the Cubans, "they stake everything on armed struggle alone," and especially on "partisan warfare." Codovilla, who served for many years as a Comintern functionary, agreed that "in certain conditions partisan action as a component of the mass movement is a form of the popular struggle," and a "justified and necessary form," but, he insisted, armed force is only one of many admissible forms of struggle, and "if the ob-

jective conditions are not favorable for waging an armed struggle, partisan action will end in failure and in the long run will damage the revolutionary movement.' This is not the language of Castroism, which had previously advocated the use of force always and almost everywhere by a handful of guerrillas even in countries with a weak Communist Party or outside the Party altogether.

In view of the existing confusion in some quarters, it may be well to emphasize that the difference between Codovilla, an outstanding representative of the Communist "old guard," and Castro, the exemplar of the Communist "new wave," is not one of "armed struggle" versus "peaceful transition" in principle. The difference is over when, where, and in what circumstances, it is necessary or advisable to use force. The "old guard," as in the case of Luis Carlos Prestes in Brazil, has painful memories of the heavy price paid years ago for the misuse of force and considers the stakes too high to be risked lightly. Soviet Russia and not Communist China has, after all, given Castro the material assistance and military equipment that have made his belligerence possible. The difference, then, is not one of abstract doctrine; thus far the "old guard" and the "new wave" have found it possible to live with it. Nevertheless, factional struggles in the Communist movement have flared up and have raged out of control for less cause. The antagonism between the "old" Communists and the "new" in Castro's Cuba should not be pooh-poohed. For historical, personal, and tactical reasons, it is one of the most divisive elements in Castro's regime and potentially one of the most explosive.

In historical perspective, then, Castroism represents a particular case of cross-fertilization, as yet difficult to assess with finality, of a Latin American revolutionary tradition and the European Communist tradition, just as Leninism represented a cross-fertilization of the Russian revolutionary tradition and the European Marxist tradition. It is "a particular case," because it is not yet certain that the Cuban phenomenon is typical or representative of Latin American Communism as a whole. It is as yet difficult to assess with finality because it is still of relatively recent vintage and in constant flux. If the Cubans should ever achieve their ambition and truly carve out for themselves a Latin American sphere of influence—which still seems to be a long way off—it will mark a further division of the Communist world into regional oligarchies. Castroism has given world Communism cause for both exhilaration and apprehension. It has created new opportunities and new tensions. It represents growing pains and growing contradictions. All that it is safe to say at present is that the end is not yet in sight.

4

LOREE WILKERSON

'I AM A MARXIST'

When Fidel Castro publicly proclaimed before a Havana rally on December 1, 1961, that he was a Marxist-Leninist, his announcement did not come as a surprise to many who had followed his public statements throughout 1961. Indeed, the December speech was in many ways the culmination of a series of hints and implications found in his speeches and actions during the preceding year.

Some observers of the Cuban scene have argued that Castro was a Marxist long before the December speech, noting that the Cuban leader himself claimed to have been a Marxist for at least a decade preceding the date of the speech. But this view is advanced less frequently ten years after the speech than it was in the early 1960s.

Few of Castro's speeches have been more studied, however, than the "I am a Marxist" speech, as the December 1961 talk is now known. One of the ablest of these studies is Loree Wilkerson's readable monograph from which the following excerpt is taken. Mrs. Wilkerson concludes that the speech is "in opposition to the political ideology" that Castro "originally expressed as he began his climb to power."

Reprinted from Loree Wilkerson, *Fidel Castro's Political Programs from Reformism to "Marxism-Leninism,"* pp. 82–92, by permission of the University of Florida Press.

In proclaiming his conversion to Marxism-Leninism at the end of his third year in power, Castro placed himself squarely in opposition to the political ideology he originally had expressed as he began his climb to power. At the beginning of that climb, he cast the 26th of July Movement in the image of the Latin American indigenous reform movement as it had been developed in Cuba through the Auténtico and Ortodoxo parties. When he called on the Cuban people to support his insurrection, he promised to carry on with integrity and new vigor the social revolution which had been sparked by the Auténticos in the mid-1930s only to bog down under a leadership which could not rise above the self-serving political practices of the past. In the Declaration of the Sierra Maestra, Castro restated the primary concepts of all Latin American democratic-reform movements; that is, nationalism, agrarian reform, industrialization, social welfare, political democracy, freedom of the press and speech, and massive public education. Nothing in his program was new to Cubans—it had all been set ˙own before in that comprehensive, particularized, social document, the Constitution of 1940. Castro recognized the likeness and promised to restore the Constitution.

Thus Castro garnered the necessary support to overcome Batista on the basis of a restatement of the social-democratic program of the Auténticos and the Ortodoxia. To what extent, then, has Castro fulfilled the program of the 26th of July Movement? There is no question that his program for political democracy with its appurtenances of free elections and opposition political parties has not materialized. His public rejection of the democratic political system embodied in the 1940 Constitution, which came in the middle of his third year in power, was no more than a delayed recognition of the de facto system which had been in operation from the onset of his regime. The Fundamental Law, which was decreed some six weeks after his take-over, effectively emasculated the elective system of the

Constitution by vesting all powers of government in an appointed Council of Ministers and granting them the power to amend laws by a two-thirds vote. In place of the system of elections and organized political opposition, Castro substituted what he termed "direct democracy," in which sanction for the policies of his regime is to come from "a constant meeting with the people." In practice the meetings have taken the form of massive, open-air rallies at which Castro announces government policies.

Fundamental to Castro's program before coming to power was the revitalization of political parties as a necessary condition for democratic government. Yet when the first signs of an organized opposition appeared, Castro moved quickly and ruthlessly to destroy the movement by imprisoning Hubert Matos. Only the Communist party was granted legal recognition by the new regime, and it was subsequently incorporated into a single government party. Freedom of the press, almost a necessity for the emergence of meaningful opposition parties, was reinstated at the beginning of Castro's regime, but when editorial criticism of some of the regime's policies occurred in the latter half of 1959, the government responded by imposing regulations which curtailed press freedom. By the end of 1960 a controlled press was in force. In the same period, professional and voluntary organizations, which could serve as a rallying point for opposition movements, were brought under government control.

Thus, by the end of its first two years in power, Castro's regime had abandoned the basic concepts of democratic action which had characterized the Cuban reform movement in its earlier stages and which had been pledged by Castro during his struggle against Batista. In their place the Castro regime developed a government based on the power of one man, virtually unchecked by constitutional guarantees or institutional restraints.

Although Castro failed to restore political freedoms in Cuba, action has been taken with respect to the agrarian and social welfare aspects of his program. When the agrarian law was enacted, however, it differed in important respects from the proposal put forth in the Sierra manifesto. That proposal, in accordance with the Ortodoxo program, called for the distribution of unused lands to the landless, with prior indemnification for any privately owned land thus confiscated. The agrarian law which Castro's regime enacted placed limitations on the amount of land any individual or corporation could own, seized the excess, and offered to provide indemnity in twenty years. The regime claimed to have given out 21,000 parcels of land to landless farmers by mid-1961 and to be continuing the program. That this phase of the agrarian law is being carried out appears to be corroborated by a recent reliable estimate that 60 per cent of the agricultural land in Cuba is privately owned.

Social welfare aspects of Castro's program have likewise been initiated since he took power. In the first months of his regime an extensive housing program was begun which aimed at providing every Cuban with the opportunity to own his own home. Health and medical facilities were extended to the rural areas, rental rates were reduced by 50 per cent, and utility costs were drastically lowered. Large-scale school construction was started, and great efforts have been made to eradicate illiteracy. Recreational facilities, which had been available to only a minority of Cubans, were opened to all Cubans, and many new facilities were provided. A campaign was launched to eliminate racial discrimination, and new opportunities for employment were extended to non-whites. Thus, a start has been made to carry out that part of Castro's program aimed at giving all Cubans a better chance in life.

In another area Castro at first appeared to be sticking to a part of the program he had fashioned for the 26th of July Movement. The concept of nationalism which had permeated the Ortodoxia was fully reflected in his own organization, and despite one attempt to reassure American investors in Cuba (in the *Coronet* article published during the guerrilla campaign), his pronouncements from the beginning of the insurrection called for native control and development of the Cuban economy. Two of the five revolutionary laws which Castro presented during his Moncada trial were designed to check and in time eliminate foreign ownership of agriculture and industry in Cuba. The very first manifesto issuing from the 26th of July Movement after the insurrectionists had retreated into the Sierra Maestra warned other nations not to intervene in the affairs of Cuba. Later on, a part of his squabble with the other opposition groups over the unification proclamation hinged on what he considered to be a weakly worded passage dealing with foreign interference. Thus, as the process of elimination of foreign ownership was completed near the end of the second year of Castro's regime, he appeared to be adhering to the nationalist orientation expressed in his program. Hence, his later advocacy of international Communism, which became official at the end of his third year in power, was an abrupt refutation not only of the earlier actions of his regime but of the deeply nationalist sentiment of the social revolution he had promised to fulfill.

From this comparison of the program Castro proposed before coming to power and the program which was initiated after he came to power, it is apparent that only those measures dealing with agrarian reform and social welfare have been implemented. In the case of agrarian reform, moreover, the enacted law was a marked modification of his original proposal for adjusting landownership patterns in Cuba. With respect to the other major planks in his platform, Castro's box score is zero. In place of the Constitution of 1940 and its guarantees of representative government based on democratic procedures, which Castro was pledged to honor, a single government party has been installed in conjunction with an appointed Council of Ministers who have unchecked legislative powers. Deserting nationalism, which was an integral part of the philosophy

of the democratic-reform movement in Cuba and fully
reflected in his own program, Castro has aligned his country with the cause of international Communism.

These reversals in ideology began only a few months
after Castro gained control of the Cuban government and
were completed by the end of his third year in power. Because of the rapidity with which these changes took place
and because they appeared to be such total refutations of
much that Castro had previously stood for, his actions
seemed inexplicable not only to many observers but to
many who had taken a stand with him in the Sierra Maestra or had supported him in other ways. However, by viewing chronologically each stage of Castro's struggle for
power in Cuba, a unifying thread of an uninhibited urge
to personal rule appears to bring the seemingly unconnected stages into harmony.

In the first stage, Castro clearly supported much of the
ideology of the indigenous reform movements throughout
Latin America. He consistently, often eloquently, set forth
a program based on democratic-social concepts from the
time he began active political life until he was well into the
first year of his regime. His debut as a professional poli-
tician was made under the auspices of the Ortodoxia,
which advocated democratic-social reforms, and when Castro became active in the opposition following the destruction of the legal political process by the Batista coup, he
supported the program of the Ortodoxia in all of his writings and pronouncements from the time of the Moncada
attack right through the guerrilla phase of the insurrection.
The Moncada manifesto declared that Castro's rebels were
in full accord with the "revolutionary program" of the Ortodoxia. Later, after the break with the Ortodoxo leadership, Castro no longer rang in the name of his former
party, but he stated categorically that the 26th of July
Movement was dedicated to the tenets of Eduardo Chibás,
founder of the Ortodoxia. In July, 1957, some months after
the rebels began their operation in the Sierra Maestra,

Castro issued the Declaration of the Sierra Maestra, which had been drafted with the aid of Eduardo Chibás' brother Raúl. This manifesto, calling for free elections under the 1940 Constitution and a program containing all the elements of the 1952 Ortodoxo platform, became the official program of the 26th of July Movement and formed the basis of the unification of the opposition groups in July, 1958.

Thus Castro spoke, but there is another side to the coin. Despite his insistence, in the Sierra declaration and other writings of this period, that he sought to restore constitutional government to Cuba, denying at the same time any political ambitions for himself, he resisted every attempt to broaden the base of the revolution's leadership. When the opposition groups sought to gain strength through unification, Castro blocked the effort until his own group was granted the dominant position under terms which he dictated from his mountain stronghold, including the provision that only his own troops would comprise the armed forces of Cuba after Batista fell. A lust for personal power in the make-up of the rebel leader was deduced by Javier Pazos while he served as an officer on Castro's staff in the Sierra Maestra. He became convinced, Pazos later wrote, that Castro was at that time a "political opportunist . . . with a firm will and an extraordinary ambition who thought in terms of winning power and keeping it." [1]

At the second attempt to challenge his supreme position, which came a few days after Batista's flight when the guerrilla forces of the Revolutionary Directorate refused to surrender their arms on Castro's order, his army quickly put down the challenge with a show of force. With respect to this incident particularly, the paradox of the sudden insti-

---

[1] Javier Felipe Pazos, "Cuba: Long Live the Revolution!" *The New Republic,* CXLVII (November 8, 1962), 15. This and several subsequent footnotes in this passage have been slightly amplified by the editor to include material not contained in the original footnotes, but found in the author's bibliography, in order to make the notes correspond with the style used throughout this volume.

gation of repressive tactics by a man who had for many years professed the utmost dedication to democratic practices bespeaks an intense desire for personal power.

In keeping with Castro's professed dedication to political freedom, there was no infringement of basic rights in the first few months after Batista fell—that is, if the numerous and rapid executions, following summary trials before a military tribunal, are excepted. These were viewed by many outside Cuba as violations of political freedom and human rights. On the other hand, the executions were justified by the Castro regime as necessary to forestall a repetition of the virtual slaughter of Machado supporters by the outraged populace when that regime fell in 1933. At least three long-time observers of Cuban events concurred at the time with the regime's justification.[2] In any event, the decisions of the tribunals, although often based on hearsay evidence, were in accord with the Napoleonic code (on which Cuban law is based), which does not require concrete evidence of guilt if it is generally believed that the accused is guilty. For example, the editor of *La Quincena,* a leading Catholic periodical in Cuba, wrote at the time: "The trials . . . , although summary, have taken into account all the formalities and guarantees to insure that the sentence be in conformity with strict justice. Those sentenced were clearly guilty of grave crimes, the proving of which was not difficult since the chain of assassinations, of torture, has been so extended and the men who committed them so well known."[3] The Cuban press reflected substantial agreement with *La Quincena*'s position.

Aside from the debatable executions of the first few weeks, Castro's regime, although disorganized to the point

[2] See R. Hart Phillips, *Cuba: Island of Paradox* (New York: McDowell, Obolensky, 1959), pp. 40–43; cf. Carleton Beals, "As Cuba Sees It," *The Nation,* CLXXXVIII (January 31, 1959), 83–85; Robert J. Alexander, *Prophets of the Revolution* (New York: The Macmillan Company, 1962), p. 277.

[3] Quoted in Beals, "As Cuba Sees It," p. 84.

of chaos, operated for several months in an atmosphere free from fear of repression. Part of the reason may have been that Castro found that he could rely primarily on his great personal popularity and his talent with the spoken word to maintain his dominance over the government. When his first cabinet expressed some disaffection for his policies, they were quickly forced out by the demonstrations of public support for Castro which he elicited in the course of several television appearances during the controversy. A single television performance was all that was necessary to obtain the resignation of President Urrutia, the man whom Castro had demanded for the position of chief executive.

It was not until the Matos affair, when Castro's hegemony was challenged by an incipient organized opposition, that he sanctioned the violation of basic guarantees of political freedom. The trial and imprisonment of Matos signaled the end of the right to dissent openly with the policies of Castro's government; from that point on internal opposition became clandestine. Matos' defection from the regime was apparently regarded by Castro as a very serious threat to his power which could not be talked away before the television cameras. In the first place, while not enjoying the degree of public worship which was accorded Castro, Matos was a popular guerrilla hero. Secondly, there appears to have been an organization building around him. Castro implied as much when he bitterly criticized three newspapers for giving support to Matos, one of which was the organ of the Auténticos Abstencionistas. A popular hero backed by a political party and three newspapers could easily be the beginning of a meaningful opposition— the sort of opposition that Castro had previously said should develop before elections could be held. But rather than allow an opposition party to develop, he used ruthless tactics to destroy it, and followed the initial repression with measures which within a year effectively eliminated all open organized opposition in Cuba. With the imprisonment of Matos, Castro made it plain that his previous guarantees of political freedom would not be honored.

An ambition to be the arbiter of the revolution, however, does not adequately explain why Castro thought it necessary to destroy the free institutions which his revolution had just restored to Cuba. Although he was encountering some resistance to some parts of his program from segments of the middle class, he still retained massive support. Even the more extreme measures he introduced, such as the agrarian law, did not diminish his popularity with the majority of Cubans. In view of the support he enjoyed, Castro's sudden negation of the democratic procedures he had advocated for so many years appears to be the result of an implacable desire for personal power in an absolutist sense. Theodore Draper has reached the same conclusion. With reference to Castro's "power complex," Draper stated that "once power came into his hands, he refused to permit anything that might lessen or restrict it. He would not tolerate the functioning of a government that was not the façade of his personal rule or of a party that might develop a life of its own." [4]

While an irrepressible drive to exercise virtually unlimited authority can explain Castro's negation of the democratic procedures he had previously advocated, his subsequent announced conversion to Marxism-Leninism appears to have little relevance to his power ambition, serving only to increase the opposition to his regime already engendered by his autocratic tactics, rather than adding strength to his position. Nevertheless, this action, too, fits into the pattern of a power complex. Castro has insisted that his new political philosophy was the result of ideological conviction, but the sequence of events suggests that he became a Marxist-Leninist because he had taken Cuba into the Soviet bloc. First, to review briefly, Castro announced this step

[4] Theodore Draper, *Castro's Revolution* (New York: Frederick A. Praeger, 1962), pp. 56–57.

at the end of his third year in power, but the event was foreshadowed in his speeches and press interviews throughout 1961. In the *Unitá* interview in the latter part of January, Castro admitted that he had been "full of petit-bourgeois prejudices and defects" during the insurrection, and he praised the Cuban Communists for withholding their support during that period. In May Castro announced that the revolution was socialistic, and he dispensed with political parties, elections, and the Constitution of 1940 in favor of "direct democracy," in which the direction of the government would be in the hands of a single party composed of members of "representative organizations of all Cuban revolutionaries," which turned out to mean members of the PSP, the RD, and the 26th of July Movement. In November Castro instructed the orientadores revolucionarios to seek guidelines for the revolution in the works of Marx and Lenin. His announcement in December of his belief in Marxism-Leninism merely clarified the pattern which had been taking shape throughout the year.

All of this took place in 1961, a year which had seen Cuban-United States relations deteriorate to the point where an attempted assault on Castro's regime by Cuban exiles had received considerable support from the United States government. The aborted invasion was merely a manifestation of the bad relations which had been developing between the United States and the Castro regime for the previous two years, beginning with the initial expropriations of American holdings in Cuba in 1959. Sometime in 1960, if not before, the United States began to plan the overthrow of Castro. Draper sets the time as "the spring of 1960." In any event, the training of invasion troops in Guatemala was already well under way when it was first revealed in the Guatemalan paper *La Hora* on October 30, 1960.[5] In all likelihood, Castro was aware of the intention of the United States to depose him some months before it was revealed. It is possible, moreover,

5 *Ibid.*, p. 69.

that Castro concluded that the United States was his implacable enemy at least a year earlier, when the United
States quietly ignored his plan for the advancement of
Latin America which he presented to the Buenos Aires
conference in May, 1959—the plan which he may well
have anticipated would catapult him into leadership of all
the Latin American peoples. Up to that time he had shown
some desire for American support, both in the *Coronet*
article and during his trip to the United States in April,
1959; but after his return from Buenos Aires, the whole-
sale expropriations of American property began, and his
denunciations of the United States became increasingly
vituperative.

The first overt step toward merger with the Soviet bloc
—the economic agreement with the Soviet Union—took
place in June, 1960. Whether this step was taken because
the United States ignored Castro's plan for Latin America
in 1959 or because the decision to depose him was reached
early in 1960—or for some other reason—remains a matter of speculation. What is clear is that once United States
policy had become set, Castro's position was in jeopardy.
An alternative, short of foregoing much of what he had
done in Cuba, was to acquire a powerful friend to protect
him from a powerful enemy. In seeking the aid of the Soviets to preserve his position, Castro's adoption of their
ideology was virtually inevitable. If he hoped to protect
himself from the United States with the threat of Russia's
armed might, he had to become sufficiently valuable in
the eyes of his protectors to offset the risk inherent in
their overt penetration into an area of vital interest to the
United States. By proclaiming to the world that he had
adopted the ideology of the Soviet Union, the welfare of
his regime became a matter of much greater interest to
them.

Other explanations for Castro's conversion to Marxism-
Leninism have been proposed, and one faction, headed by
Nathaniel Weyl and Daniel James, holds that he was a

convert from his student days and planned from the beginning to make Cuba into a Communist state. This position seems unlikely in view of Castro's denunciation of Communism during the insurrection and particularly in view of his earnest appeal to the other American states at the Buenos Aires conference to act to prevent both Communist and militarist coups in the Latin American countries.

Another theory envisions Castro trustingly accepting the aid of Cuban Communists in the early days of his regime, only to become the victim of their machinations. For this to have happened would, as Draper points out, have called for a high degree of gullibility, a quality which Castro had never displayed in the past, especially in his maneuvers to dominate the revolution. Draper refutes this "trap" theory, contending that "the Communists and Fidel walked toward each other, each with his eyes open, each filling a need in the other." In Draper's analysis, an ideological and organizational vacuum in the 26th of July Movement was filled by the experienced cadres of the PSP. That an organizational vacuum existed was readily apparent in the frenzied chaos that characterized the early months of Castro's regime, but the 26th of July Movement had formulated a workable program. Moreover, Castro has never exhibited any deep psychological need for a doctrinaire ideology; instead, as Draper himself observes, "He has never operated from a firm political center but has always associated himself with ideas and movements that seemed most able or willing at different times to serve him." [6]

Probably Castro was influenced by the Communists he had taken into his government, but once the United States embarked on a policy aimed at his removal, his need for Russia's support emerges as an overriding factor. The best insurance of his protector's continued interest in maintaining his regime in power was to subscribe to the Com-

[6] *Ibid.,* p. 107; Draper, "Castro and Communism" *The Reporter,* XXVIII (January 17, 1963), 35.

munist ideology. The validity of this conclusion is substantiated by his previous actions to maintain his personal power at the cost of violating the very principles for which he had begun the revolution in the first place.

Castro's rise to power in Cuba presents the picture of a democratically inclined idealist who succumbed to an intense desire to reign rather than lead.

5

DEPARTMENT OF STATE

THE UNITED STATES BREAK

Relations between the United States and Cuba throughout 1959 and 1960 deteriorated steadily. As the months wore on, there was a certain inevitability about an eventual break between the two governments. Apologists for one side or the other, of course, place the blame on the other country for the deterioration in relations and the eventual break.

There can be no question that the Eisenhower Administration in Washington had little sympathy for the Castro government. Likewise the Castro regime in Havana, for reasons it considered quite proper, embraced both political and economic policies that were bound to cause friction with Washington. Whether a more sympathetic attitude on the part of Washington could have prevented the break, however, is doubtful. The two nations were clearly on divergent courses from which neither would pull back. The break came on January 3, 1961.

It is interesting to note that Washington took care the following day to reassert its treaty rights to the United States naval base at Guantánamo. James C. Hagerty, press secretary to President Eisenhower, read a statement that said, in part, that the termination of relations "has no effect on the status of our naval station at Guantánamo. The treaty rights under

Reprinted from "The United States and Cuban Notes on Breaking Relations," *Department of State Bulletin*, XLIV, 26 (January 23, 1961), 103–104.

which we maintain the naval station may not be abrogated without the consent of the United States."

Cuban Note

Habana, January 2, 1961, *Year of Education*

Mr. Chargé d'Affaires: I have the honor to inform you that the Revolutionary Government has decided that under present circumstances the personnel of the Embassy and Consulate of Cuba in the City of Washington, whether diplomatic, consular, or of other character, whatever their nationality, should not exceed eleven persons. Likewise it has been decided that the personnel of the Embassy and Consulate of the United States in the city of Habana, whether diplomatic, consular or of other character, whatever their nationality, should likewise be limited to eleven persons.

For the purpose of facilitating the departure of the persons who for this reason must abandon the national territory, a period of forty-eight hours has been fixed from the time of receipt of this note.

I take the opportunity, Mr. Chargé d'Affaires, to reiterate to you the assurance of my reciprocity of your considerations.

Carlos Olivares

United States Note[1]

January 3, 1961

Sir: I have the honor to refer to a note dated January 2, 1961, from the Government of Cuba to the Chargé d'Affaires of the United States Embassy in Habana stating that the Government of Cuba has decided that personnel of the Embassy and Consulate of the United States in the City of Habana, regardless of nationality, shall not exceed eleven persons.

[1] The United States note, signed by Secretary of State Christian A. Herter, was addressed to Dr. Armando Flórez Ibarra, chargé d'affaires ad interim at the Cuban Embassy in Washington [—J.N.G.].

This unwarranted action by the Government of Cuba places crippling limitations on the ability of the United States Mission to carry on its normal diplomatic and consular functions. It would consequently appear that it is designed to achieve an effective termination of diplomatic and consular relations between the Government of Cuba and the Government of the United States. Accordingly, the Government of the United States hereby formally notifies the Government of Cuba of the termination of such relations.

The Government of the United States intends to comply with the requirement of the Government of Cuba concerning the withdrawal of all but eleven persons within the period of 48 hours from 1:20 a.m. on January 3, the time of the delivery of the note under reference. In addition, the Government of the United States will withdraw its remaining diplomatic and consular personnel in Cuba as soon as possible thereafter.

The Government of Cuba is requested to withdraw from the United States as soon as possible all Cuban nationals employed in the Cuban Embassy in Washington and in all Cuban Consular establishments in the United States.

The Government of the United States is requesting the Government of Switzerland to assume diplomatic and consular representation in Cuba on behalf of the Government of the United States.[2]

I take this opportunity to reiterate to you the assurances of my reciprocity of your considerations.

Christian A. Herter

[2] The Government of Switzerland assumed responsibility for representation of United States interests in Cuba on January 7, 1961. Subsequently, the Government of Czechoslovakia assumed similar responsibility for Cuban interests in the United States [—J.N.G.].

6

KARL E. MEYER AND TAD SZULC

BAY OF PIGS:
A PERFECT FAILURE

The Bay of Pigs landing by Cuban exiles, supported and organized by the United States, may well have been the greatest military blunder since the Charge of the Light Brigade. In addition to being a military blunder because of the half-hearted manner of execution, it was also a major political disaster.

"It was a failure of mechanics and imagination—and it was a moral failure," conclude Karl E. Meyer and Tad Szulc, the authors of the following excerpt. The pair, two seasoned reporters on the Latin American scene, take a critical look at the whole Bay of Pigs scenario a year after it took place in 1961.

A few minutes before three o'clock on the morning of Monday, April 17, 1961, a landing craft filled with silent men in jungle camouflage uniforms nosed into the sand of Playa Girón, just east of the entrance to the Bay of Pigs on the swampy coast of southern Cuba. About thirty minutes later, other landing craft touched land at Playa Larga, a tree-bordered beach at the apex of the Bay. Within minutes, the dry crackling of M-1 rifles and the staccato fire of Thompson submachine guns echoed along the dark

Reprinted from Karl E. Meyer and Tad Szulc, *The Cuban Invasion: The Chronicle of a Disaster* (New York: Frederick A. Praeger, 1962), pp. 7–8, 146–156, by permission of the authors.

beaches, punctuated now and then by the thud of bazooka rockets hitting the high ground.

The air waves of the Caribbean came alive with weird, exciting words about the rising red moon and the running fish. At hidden strips in Nicaragua and Guatemala, B-26 bombers and C-54 transport planes revved up their engines, ready to take off with their load of bombs and paratroopers. And when daylight broke over the Cuban shores, a full-scale miniature invasion, materializing from phantom bases, was underway.

For the next 72 hectic, incredible hours, Operation Pluto —the attack on Fidel Castro's fortress by a band of brave but totally unprepared Cuban exiles—ran its inexorable course toward defeat. When it was over, the incident on the Bay of Pigs earned its place in the annals of modern history as one of the great fiascos in military leadership, intelligence gathering, and psychological preparation and execution.

Invasions had failed before, but seldom had a great power like the United States allowed itself to be caught in so embarrassing a predicament as in the attack on Cuba, mounted, financed and executed by the Central Intelligence Agency. The military implications of the disaster were obvious: an operation bearing the stamp of approval of the Joint Chiefs of Staff of the world's most powerful nation was destroyed in less than three days by half-trained, part-time militia troops of a disorganized, revolutionary state led by a bearded guerrilla leader who had somehow taught his men to use with devastating effect the most modern Czech and Soviet weapons.

But the political repercussions were even more humiliating. As the invasion approached its tragic denouement, the United States buried itself deeper into the white lies, contradictions and deceptions stemming from its own confusion and uncertainty. There was the poignant spectacle of Adlai E. Stevenson, the respected Ambassador to the United Nations, telling the world forum that the planes that had bombed Castro's airfields—and missed their targets—were defecting Cuban aircraft, when it was painfully evident that they had come from the United States-built Guatemalan bases. There were the words of Secretary of State Dean Rusk declaring on the morning of the landing that it was a purely Cuban undertaking.

And, as perhaps the strangest counterpoint to the drama that was unfolding in the Cuban marshes, there was the stunned bewilderment of the Cuban Revolutionary Council —the men in whose name the invasion was being carried out—as they learned from a portable radio in a shack at the abandoned airfield of Opa-Locka in Florida where they were being held in friendly custody that their troops had gone ashore.

The backdrop was in accord with the rest of the phantasmagoric operation. A New York press agent was handing out war communiqués, drafted in the style of a great army's headquarters, that were telephoned to him by an exiled Cuban judge, who in turn was receiving them from the CIA. His assistants were signing up news correspondents for the trip to the beachhead that was to start any minute, but they never left the lobbies of Miami hotels. In a private house in Georgetown, ten minutes away from the White House, a small dinner celebration was underway— until the news from the elusive front, relayed by walkie-talkies from the bloody and swampy beach to a United States destroyer laying offshore, turned the party into a mournful wake.

No melodramatic and tragicomical touch was missing in the hours that Operation Pluto lived its short life as the strangest tragedy of errors in which the United States was ever involved.

When it was all over and only the tears, the anger and the recrimination were left, the great question arose of how such a debacle could have occurred.

.   .   .

Looking backward through the telescope of retrospect a year later, the Cuban invasion seems a less implausible catastrophe than it did in the cruel April of 1961. Time, however, has not scaled down the dimension of the fiasco. The Cuban invasion was, as Theodore Draper has remarked, one of those rare events in history—a perfect failure.

It was a failure of mind, of imagination, of common sense—a failure that seems all the more grotesque now as the bright insiders in the Kennedy Administration discuss it with a certain mordant relish. It solved nothing. It won nothing—indeed, perhaps its one redeeming virtue was that it was settled with blessed speed before thousands of brave men rounded up in Cuban jails were slaughtered by a panicky regime.

As a mechanical failure, defeat was built in by the very flimsy pretense on which the invasion was based. For political reasons, and surely not unreasonable ones, President Kennedy felt that overt involvement by the United States was out of the question. Mr. Kennedy did not want what his aides described as a "Hungary in reverse" in which it would seem to the world that Washington was no different from Moscow and would act just as ruthlessly to crush a rebellious neighbor.

From beginning to end, therefore, the pretense was officially maintained that the invaders had the hearty good wishes of the United States, but little else. The seemingly obvious fact that it would be impossible to conceal American complicity—at least in a free society with a free press able to hear the gossip of loquacious Cubans—this fact never seemed to dawn on the operators at the top.

Mr. Kennedy set the ground rules by proscribing any direct United States support. Both the CIA and the Joint Chiefs of Staff, let it be stressed again, accepted this limitation—and acquiesced in every modification aimed at preserving the fiction of a "spontaneous" Cuban invasion.

Yet these modifications had the effect of perhaps fatally impairing the military feasibility of an already risky plan.

The key to the military outcome, in terms of holding a beachhead, was largely control of the air. In order to conceal the United States role, it was agreed that no American pilots would participate, that no planes would fly from either mainland United States or Puerto Rico, and that only obsolete prop-driven planes would be supplied to the invaders. Finally, at the last minute, a second air strike aimed at crippling Castro's air power was canceled. The net effect of these self-imposed restraints was to enable Castro to sink a good part of the invasion armada before the fight had really begun. In the air battles over the Bay of Pigs, the lumbering rebel B-26s had no protection against the faster Castro T-33 trainer jets and Sea Furies. Yet within the limitations of operation, it was impossible to supply the invaders with fighters because the base in Guatemala was beyond fighter range.

As a military failure, the debacle might have been prevented *if* the Joint Chiefs had frankly advised that the self-imposed limitations robbed the venture of a chance to succeed. The Joint Chiefs approved the plan, apparently without looking ahead to the next moves in the chess game based on Castro's capabilities. They did not insist on contingency plans based on the possibility of partial or total failure.

Mechanical failure was also built in by the very assignment to the CIA of a military-political task beyond its competence. With no independent checks operating on the CIA, the Agency quickly became the captive rather than the master of its own operation. Lulled by its easy earlier success in Guatemala, the CIA over-estimated its ability to manipulate history. Step by step, the Agency became infatuated with its own judgment as it plunged deeper into a labyrinth of its own making. Instead of a hard-headed, realistic plan, the Agency opted to gamble.

In February 1960, President Eisenhower gave the

Agency authorization to proceed with the training of an exile force. By early fall, the camps in Guatemala were in full swing and an army of about 500 was in existence. At this point, the CIA thought in terms of a multiple operation involving a series of scattered landings tied in with an underground insurrection. But the Agency had little patience with or knowledge of the Cuban underground, and as time went on more and more reliance was placed on a single, all-or-nothing invasion strike. Indeed the steady expansion of the exile army had the effect of predetermining the way it would be used.

The CIA's misadventures in political policies tied in closely with its military preconceptions. Distrusting the underground, wary of the left-liberal MRP, CIA agents placed their main reliance on aging Cuban politicians of honorable intentions but limited appeal and on an adventurous youngster with conservative leanings who was cast in the role of Guatemala's Castillo Armas. If the invasion had succeeded, the government literally glued together by the CIA would have seemed to all the world like pliant proxies for Washington, in the pattern of Colonel Castillo Armas in Guatemala.

Taken together, the CIA operation was like a car decked out with flashy accessories—a musical horn, a two-way radio and tailfins three feet high—but lacking a motor. The motor could not be installed by outside mechanics— the vital missing part was the participation of the Cuban people in whose name the invasion was fought. From the beginning, there was a preconception that Cubans so loathed Fidel Castro that they would jump to the barricades at the first opportunity and throw the rascal out. But there was more to the Castro revolution than a simple question of communism. Although many of the Cubans in Miami lost because of Castro, hundreds of thousands of Cubans on the island gained. A meaningful insurrection would have to come from within, and the incentive for revolt would have to be stronger than diatribes, no doubt deserved, about a Red specter that meant little to *guajiros* in the hills. Even if American air power had enabled the rebels to hang on a while longer on the beach, it is highly debatable whether there would have been any mass defections from Castro. External invasion was the form of attack that would best enable Castro to rally even wavering supporters. And the fact that the CIA failed to alert the underground neutralized the one internal group that might have altered the outcome.

Thus, the invasion accomplished just the reverse of its objectives. Instead of eliminating Castro, it strengthened his hold on his people and inflated his prestige in the world. Instead of isolating Castroism, it ended up by momentarily isolating the United States. And in place of dramatizing the aggressive intent of Castroite communism, it seemed to dramatize the bullying tactics of the United States.

It was a failure of mechanics and imagination—and it was also a moral failure. The immorality, in our view, did not lie in assisting the genuine democrats who opposed the perversion of the Cuban revolution. Rather, it lay in the way the assistance was rendered, leaving this country with only a few shreds of defense against the charge of violating national, hemisphere and international laws. Yet, in fact, the United States was not willing to go the limit, so that America earned the opprobrium for transgressing without winning any of the benefits.

Some feel that the United States should hew to the strictest letter of nonintervention pledges, withholding either overt or covert help for democrats who are struggling against some odious foreign despot. But adherents of this view must contend with an argument made more than a century ago by John Stuart Mill, the unimpeachable apostle of liberal political philosophy. In his little-known essay, "A Few Words on Non-Intervention," first published in 1859, Mill wrote:

The doctrine of non-intervention, to be a legitimate principle of morality, must be accepted by all governments. The despot must consent to be bound by it as well as the free states. Unless they do, the profession comes to this miserable issue—that the wrong side may help the wrong, but the right must not help the right.

Intervention to enforce non-intervention is always rightful, always moral, if not always prudent. . . . It might not have been right for England (even apart from the question of prudence) to have taken part with Hungary in its noble struggle against Austria, although the Austrian government in Hungary was in some sense a foreign yoke.

But when, the Hungarians having shown themselves likely to prevail in this struggle, the Russian despot intervened, and joining his forces to that of Austria, delivered back the Hungarians, bound hand and foot, to their exasperated oppressors. It would have been an honorable and virtuous act on the part of England to have declared that this should not be; and that if the Russians gave assistance to the wrong side, England would aid the right.

A great deal has changed in the world since 1859, although the Russian despot still binds Hungary hand and foot. In the military sphere, nuclear weapons have given more importance to the question of the prudence of intervention. In world diplomacy, treaties now set some limits on overt intervention.

But in Cuba, would it have been more "moral" if the Russians gave assistance to the wrong side while the United States turned its back on the right? The Cuban people have by now become the victims of what Mill called a "native tyranny upheld by foreign arms." Surely it is dissembling to invoke the phrase "self-determination" in discussing the plight of a people who since Castro took power have never had a chance to cast a vote, despite the most explicit promises that elections would be held. When Raúl Roa sanctimoniously lectures the United States on nonintervention, it is well to remember that his own government refuses to respect the same principle.

We have attempted in our narrative to point out that United States blunders abetted Castro's communization of Cuba. But we cannot accept the argument that the United States "drove" Castro into Khrushchev's arms. Getting the "Maximum Leader" to embrace the Russians was like bribing Don Juan to have a date with Venus.

In the light of the foreign-backed autocracy that Castro has imposed on Cuba, in our view there was nothing immoral about helping the dictator's opponents. But surely prudence should have indicated a quite different method of aid. The United States is party to a series of treaties that proscribe overt intervention into a neighbor's affairs. These were the same treaties cited repeatedly by the State Department in condemning Castro's own attempts to "export" his revolution.

Moreover, in Latin America, the United States has yet to live down the long era when a squadron of Marines and a gunboat were regarded as the indispensable tools of Caribbean diplomacy. Latin Americans are hypersensitive to the question of intervention, and the invasion was an affront to those sensibilities. Remember that in April 1961, Castro was also an unsullied idol to millions of Latin Americans, who saw events in Cuba from a quite different perspective than they were seen in Washington.

For all these reasons, the United States approach to helping the forces of freedom in Cuba ought to have taken a different and more sophisticated form. In the long run, no communist satellite can flourish only 90 miles from the soil of Florida. Not even the euphoria of revolution could forever blind the Cuban people to the simple reality that their island has no future in trading its major crop halfway around the world to a country that has ample sugar stocks of its own. Finally, few people in the world have shown a more persistent willingness to rise up again and again to oppose odious tyrants. Indeed, Mr. Khrushchev, with a peasant's shrewd sense, was smarter in this respect than the CIA. While Moscow has found it useful to provide help for Castro, the Russians have refused to invest their rubles heavily in a country with so uncertain a future and such effervescent leadership.

The invasion was an attempt to hurry history; a slower, surer, more politically defensible course would have been to provide discreet help to the Cuban underground. Such assistance could have been genuinely covert, and even if detected, could have been disclaimed officially by the United States. Castro himself, it should be recalled, smuggled guns from Florida.

Intelligence sources maintain that the underground was not sufficiently "security" conscious, that the Castro police was too efficient, and that it was difficult to smuggle "communicators" with radio equipment into Cuba. Strangely, the CIA was able to overcome the logistic problems of organizing an entire miniature army in Guatemala, but was seemingly unable to manage sneaking a few men, radios and explosives into an island 90 miles from Florida.

In any event, this course was not followed before (or after) the invasion. Three times, within the space of a decade, the United States has managed to undercut its best democratic friends in Cuba. The first time was during the Batista era, when Washington paid little attention to the embattled, and noncommunist, opposition groups; the second time was after the Castro revolution, when clumsy United States policy seemed time and again to play into Castro's hands and to impair the influence of moderates; finally, there was the invasion, in which the United States engendered a sense of betrayal among Cuban democrats in exile and in the underground.

It is not a happy record.

Who, in the end, was responsible for the Cuban calamity? It is difficult to single out villains, because the tragedy sprang from a conspiracy of circumstance. Clearly, the

President of the United States must accept the responsibility for approving the venture and for failing to heed the counsel of his own common sense. And whatever the reason, the President's decision to cancel the second air strike before the invasion was a serious blow to an already risky plan—although those who talk only about this decision often conveniently overlook the other mistakes for which the President bore more limited responsibility.

The men around Mr. Kennedy, too, must share in the blame. These bright and able aides failed to see that the scale of the invasion was too big to conceal United States complicity. Strangely, no effort was made to probe deeper into the Miami operation despite the warnings that American prestige was hinging on the work of men miscast for their role. And the Joint Chiefs, as we have pointed out, also failed to apply the brakes by using some foresight about the capability of an adversary.

In essence, the invasion was rooted in a military miscalculation compounded by political miscalculations that in turn rested on intelligence miscalculations. The burden of the institutional blame falls most heavily on the Agency that conceived and directed the invasion itself. The CIA was simply not equipped to make the military and political decisions thrust upon it. The Agency, in building up the invasion force, became involved in questions of almost metaphysical nicety in trying to conceal its own hand. Obsolete bombers were permitted the invaders—presumably because they could be purchased on the open market—but obsolete aircraft carriers that might have assured air support were withheld because that might give the show away.

In the command strategy, CIA operatives seemed to pass over the points of psychological preparation that are as vital as military preparation. The island itself was not thrown into confusion by preparatory sabotage; and the invaders themselves landed on the beach with the complete confidence that air support would shelter them. Thus the island was not prepared for the invasion—and the invaders were not prepared for the devastating blow to morale that came when Castro's planes dominated the air.

Yet the CIA was not behaving idiotically; it was in many senses responding to the insulated rationalism that infects a sheltered bureaucracy. Indeed, if there is an institutional villain, it is bureaucracy itself—that hulking, stubborn giant that seemingly can only look where it has been and not whither it is tending.

Max Weber, the German sociologist and great natural historian of bureaucracy, would not have been overly surprised by the Cuban invasion. Glance at these attributes that Weber detected in the modern bureaucracy (quoted from H. H. Gerth and C. Wright Mills, translators of *From Max Weber: Essays in Sociology*):

> Under normal conditions, the power position of a fully developed bureaucracy is always overtowering. The "political master" finds himself in the position of the "dilettante" who stands opposite the "expert," facing the trained official who stands within the management of administration. . . .
>
> Every bureaucracy seeks to increase the superiority of the professionally informed by keeping their knowledge and intentions secret. Bureaucratic administration always tends to be an administration of "secret sessions": in so far as it can, it hides its knowledge and action from criticism. . . .
>
> The concept of the "official secret" is the specific invention of bureaucracy, and nothing is so fanatically defended by the bureaucracy as this attitude. . . . In facing a parliament, the bureaucracy, out of a sure power instinct, fights every attempt of the parliament to gain knowledge by means of its own experts or from interest groups. . . .
>
> The absolute monarch is powerless opposite the superior knowledge of the bureaucratic expert—in a certain sense more powerless than any other political head. All the scornful decrees of Frederick the Great concerning the "abolition of serfdom" were derailed,

as it were, in the course of their realization because the official mechanism simply ignored them as the occasional ideas of a dilettante.

Max Weber was propounding the traits of bureaucracy in general; the case of a secret bureaucracy raises special questions even more difficult to answer because the bureaucrat is free from the normal controls of parliamentary inquiry or press comment. Once it has ventured down a blind alley, there is little built into our system that can redirect the secret bureaucracy on a different course.

In the case of the Cuban invasion, a segment of a powerful bureaucracy committed itself to a specific approach to a particular problem. Its money, its prestige, its *esprit de corps* were enrolled in a project the bureaucratic experts adjudged to be sound. The wheels ground forward and the momentum of the bureaucracy seemed to become irreversible as it swept along an entire government behind a plan that rested on the secret knowledge of those who were steering in darkness. One overall lesson of the Cuban invasion is that in the cathedral of bureaucracy an outspoken atheist can perform an essential function.

But there are further "sobering lessons for us all to learn," as the President said on April 20, 1961, when the gall of defeat was bitterest. Surely a few general reflections on the role of the CIA are in order. Palpably, the Agency is in a difficult position. Its officers cannot—or at least should not—engage in public debate in defending the CIA's deeds. Obvious blunders receive sensational headlines; quiet successes go (as they should) unreported. At the higher levels, the Agency is staffed by men of probity and experience, and one can assume that the CIA does a competent job in gathering information.

Yet during the past years, the Agency has tended to assume an activist role in many areas of the world—a tendency that was especially marked during the Eisenhower years when a passive Chief Executive allowed the CIA wide latitude. The result of the near-autonomous status was not always happy. American ambassadors complained that at times the CIA seemed to be running its own foreign policy in the field; reporters exchanged horror stories about what CIA operatives were doing in scattered corners of the world, notably in Southeast Asia. A recurring theme was the tendency of CIA agents, often working with military mission officers, to gravitate to the right and support the most effusive but often least effective anti-communists.

Some of this bias may spring from a selection process that frequently brings into the Agency covert operators whose patriotic zeal does more credit to their hearts than heads. To this can be added the inherited legacy of the CIA from its predecessor agency, the Office of Strategic Services. When World War II was over, most of the abler veterans of the OSS returned to civilian work. But those who found a vocation in the conspirational twilight world of the "black" service tended to stay on, and many later joined the CIA.

The conspiratorial personality at its worst is memorably described by Rebecca West in *The Meaning of Treason:*

> Sweet it is to be not what the next man thinks one, but far more powerful . . . to charm the confidences from the unsuspecting stranger; to put one's finger through the whimsical darkness and touch the fabric of state . . . and to do all this for nobility's sake.
>
> It is the misfortune of our age . . . that the life of the political conspirator offers the man of restricted capacity but imaginative energy greater excitement and satisfaction than he can ever derive from overt activities.

The description snugly fits the bizarre cast that romped around Miami, making and breaking future governments of Cuba. At one point, reportedly, Captain Artime jokingly offered the job of Cuban Sports Commissioner to Mr. Bender who, with equal hilarity, accepted. "They come by plane, by train and by bus," one exile in Miami observed, "and in half an hour everyone knows who they are." Indeed, Mr. Bender's telephone number was casually offered to a reporter in a bar by a Cuban friend within an hour of the newspaperman's arrival in Miami in March 1961.

Power corrupts; secret power intoxicates. Our men in Miami lived beyond the law's reach, spent vast and unaccounted-for funds; posted satisfying cryptic reports to Washington; and savored to the hilt the giddying sense of being the secret makers of history.

This is not a cast of characters to whom one would confidently entrust the most delicate mission of making foreign policy in a controversy close to home but with ramifications around the world. Here, ultimately, rests one of the mainsprings of the Cuban tragedy: the delegation of American prestige into the hands of agents who by normal personnel standards might be adjudged misfits or adventurers.

One painful lesson of the Cuban invasion is that there must be limits to the kind of clandestine ventures that the CIA may sponsor. Put succinctly, the Agency should be an instrument and not an originator of foreign policy, and the scale of its operations ought not to compromise the free institutions the CIA is defending. It is one thing to tailor covert operations to fit within the framework of a free society, and quite another to try and remake the free society to suit the convenience of a secret bureaucracy. In organizing a miniature army recruited from American soil, the CIA was counting on a degree of collaboration for essentially lawless activities that only a monolithic despotism can exact. That it was done so badly suggests that this kind of clandestine operation is not one that Americans can do well. That so many political blunders were made suggests that the founding fathers were wise to delegate the administration of foreign affairs to the Department of State.

A larger lesson involves the total American reaction to

the Cuban revolution. The invasion plan was in some sense a logical extension of prevailing attitudes to a revolutionary situation. Like it or not, Americans must learn to work within the swift currents of change that are sweeping through the world. In terms of simple realism, it is impossible to emulate King Canute and order the waves to recede.

If the CIA plan, based on its Guatemala success, was not an attempt to reverse the wave,—it was clearly carried out in a fashion that implied the tide did not exist. Like so much of the American reaction to the Cuban revolution, the CIA did not take seriously enough the depth and breadth of the change signified by the emergence of Fidel Castro. There was a reluctance to face the fact that Cuba was in rebellion against the past—a past in which American interests were deeply implicated. What happened in Cuba, in its initial phases, was a declaration of independence; if subsequently Castro perverted the revolution, he has not stifled the demand for independence. Indeed, the same impulse that he once encouraged may yet turn against him and bring about his downfall. The Cuban drama has not yet ended, and the island's genuine partisans of freedom will surely still have the last word.

7

U.S.S.R. FOREIGN MINISTRY

THE SOVIET TIE

Growing Cuban-Soviet friendship in 1959 and the first half of 1960 led to the signing of a joint communiqué by Cuban and Soviet officials in June 1960, following a three-week visit to the Soviet Union by a team of seven Cuban economic planners, headed by Antonio Núñez Jiménez, the head of the Instituto Nacional de Reforma Agraria (the National Agrarian Reform Institute). The communiqué stresses the growing friendship between the two countries and outlines a number of agreements strengthening economic, trade, and cultural ties.

The 1960 treaty was the first in a series of major agreements that brought Cuba increasingly into the socialist orbit during the 1960s.

A Cuban republic government economic mission headed by Ambassador A. Núñez Jiménez, director of the National Agrarian Reform Institute, was in the Soviet Union from June 1 to June 19, 1960. Members of the mission were: R. Maldonado Ortega, O. Borrego Díaz, A. Rodríguez Saenz, E. Sitra Mata, J. Paglieri Pérez de Alderete, and E. Méndez Pérez.

During the stay of the Cuban government economic

Reprinted from *Pravda* (June 20, 1960), by permission of *The Current Digest of the Soviet Press.* Translation copyright 1960 by *The Current Digest of the Soviet Press,* published weekly at The Ohio State University by the American Association for the Advancement of Slavic Studies.

mission in the Soviet Union, A. Núñez Jiménez was received by N. S. Khrushchev, Chairman of the U.S.S.R. Council of Ministers, and A. I. Mikoyan, First Vice-Chairman of the U.S.S.R. Council of Ministers, and held negotiations with them. In the course of these negotiations, which proceeded in a spirit of cordiality and complete trust, an exchange of opinions on questions of Soviet-Cuban relations took place.

A. Núñez Jiménez invited N. S. Khrushchev on behalf of Fidel Castro, Prime Minister of the revolutionary government of the Republic of Cuba, to visit Cuba; the invitation was gratefully accepted. The time of N. S. Khrushchev's visit to Cuba will be agreed upon later.

Those who participated on the Soviet side in the talks with the Cuban government economic mission on questions of trade and economic cooperation between Cuba and the U.S.S.R. were: V. N. Novikov, Vice-Chairman of the U.S.S.R. Council of Ministers and Chairman of the U.S.S.R. State Planning Committee; N. S. Patolichev, Minister of Foreign Trade; S. A. Skachkov, Chairman of the U.S.S.R. Council of Ministers' State Committee on Foreign Economic Relations; U.S.S.R. Minister V. P. Zotov, Vice-Chairman of the U.S.S.R. State Planning Committee; M. P. Kuzmin, Deputy Minister of Foreign Trade; P. A. Maletin, Vice-Chairman of the State Committee on Foreign Economic Relations; and Ya. V. Yushin, member of the U.S.S.R. State Planning Committee.

At these talks, questions of expanding the variety and volume of Soviet-Cuban trade in 1960–1961, and questions of U.S.S.R. cooperation in the construction of a number of enterprises for various branches of industry in Cuba and in the development of the electrification of the country on the basis of previously signed agreements on trade and payments and agreements on offers by the Soviet Union of credit and technical aid to Cuba were discussed, as were some other questions of trade and economic cooperation of interest to both sides.

At the request of the revolutionary government of the Republic of Cuba, the Soviet government consented to the delivery of oil and petroleum products from the U.S.S.R., and in connection with this N. S. Patolichev, U.S.S.R. Minister of Foreign Trade, and A. Núñez Jiménez, the head of the mission, signed an appropriate agreement.

During the mission's stay in Moscow, agreements were signed between the U.S.S.R. State Bank and the National Bank of Cuba on a number of accounts for goods deliverable under the agreement on trade and payments and under the agreement on offers by the Soviet Union of credit to Cuba.

A contract was signed for the delivery of 425,000 tons of sugar to the U.S.S.R. in 1960, thereby completely fulfilling the Soviet Union's obligation to buy 1,000,000 tons of Cuban sugar in 1960, as this total is added to purchases made earlier.

The head of the Cuban government economic mission and S. G. Lapin, First Vice-Chairman of the U.S.S.R. Council of Ministers' State Committee on Cultural Ties with Foreign Countries, held talks on questions of cultural relations. These talks were directed toward the development of cultural ties between the Soviet and Cuban peoples, and both sides decided that an agreement on a cultural exchange would be signed.

Negotiations on questions requiring further study by Soviet and Cuban specialists were successfully started and the parties arranged to continue them at the level of the appropriate organizations of both countries.

Both sides expressed complete satisfaction with the results of the negotiations and took note of the fruitful development of trade, economic and cultural relations between the Soviet Union and Cuba. The sides also expressed the conviction that these ties would develop in the future on the basis of existing relations of sincere friendship and mutual understanding between the peoples of both countries.

In the Soviet Union, the Cuban government economic mission became acquainted with the work experience of various organizations and enterprises and visited the Exhibition of Achievements of the U.S.S.R. National Economy, the Likhachev Automobile Plant in Moscow, the First Bearings Plant, the Electric Lamp Plant and other industrial enterprises, the Lenin's Ray Collective Farm outside Moscow, Gorky State Farm No. 2, Moscow State University and the U.S.S.R. Academy of Sciences' Geography Institute. The Cuban government economic mission also was shown a number of cultural institutions in Moscow and Leningrad.

A. Núñez Jiménez, the head of the mission, delivered lectures on the Cuban revolution at the Moscow State University, at the U.S.S.R. Academy of Sciences' Geography Institute and in the House of the Union.

The Cuban government economic mission was met everywhere with hospitality and demonstrations of the warm, friendly feelings of the Soviet people.

8

W. RAYMOND DUNCAN

THE COMMUNIST PARTY
AND MARXISM

✳

Cuba's old and well-established Communist party be-
gan playing an increasingly important role in the
early years of the Castro government. In the process,
the party underwent a number of significant organ-
izational changes *as W. Raymond Duncan outlines in*
the following reading. By 1965 Castro fully asserted
his dominance over party machinery.

Professor Duncan, a political scientist at the State
University of New York, Brockport, is a specialist in
Soviet affairs in Latin America.

Cuba is the first Latin American country in which the
Communist Party, under Castro's direct control, plays a
dominant institutional and organizational role in the political system and in which Castroized Communism is the
central ideological tenet. In terms of Party membership,
relations between old-line pro-Soviet Communists and
Fidelistas have undergone three major organizational
stages—merger of the old Cuban Communist Party (PSP)
with Castro's July 26th Movement into the Integrated

Reprinted from W. Raymond Duncan, "Moscow and Cuban Radical Nationalism" in W. Raymond Duncan (ed.), *Soviet Policy in
Developing Countries,* pp. 116–118, by permission of Xerox College
Publishing. Copyright © by Ginn and Company, a Xerox Company,
1970. All rights reserved.

Revolutionary Organization (ORI) in 1961; replacement of the ORI with the Castro-dominated United Party of the Socialist Revolution (PURS) in 1963; and transformation of the PURS into the Cuban Communist Party (PCC) in 1965, which increasingly strengthened Castro's dominance over the Party machinery.

The final stage of this organizational transition in 1965 left the Party structure tightly under Castro's personalist direction. At that time old-line Communists were given a respectable number of seats on the 100-man Central Committee, but the real decision-making body—the eight-member Politburo—was composed of Castroites. While much can be made about Castro's personalist ascendance over old-line Communists in terms of Moscow-Havana relations (a point examined later in this essay), an objective assessment must emphasize that notwithstanding Party membership, it is a modernizing single-party system that coordinates revolutionary goals with the process of mass mobilization and political integration. This situation represents a remarkable expansion of the State into all walks of Cuban life since Batista's demise, a trend which the Soviets can hardly fail to miss.

More specifically, Party cadres are given heavy responsibility to coordinate Cuba's mass organizations with State production and development plans. In areas of agricultural and industrial expansion, general administration, local governance, mass education, and ideological and political indoctrination, the active organizations include the National Association of Small Farmers (ANAP), the Cuban Workers Organizations (CTC), the Committees for the Defense of the Revolution (CDR), and the Communist Youth Union (UJC). Party cadres are assigned tasks of directing and regulating production plans as well as working to instill a sense of responsibility and revolutionary zeal among the working class. In the words of the official news media of the Central Committee of the Cuban Communist Party, *Granma,* in September 1966:

There are four basic aspects pertaining to the work of the nucleus of militant communists in a work center: first and foremost, the work of production or of service. The nucleus, the militant communists of the work center, must analyze what they can do, what ought to be done, what to do, and what they are doing to promote the work of the center. Secondly, the political, cultural and technical excellence of the communists is to be achieved. This is another sphere of basic activity in the work of the nucleus. Thirdly, the ideological struggle, the development of the Party line, and its discussion and analysis must be undertaken. And fourthly, it is our opinion that a nucleus must also analyze and study the attitudes and status of all personnel with regard to their activity as workers, and as communists.

This organizational activity is the product of Party ideology, which acts as a catalyst in stimulating new attitudes toward work and nation-building.

As the unifying ideology in contemporary Cuban political integration, Marxism-Leninism is taught principally in Revolutionary Training Schools (*Escuelas de Instrucción Revolucionaria*—EIR), established in December 1960 to train militants and cadres. From exposure to Marxism-Leninism in these schools, where "activism," "emulation," "overfulfillment," class struggle, economic determinism, and imperialist exploitation are central themes, leading Castroites are determined to instill in students absolute fidelity to the Revolution, a working class spirit and a revolutionary sense of life—required attitudes to produce total transformation in the traditional Cuban political culture which underlay years of underdevelopment. During its first six years of operation, the EIR trained 144,378 members of the Party and of the Communist Youth Union (UJC). In 1966 approximately 66 per cent of Party trainees were industrial and agricultural workers; 9 per cent, peasants; the balance, teachers, specialized technicians, and university graduates. This intensified training program in Marxism-Leninism, combined with other expanded State activities including increased nationalization of private industry in 1968, mobilization of young people between the ages of 7 and 14 years into the Cuban Pioneers Union (UPC) and establishment of giant work brigades in road, reservoir, and agricultural development, are empirical evidence of Castro's drive to build his own brand of "communism and more communism, real communism."

Despite the uniqueness of Castro's communism, a point examined below, the process of national political integration through a new Party structure and communications network has been locked in closely with a Marxist-Leninist ideology. This contribution of nation-building and communism dramatically expands into Latin America the "world socialist system," so critical in the Soviet power and ideological matrix; indeed it reached almost to the very shores of the leader of the "imperialist" camp. This vital link of Cuba with the "world socialist system" was spelled out clearly by the Soviet Ambassador to Cuba, Aleksandr Alekseyev, at a Cuban ceremony in early November 1966 dedicated to the 49th anniversary of Russia's October Socialist Revolution:

> The achievements of socialism are a magnificent testimonial of its invincibility and vitality. Socialism, on emerging from the limits of a single country, became a world system embracing more than a third of humanity. Socialism triumphed in several countries in Europe, Asia, and it waved its banners over the Western Hemisphere in Cuba. All these facts demonstrate the international significance of the October Revolution and prove the power of socialism and its great force to attract.

It would be inaccurate to underestimate the significance of this ideological bond in Moscow-Havana relations.

9

ANDRÉS SUÁREZ

THE MISSILES ARE REMOVED

*The Soviet Union's decision to place ground-to-air
missiles in Cuba in 1962 brought the United States
and the Soviet Union to the brink of war during the
tense, chilly days of October of that year. When the
Soviets finally backed down and removed the missiles,
there were many effects. Fidel Castro was embittered
over the Soviet action. Complaints appeared in Cuban
newspapers and on Cuban radio concerning the way
the big powers treated a small nation, such as Cuba.
In the end, the crisis and its effect on Cuba's internal
situation led to Castro's full entry into the Soviet
bloc.*

*The missile crisis events are detailed in this read-
ing by Andrés Suárez, who served a time in the ministry of the treasury under Castro before going into
exile. Professor Suárez is on the faculty of the University of Florida.*

At the end of July and the beginning of August [1962]
substantial quantities of arms and Soviet troops began
arriving in Cuba. On August 29, U.S. reconnaissance
planes discovered ground-to-air missile bases in Cuba.
On September 4, Washington accepted the "defensive"
fortification of Cuba—rejecting the invasion that had been

Reprinted from Andrés Suárez, *Cuba: Castroism and Communism,
1959–1966*, pp. 167–171, by permission of The M.I.T. Press, Cambridge, Massachusetts. Copyright © 1967 by The Massachusetts Institute of Technology.

suggested by more impatient circles—and laid down the conditions that would raise "the gravest issues": an organized combat force in Cuba from any Soviet bloc country, Soviet military bases in Cuba, violation of the 1934 treaty relating to Guantánamo, the presence of offensive ground-to-ground missiles or "other significant offensive capacity either in Cuban hands or under Soviet direction or guidance." Three days later the President requested authorization from Congress to call up 150,000 reservists. On September 8, according to Secretary McNamara, the first offensive missiles, as described in Washington, arrived in Cuba. On September 11, the Soviet government replied to the American statement distinguishing between defensive and offensive capability by stating that the arms and "specialists" sent to Cuba would serve "exclusively defensive purposes"; but at the same time it declared that "there is no need for the Soviet Union to set up in any other country (Cuba for instance) the weapons it has for repelling aggression" and warned that "one cannot now attack Cuba and expect that the aggressor will be free from punishment. . . . If this attack is made, this will be the beginning of the unleashing of war." At that time and, indeed until October 14, when, as we know, the first photographs of the launching pads were obtained, Washington was not convinced of the existence of offensive missiles in Cuba even though an attentive reading of the speeches of the Castro brothers would have helped to confirm the suspicions already held by some, among them, the director of the CIA. On September 12, Raúl, for instance, had shouted: "If they shoot, it will be the end of imperialism!" A few days later Fidel warned that "if the imperialists underestimate the solidarity of the Soviet Union, if they make a mistake—and let us hope they do not—if they do not believe, if they do not know, we, for our part, do know just how far that support will go!"

On October 22 President Kennedy initiated the confrontation: he denounced the presence of ballistic missiles on Cuban territory, called upon Khrushchev to remove this threat to world peace under the inspection of the United Nations, ordered a blockade of all shipments of offensive military equipment to Cuba, and warned that any nuclear missile launched from Cuba would be countered by one directed at the Soviet Union. The following day the Soviet government rejected the American President's demands and declared that his insistence on the withdrawal of the military equipment "necessary" for Cuba's "defense" constituted a demand that "of course no state that respects its independence can satisfy." However, instead of making the customary threats, the Soviet government limited itself to announcing that Moscow had instructed its representative in the U.N. Security Council to accuse the United States of endangering peace.

Castro, who had put his country on a war footing at 5:40 in the afternoon of October 22, that is, before President Kennedy made his speech, also responded during the night of October 23. He insisted on Cuba's right to possess all the arms it thought necessary and rejected any attempt at supervision or inspection. He demonstrated his determination in the following words: "It calms us to know that the aggressors will be exterminated. It calms us to know this." Even though he was not especially effusive about the attitude of the Soviets, he did not show any lack of confidence, describing it as "serene . . . exemplary," a "genuine lesson to imperialism, firm, serene, laden with arguments, with correct thinking."

A *Pravda* editorial of October 24 revealed that the Soviet leaders did not contemplate with the same "calmness" the grim fate that would also be that of their own people in the event of a nuclear war. *Pravda* clung almost desperately to the hope of the United Nations. "In the situation that has arisen," it said, "a special responsibility falls on the U.N. . . . The question is whether it will show itself capable of fulfilling the mission to which it has been called . . . or whether there will be reserved for it the fate that

befell the League of Nations. . . . There is no third solution."

On that same date U Thant initiated his mediation. On
October 26 Khrushchev gave orders for the Soviet ships
on their way to Cuba to turn back, and U Thant addressed
a letter to Castro requesting suspension of the work on
the launching pads, which, as aerial observation showed,
had been continuing. On this same day at 1:30 P.M. John
Scali, an American Broadcasting Company correspondent
in Washington, received a telephone call from "a senior
Soviet official" urgently requesting an immediate meeting.
Shortly afterward he heard from the official's own lips the
Soviet proposal for the solution of the crisis: withdrawal
of the missiles under U.N. inspection, a Soviet promise
not to reintroduce them, and a U.S. promise not to invade
Cuba.

At 7:30 P.M. Scali had another interview with the Soviet
official to tell him that the U.S. government saw "real
possibilities" in this offer; at the same hour Kennedy received a telegraphed letter from Khrushchev, the text of
which we do not know but which according to American
sources "indicated a willingness to negotiate." Everything
seemed to be on the road to a solution.

On October 27, however, the scene changed. That day
Castro rejected U Thant's request, insisting again on Cuba's
right to possess all the arms it thought necessary; he warned
that any combat plane that invaded Cuban air space would
be met with "our defensive fire." Following this warning
a U-2 airplane was shot down and others were fired upon.
That the Cubans and not the Soviets were responsible for
the shooting down of the U-2 was later publicly admitted
by Castro in his speech of May 1, 1964. And at 10:17 on
the morning of October 27 a new letter from Khrushchev
came in by broadcast. It set the withdrawal of American
missiles from Turkey as the condition for the withdrawal
of Soviet missiles from Cuba.

Why did Khrushchev thus go back on the much milder

proposal that had been communicated to Scali? Scali's Soviet contact later explained this change of position by saying that his communication reporting the favorable reaction of the American government had arrived in Moscow only after Khrushchev's second, stiffer, letter had already been sent off. Henry Pachter, in his book *Collision Course,* supposes that the stiffer letter, though received later, had been written earlier than that of October 26 which was more in line with the proposal to Scali.

To me, a more logical explanation would seem to be that late on October 26 Khrushchev communicated to Castro his willingness to negotiate on the basis of the proposals to Scali, that Castro's reaction was violently negative, as is reflected in his refusal to accept U Thant's request and in his order to shoot down American planes, and that this caused Khrushchev to change his mind and adopt a stiffer attitude.

Whatever the true reason for Khrushchev's change of attitude in his second letter, President Kennedy decided to disregard it and answer the first in the affirmative. On October 28 at 9:00 A.M., Radio Moscow broadcast a third letter by Khrushchev in which it was made known that the Soviet government had given orders for the missiles placed in Cuba to be dismantled, packed up, and sent back to their place of origin. This ended the first confrontation of the atomic age.

10

CECIL JOHNSON

THE CHINESE TIE

*China viewed Fidel Castro's victory in 1959 with
enthusiasm. Although Castro was not at the time a
Marxist-Leninist, the early Chinese comment on Castro's rise to power indicated that China hoped to forge
solid links with the Cuban leader anyway. Indeed,
the Chinese apparently saw the possibility that Castro
might become "their chief ally in the Latin American
revolutionary movement" as the following excerpt
indicates.*

*Peking's relations with Havana have had their ups
and downs over the years. China's leaders, for example, found it increasingly difficult by the mid-
1960s to deal with Castro. Although they showed
signs of pleasure at Castro's independence from Moscow on frequent occasions, they also soon learned
that his independent attitude included them, too. At
the same time, Peking's abiding interest in Latin
America and what it saw as the area's potential for
revolution played a role in the 1960s in keeping at
least tenuous ties with Havana.*

*In the following passage Cecil Johnson, a specialist
in Chinese affairs, looks at the initial contacts between Havana and Peking before the disagreements
got underway.*

Reprinted from Cecil Johnson, *Communist China and Latin America, 1959–1967* (New York: Columbia University Press, 1970), pp.
129–132, 145–146, by permission of the publisher.

The victory in January, 1959, of Fidel Castro and his July 26 Movement over the discredited Batista regime elicited a prompt and enthusiastic response from the leaders of the Chinese Communist Party. The Chinese, who had been following closely the course of events in Cuba, seemed to perceive almost instantly in the charismatic young Cuban leader the potential for becoming their chief ally in the Latin American revolutionary movement. That he was not a professed "Marxist-Leninist" at the time of his advent to power did not appear to be a major source of concern for the strategists of the CPR. The policy adopted by them in regard to the "historical significance" of the Cuban Revolution reflected more flexibility on their part than China specialists often attribute to them. It is contended that the Chinese here, as elsewhere in the Third World, made revisions in their ideological framework in order to promote their national interests in Latin America.

.   .   .

The Chinese came to regard Fidel Castro as the man best suited to help them implement their strategy for Latin America, although he was not to declare himself a "Marxist-Leninist" for some time. For reasons that I shall disclose below, I am convinced that the Chinese did not think of him as a "Communist" at least until the end of the first stage of the Cuban Revolution. Their attitude toward him was in sharp contrast with their attitude regarding bourgeois nationalist leaders in some Asian and African countries. As Donald Zagoria points out, the Chinese felt that leadership of the national democratic revolution could not be entrusted to them, for they could not be depended on to accomplish fully all the tasks of that revolution. Wang Chia-hsiang, a secretary of the CCP, expressed in *Hung Ch'i* the distrust of the Chinese for such leaders:

> The bourgeoisie which is in power in these countries has played to a certain degree a historically progressive role. . . . It may to a greater or lesser degree go part of the way in *opposing imperialism and*

feudalism. . . . But after all the bourgeoisie is the bourgeoisie. When in power, it does not follow resolute, revolutionary lines; it *oscillates* and *compromises.* Therefore it is out of the question for these countries to pass to socialism, *nor is it possible for them to accomplish the tasks of the national-democratic revolution.* What is more, even the national independence they have achieved will not be secure . . . there may emerge bureaucrat-capitalism, which gangs up with imperialism and feudalism. . . . Thus, *in the final analysis, they cannot escape the control and clutches of imperialism.*

The evidence available suggests that the Chinese trusted Castro to carry the revolution forward. In the case of Cuba, then, they indicated a willingness to allow a non-Communist nationalist leader to perform the "national" and "democratic" tasks of the revolution. To realize fully the significance of their position vis-à-vis Castro's leading the revolution through the extremely crucial first stage of the revolutionary process, one must recall that Mao Tsetung had held in the case of the Chinese Revolution itself that the first stage, the new democratic one, must be under the leadership of the proletariat: "the Chinese democratic republic which we desire to establish now must be a democratic republic under the joint dictatorship of all anti-imperialist and anti-feudal people *led by the proletariat.*" In view of this longstanding insistence by the Chinese on the leadership of the first stage by the proletariat (the Communist Party), why did they make an exception in Castro's case?

Apparently they believed, on the basis of their observation of the strategy used by him in attaining state power, that his road to power was, in many ways, similar to their own. They were undoubtedly impressed by his alleged reliance on the peasantry as the main force of the revolution. Equally impressive to them was the fact that he gained state power via the path of armed struggle. Furthermore, he and his comrades established bases in the countryside, engaged the enemy in guerrilla warfare there, and finally encircled the cities from these bases in the countryside. Once in power, he assumed a militantly "anti-imperialist" posture in regard to the United States, clashing on many occasions with the "number 1 enemy of mankind," U.S. imperialism. Moreover, his domestic reforms such as land reform and nationalization of U.S. properties in Cuba and later those of wealthy Cubans as well must have persuaded the Chinese that he was committed to the implementation of the democratic tasks of the revolution. In the realm of foreign policy, he established political and economic ties with the socialist bloc after a series of incidents led to a rupture of diplomatic and commercial relations with the United States. These and similar acts by the Cuban revolutionaries persuaded the Chinese that the Cuban Revolution was developing in the direction of a socialist revolution, the second stage in the revolutionary process, and hence could be held up by them as a model to be emulated by revolutionaries throughout Latin America.

. . .

Fidel Castro's television speech of December 1, 1961, declaring that he had always been a Marxist-Leninist and that he would remain one as long as he lived, elicited no comment from the Chinese, but they responded most favorably to his Second Declaration of Havana proclaimed on February 4, 1962. The Soviet leaders, on the other hand, reacted rather coolly to the Declaration. The contrasting reactions of the Soviets and the Chinese stemmed from the fact that the dominant theme of the statement was that the road of armed struggle represented the only viable path to power. Castro's view coincided with that of the Chinese rather than with that of the Russians, who were then advocating, whenever possible, that peaceful means be used in the effort to obtain state power.

Hailing the Second Havana Declaration as a "militant banner of unity of the Latin American Peoples," the Chinese contended that there were only two roads available for the Latin Americans: (1) the anti-imperialist and anti-feudal road advocated by the Cubans, and (2) the path of continued submission to "exploitation" by U.S. imperialism. Arguing that "the burden of U.S. imperialism and the reactionary Latin American *latifundia* weighs like two mountains on the masses of these countries," the Chinese concurred in the position expressed in the Declaration that the struggle against U.S. imperialism and feudalism was the current militant task confronting the peoples of Latin America. They also supported the Cuban's statement that: "Today, Latin America is under the control of an imperialism more cruel, more powerful and ruthless than the Spanish colonial empire."

.   .   .

11

ALDO J. BÜNTIG

CHURCH AND STATE

The importance of the Roman Catholic Church declined markedly after Fidel Castro came to power. Although relations between Havana and the Vatican were maintained throughout the 1960s, relations between the government and the church in Cuba grew worse steadily. While church property was left largely untouched, there was a general exodus of churchmen and attendance at church services dropped sharply.

Early in the Castro years the church adopted an attitude of "the silent church," as Aldo J. Büntig, Argentine priest and sociologist, wrote following a visit to Cuba in 1969. This posture continued through the decade, but by the time Father Büntig visited Cuba, there were signs that the church was beginning to emerge from this protective shell and that relations between the church and the government were improving slightly.

The frustrated invasion at the Bay of Pigs apparently strengthened the revolutionary regime. And, as was foreseeable, the reprisals against those responsible and their accomplices—presumed or real—were not long in coming.

As far as the church is concerned, there were mass de-

Reprinted from Aldo J. Büntig, "La Iglesia en Cuba: Hacia una Nueva Frontera," *Revista del CIAS,* Vol. 193 (June 1970), by permission of Centro de Investigación y Acción Social.

tentions of priests, the religious, and lay Catholics. Local
Catholics were closely watched. The Auxiliary Archbishop
of Havana, Monsignor E. Diaz and one of his auxiliaries,
Monsignor Boza Maspidal, were detained for three days in
the Secret Police Building. Cardinal Arteaga, an octo-
genarian, took refuge in the Argentinian embassy.

But in all the ups and downs of this process, May 1,
1961, is a key date. On that day Castro officially declared
Cuba to be a socialist republic. The same day, by a "ukase"
incapable of being appealed, all the private schools of
Cuba were confiscated; of these the majority were Catholic. The Catholic University of Villanueva, described
contemptibly by the regime as "a university of Yankee-
land," shared the same fate.

There was in these gestures an attitude of elemental
consistency with the proclaimed official identification of
Cuba with socialism. Nevertheless, it is easy also to see in
such determination a clear and definitive expression of the
triumph of the regime. In all confrontations out of the
progressive dialectic of the events, a victor emerges. Here,
humanly speaking, the undeniable victor was the revolutionary regime. Then a mass exodus of members of religious orders and priests occurred. Except in cases of
direct deportation—which were not many—they seem
to have suffered from a desperate escape psychosis.

Today, with another perspective, another historical context and another attitude in the face of socialism, it pains
us that all this happened. Nevertheless, the situation of
collective panic that existed—the psychological pressures
and, in some cases, the direct aggressions—adequately explain the events. For the rest, the Mexican and Spanish
experiences were too recent and close to be able to invent
illusions about future events. In fact, in September of that
year, after another civic-religious demonstration for the
Patroness of Cuba, the Auxiliary Bishop of Havana, Boza
Maspidal, was expelled and all religious acts outside
churches were prohibited. The Cuban church was then

left virtually undone and maintained an attitude of "the silent church."

According to trustworthy statistics, not more than 230 diocesan priests and religious priests still remain in Cuba. There were 745 in 1960. The greatest exodus was, without a doubt, that of the nuns, most of whom had taught in the Catholic schools. From 2,225 in 1960, their number was reduced to 191 in 1965, then went to 198 in 1966, and hovered around 200 in 1970. There are currently an insignificant number of non-priest religious.

The revolutionary regime, for its part, continued its accelerated transformation. On December 1, 1961, Fidel Castro identified the system as Marxist-Leninist and defined himself as such. Thus, Marxist-Leninist ideology officially defines the revolutionary process. But it is a Marxism poured into Cuban molds and bearing the unmistakable stamp of Fidel, as we will see later. A Marxism that depends economically on Russia, but that is profoundly in tune with the Maoist line on exporting revolution. Thus, with Che Guevara in full guerrilla action on Bolivian soil and encouraging hopes that would later, in part, be frustrated with his death, Fidel Castro announced at the meeting of the O.L.A.S. (Organization of Latin American Solidarity) (July–August, 1967) the Cuban desire to encourage revolutionary movements in the whole continent. Consistent with that, he could well say upon emotionally announcing the death of Che on October 15, 1967: "Those who believe that his death signals the defeat of his ideas are mistaken."

The internal structure of the revolutionary regime has been strengthened over the years. Its key organizations (Association of Rebel Youth, later the Union of Communist Youth; the "Pioneers" for children under twelve years of age; the Federation of Cuban Women, and so on) were consolidated. The functions of the Committees for the Defense of the Revolution (C.D.R.) were beefed up. One such organization was to be organized on each block in the urbanized zones for the permanent control of its residents and to ward off any suspected anti-revolutionary activity.

The State, for its part, progressively assumed—extensively and intensively—more of the fundamental activities of the country: economic, educative, health, welfare, recreational.

The specific characteristics original to the regime were internally affirmed in January 1968. Fidel Castro then consolidated his position as leader and sole interpreter of the Cuban Revolution after throwing out the Soviet-leaning faction, whose leader, Aníbal Escalante, was condemned to 15 years in prison.

At the beginning of this stage, the conquered church, threatened because of its counterrevolutionary stance and with its full-time personnel decimated, turned in upon itself in a spontaneous mechanism of self-protection and defense. At first, it objectified the image of the silent victim. The hierarchy, the priests, the religious, and the Christians who stayed knew that they had to be prepared for any eventuality. They kept quiet, they lived, they waited.

In fact, the revolutionary regime did not pretend to reproduce the bloody persecution of other countries with Marxist-Leninist ideology. Furthermore, the Government addressed itself to the country on March 19, 1962: "There are hot-headed, extremist, immature elements who want to declare war on religion; who sometimes do not respect the religious feelings of believers. The Revolution does not approve of these tendencies. The Revolution has taken serious measures to break up the conspiracy of the Catholic hierarchy, but it has done nothing to offend a sincere Catholic of the people. On the contrary, it has guaranteed the right of the believers to their worship and to their religion."

Nevertheless, its activity controlled and reduced to the

grounds of the churches and adjacent locales, sacristies and parish houses, the church not only encouraged mechanisms of self-protection, it instinctively fed on the strategy of the ghetto. However understandable that may have been, the risk that this isolation from Cuban society entailed was highly serious. So much the more so when many Catholics and ecclesiastics lived with the illusion that the situation was a temporary one. "This will fall," was the phrase that was repeated, despite the defeat of the Bay of Pigs, as a rumor generating illusory hopes. Today, the great majority admit that the revolutionary phenomenon is irreversible.

In spite of everything, diplomatic relations with the Holy See were never broken. Without a doubt, the great sense of reality and the prophetic intuition of John XXIII were influential in that decision. (Today, the Cuban Ambassador to the Holy See is the dean of his colleagues.)

The Papal Nuncio during the difficult moments, Monsignor Sentos, was relieved of his duties in 1962. Monsignor César O. Zacchi succeeded him as chargé d'affaires. This man has been providential in his lucidity and in the breadth of his vision. Without being naive, he enthusiastically recognizes the positive values of the Revolution and is the key man, in our judgment, in the Church-Government dialogue. The reciprocal friendship and respect that links him with Fidel Castro is well known.

For some—above all, the Cuban exiles—his person is placed in the context of a deplorable diplomatic "careerism." The author of these reflections, however, who was able to speak at length with Monsignor Zacchi and share his table on various occasions, considers such an evaluation totally unjust. As sociologists, we should say that his attitude springs from a dynamic attitude toward the church and from a long and rich experience in contact with socialist regimes.

In reality, whether it is due to the able mediation of Monsignor Zacchi or to the silent attitude of the church, the tensions progressively subsided during the years 1962–

65. Some events demonstrate this. Several bishops were able to participate normally in Vatican Council II. A group of Cuban priests who were studying abroad were permitted to return; even some priests who had been expelled during the period of confrontation (1960–61) were re-admitted. Today, one of them occupies a prominent position in the Cuban hierarchy.

In that way, a modus vivendi was established that allowed the church to heal its wounds and serenely re-establish its old positions in light of the new events that took place, as much inside the revolutionary regime as in the church and after Vatican Council II.

Even one of the figures best known for his combative attitude during the difficult years, Monsignor Pérez Serantes, confided to a foreign religious shortly before his death: "All that is happening to us is providential. . . . We believed more in our schools than in Jesus Christ."

Nevertheless, in this period there were numerous Christians who chose voluntary exile, using the so-called "Freedom Flights." Apparently, the church silently favored exile. What seems to us somewhat incomprehensible had many explanations. Among the explanations most often used we find that of the Marxist orientation of the teaching. Many parents resisted accepting a systematic Marxist indoctrination for their children. (It is important to note that it is in education where Marxist orientation is most systematically in evidence.) In all, the results are not the expected. Fidel Castro thoroughly intuited the problem.

In this situation of reciprocal tolerance, the tensions and suspicions were unexpectedly renewed in 1965. A circumstantial and unexpected event came to poison anew the relations. A young Cuban priest, ordained in Miami, had been admitted to the country, taking advantage of the opening offered by the regime during the previous year. But, incomprehensibly, this young man had accepted—although he had never engaged in a specific act of espionage—a mission of collaboration with the CIA in Cuba. Once the fact was proven, the man was immediately expelled at a decisive time. His function as a priest undoubtedly prevented a more severe sanction.

Then the entrance of all Cuban priests who may have been residing abroad was decisively prohibited. Only some foreigners, especially Canadians, were able to come in, with the necessary precautions. Nevertheless, this event—together with the constant exodus of Catholics—renewed the suspicions and mistrust of the regime toward the church.

In many sectors of the revolutionary regime, the impression that the Catholics, along with believers in general, were potential, if not actual, enemies of the Revolution was ratified. One could not seriously count on them to advance the revolutionary process. Consequently, on all fronts the regime acted in the same way. From then on, Catholics, particularly those defined by their militancy, could not occupy important or strategic positions within the revolutionary structures, much less in the Party.

Thus, a principle of discrimination, objectively painful, especially for young believers who would have liked to participate more actively in a revolutionary process that more and more took on Cuban characteristics, was established. This discrimination was also felt among teachers in secondary schools and universities and in access to careers in the Humanities (Philosophy, Letters, History, etc.) or strategic fields (nuclear physics, a dependent of the FAR: Revolutionary Armed Forces).

In various contacts with professional and university youth throughout the island, we have listened more than once to the rising complaint of this discrimination. In spite of that, the attitude of the regime is consistent: Christians will have to earn with deeds their right to live under the sun. It would be naive to expect the revolutionary regime suddenly to change its attitude, if a systematic sequence of events, and not purely sporadic ones, did not justify such a change.

It is this context of mutual reserve and distrust which explains such events as the condemnation of the Franciscan Loredo (the only priest in prison in Cuba today) for the crime of concealment: an act which has not yet been proved, and which in fact never happened. The sectarianism of certain leaders of the Party at the local level is also explained. There are numerous anecdotes that show how at this level especially one wants to be more Fidel than Fidel, with a rigor that does not admit variations.

Nevertheless, 1968 was a very fruitful year for the People of God in Cuba. It was a year of opening up, searching, development and maturation. These processes were facilitated, thanks to the contacts established by Cuban bishops and priests, in Bogotá and Medellín, with the reality and the experiences of the rest of the churches in Latin America.

The church prepared the "Communiqué" of April 10, 1969, that opened a totally new stage in Church-Cuban Reality relations. In this preparation the lines for a "Today" for the Cuban Church were rather clearly outlined having its own characteristics, just as the regime and the Cuban society in which it is placed have theirs.

.   .   .

12

JAIME SUCHLICKI

TAKING CONTROL
OF THE STUDENTS

The student movement in Cuba gave considerable support to Fidel Castro's struggle against the Batista dictatorship. After all, the students wanted the same thing Castro did: the downfall of Batista. But the student movement was not totally Fidelista, nor were the many Castro supporters among the students ready to follow Castro blindly.

Jaime Suchlicki, a Cuban who teaches at the University of Miami, was active in the student movement. In the following reading Suchlicki shows how Castro little by little took over the movement, ousting many of the leaders who had originally supported him.

The crumbling of Batista's regime on January 1, 1959, marked a turning point in the history of Cuba's student movement. Advocating unity among the revolutionary forces that had fought Batista, and claiming that State and University were now identical, Castro proceeded to seize control of the student movement and the University of Havana, expelling dissident students and professors.

Reprinted from Jaime Suchlicki, "Cuba" in Donald K. Emmerson (ed.), *Students and Politics in Developing Nations,* pp. 315–349, by permission of Praeger Publishers, Inc., New York, and The Pall Mall Press, London. © 1968 by Frederick A. Praeger, Inc.

. . . Of the several groups that had fought Batista, the July 26th Movement had an almost undisputed claim to fill the vacuum left by the dictator. Castro's charisma and his revolutionary prestige made him in the eyes of the Cuban people the logical occupant of Batista's vacant chair; he was the man of the hour, the new messiah. The other insurrectionary organizations lacked the mystique, the widespread support, and the organized cadres of Castro's movement. . . . Castro's bid for power seemed unchallenged.

The *Directorio Revolucionario,* however, had a chance to confront the national hero from a position of strength. Prior to Castro's triumphant arrival in Havana, the *Directorio* underground, led by Faure Chomón, occupied key positions in the city, including the presidential palace and the University of Havana. The students also took large quantities of weapons from a military base near the capital and moved them to the University. "Some *Directorio* leaders, and especially Chomón," *Directorio* activist Jorge Nóbrega said later, "wanted an active role in the new government." Angered because a provisional government had already been formed in Santiago de Cuba without its participation, the *Directorio* demanded that the other insurrectionary organizations be allowed to share power. "The victory belongs to all," emphasized Chomón at the time, "and none should try to impose his will."

As soon as he arrived in Havana, Castro demonstrated his tactical ability by outmaneuvering his young rivals. In his first victory speech, he pleaded with the students' mothers to take their weapons away. "Arms for what?" asked Castro. "The time to fight is over. What we now need is unity." In a televised appearance the next day, he criticized the *Directorio* leaders, particularly Chomón. Portraying the students as ambitious divisionists, he was able to turn public opinion against them. Faced with mounting pressure, the *Directorio* had no choice but to end its defiance and turn over its strongholds to the July 26th Movement.

Castro immediately rewarded those willing to support him. Former *Directorio* leader Major Rolando Cubela was appointed military attaché to the Cuban Embassy in Spain and later Under Secretary of the Interior. José Naranjo, who had worked closely with the July 26th Movement while he was *Directorio* coordinator in the United States in 1958, was appointed Minister of the Interior. Although remaining outside the government in 1959, Chomón decided to support Castro's move to the left and endorsed the ensuing purge of anti-Communist elements within the revolution. Castro rewarded Chomón with an ambassadorship to the Soviet Union in 1960 and later with a cabinet post. A host of minor governmental positions went to less prominent *Directorio* members. Some students, however, were alienated by Castro's accelerating shift leftward throughout 1959; others quietly resumed their studies.

The University of Havana reopened its doors early in 1959. Old student leaders and new ones, emerging out of the insurrectionary struggle, took provisional charge of FEU. They saw as their first task the transformation of an archaic university into an academically modern, politically progressive institution. To that end, students and faculty formed a University Reform Commission. The Commission immediately organized revolutionary tribunals to purge professors, students, and employees who had collaborated with Batista. Once the Alma Mater had been "purified," the Commission drew plans to reform the University's structure and curriculum, and called for student elections in October 1959 to renew FEU's leadership.

The approaching elections prompted the government to intervene. To mobilize and indoctrinate the students, control of FEU was essential. Castro advocated unity among the various student factions and urged the "election" of one candidate by acclamation. In a meeting held with Rolando Cubela and Pedro L. Boitel—the two candidates for President of FEU—and with other students, Castro's brother Raúl backed Cubela.

There were several reasons for this choice. Cubela worked with the government and supported the Castro brothers. Although he was not directly involved in student affairs, he enjoyed great popularity at the University. The Castros may also have seen in Cubela personality weaknesses to be exploited to their own advantage. Finally, the alternative to Cubela, Pedro Boitel, opposed and was opposed by the Communists. To ensure complete control, Raúl placed three unconditional Castro supporters as Cubela's running mates: Major Angel Quevedo, Ricardo Alarcón, and José Rebellón.

As the election approached, government pressure increased. The day before the voting, Fidel asked Boitel to resign his candidacy. The next morning, October 17, 1959, the official government newspaper *Revolución* carried on its front page Castro's exhortation to the students to unite and name the FEU President by acclamation rather than by election. "All students," the paper quoted Fidel, "should proclaim one President unanimously. That will really be a victory for all and not the Pyrrhic triumph of one group." Then Raúl Castro, to leave no doubt where the government's support lay, accompanied Cubela to the University and spoke to the students on Cubela's behalf. In addition, Minister of Education Armando Hart met with the two candidates and asked Boitel to withdraw from the race.

Under these pressures, Boitel called a student assembly and offered not to run. But the students demanded an election. Their insistence should not be interpreted as a rebuke of Fidel, but rather as part of the student political tradition at the University of Havana, where elections had been held every year prior to 1956.

The revolutionary regime enjoyed the support of a great majority of the students and, for that matter, of the Cuban people. The students were largely unaware of the pressures and maneuvers going on behind the scenes. Many, reading

Castro's appeal in the newspapers on the morning of the election and hearing rumors that Boitel had withdrawn his candidacy, expected no elections and stayed away from the polls. With approximately half of the student body voting, Cubela won the election. He received 52 per cent of the votes to Boitel's 48 per cent. There were no other elections until 1962, when José Rebellón was "elected" President of the FEU. He was the sole candidate. Pedro L. Boitel had been sentenced to forty-two years in prison in 1960 for "counterrevolutionary activities."

Cubela's election gave Fidel Castro only partial control of the University. Its autonomy still sheltered the campus from further interference; the University Council could still decide internal matters. Castro's desire to direct the university reform movement became the issue over which State and University clashed. Autonomy was the obstacle, and control the prize.

An early attempt to subvert the University's autonomy occurred simultaneously with the FEU election campaign in 1959. On October 7, Professor Raúl Roa, Minister of Foreign Relations, proposed that the University Council ask the government to appoint several cabinet members to form a joint committee with the deans of the faculties to plan university reform. The Council, pretending that this proposal was not contrary to university autonomy, adopted Roa's proposal and petitioned the government accordingly. The uproar this request produced among teachers and students and the regime's stake in the approaching student elections, however, convinced the government that the time was not yet ripe for such a move. Castro shelved the Council's petition.

A second assault on the University's autonomy occurred in 1960. At a time when the government's power was expanding into every sector of Cuban society, the University still enjoyed relative independence. Arguing that autonomy had special significance when State and University clashed, but was anachronistic when they coincided, Castro's cabinet proposed to participate in planning university reform and sent representatives to explain this view to the student-faculty University Reform Commission established early in 1959. The government demanded a role for the Ministries of Education and Finance and the National Institute of Agrarian Reform in shaping university policy. But this threatened intervention again met with the professors' stern opposition.

The government then made a final attempt, this time through the Student Federation. In a joint declaration issued in April 1960, FEU in Havana and its counterparts at the Universities of Las Villas and Oriente requested the creation of a "Higher Council" composed of government representatives and faculty members and students from the three state colleges to coordinate Cuba's university education. Although opposing this new attempt, the University Council did agree that two students and two faculty members from each university should form a committee—without government representation—to coordinate reform plans.

Despite this concession, the University Council remained in control. But the government-controlled FEU refused to cooperate and the new committee soon died out. Meanwhile, the 1959 University Reform Commission had lapsed into inactivity. The Federation needed an incident to justify the government's complete intervention in university life. This occurred in mid-1960. The crisis was provoked after the University Council refused to approve the actions of several engineering students, led by José Rebellón, who had accused two professors of being "counterrevolutionary"; the students had ejected the professors from the University of Havana, barred them from their classrooms, and—without any legal authority—advertised in the press for replacements. The Council sided with the two professors while FEU, although it apparently had not been formally involved in the "expulsion," supported Rebellón's action.

Verbal attacks and counterattacks followed. Castro's official press began a defamatory campaign against the Council. Charging that "reactionary" professors were attempting to provoke a crisis to damage the revolution, FEU demanded that Council members resign. Several professors resigned. Pro-Castro students occupied university buildings. Finally, on July 15, a group of about fifty professors and the leadership of FEU organized a new revolutionary council. The professors who refused to accept the new junta were expelled, forced to resign, or pensioned off. The government soon sanctioned this university coup and at the request of the new Council passed legislation legalizing its functions. Nearly 80 percent of the old faculty members were replaced with professors favorable to the revolution. The regime dealt a final blow to university autonomy on December 31, 1960, when it created a Higher Council of Universities, patterned after the Higher Council proposed by the students in April and headed by the Minister of Education, to rule the three state universities.

The students' coup converted the autonomous University of Havana into an extension of the state. Credit for this transformation must also be given to Carlos Rafael Rodríguez, one of the PSP's top theoreticians. In March 1960, Rodríguez became Professor of Political Economy at the University. Working together with Héctor Garcini —a law professor and legal adviser to Cuba's President, Osvaldo Dorticós—and with FEU leaders, Rodríguez helped plan the take-over. Minister of Education Armando Hart and two student leaders, Ricardo Alarcón and Isidoro Malmierca, also played key roles in the July crisis.

Rodríguez remained in the background, allowing others to occupy important positions. By the end of 1961, however, he became the University's representative on the Higher Council of Universities and the guiding force behind plans for reform. At the time of the July events, Rodríguez explained to a reporter, the Communists' tactic had been "thorough cooperation with Castro"; the government and the PSP had agreed that non-Communists as well as Communists could teach at the University, but that the institution would have to be dedicated "to the complete service of the revolution." Having fulfilled his mission at the University of Havana, Rodríguez moved in February 1962 to the presidency of the National Institute of Agrarian Reform. In January of that same year the President of the PSP, Juan Marinello, became Rector of the University.

.   .   .

Student opposition to the Castro regime was at first amorphous, but as the tempo of the revolution increased and the Communists gained in strength, it took on definite form. Late in 1959 and throughout 1960, anti-Castro organizations established branches within the University of Havana. One group, known as *Trinchera* (the Trench), soon acquired some prestige and importance. . . .

In February 1960, they demonstrated against Soviet Vice Premier Anastas Mikoyan's visit to Havana. Minutes after Mikoyan had placed a wreath on the statue of José Martí in the city's Central Park, the students attempted a similar ceremony to show their discontent. Police fired shots into the air and arrested twenty students. The following month, while *Trinchera* students marched from the University in support of Luis Conte Agüero, a popular radio and television commentator then waging an anti-Communist campaign, FEU leaders and student militias recently organized by FEU gave them a brutal beating.

Soon after these events, seeking to organize and lead an active struggle against the regime, the *Trinchera* group joined the Revolutionary Recovery Movement (MRR). The MRR's origins dated back to the insurrectionary era, when it was called the Legion of Revolutionary Action. One of its military leaders, Manuel Artime, had fought briefly against Batista in the mountains and had later worked with the revolutionary government. After break-

ing with Castro, he and other rebel army officers organized the MRR. Several student leaders had belonged to
and kept in close contact with Artime's organization;
after the anti-Mikoyan demonstration, they formed the
Revolutionary Student Directorate (*Directorio Revolucionario Estudiantil,* or DRE) of the MRR within the University of Havana and tried to build a student underground.

The activities of the DRE and other anti-Castro groups
interfered with the government's attempts to control the
University. Castro and the controlling group within the
FEU recognized the danger and acted accordingly. The
Federation set up disciplinary tribunals to judge and expel
"counterrevolutionary" students and suspended some of
its own officials who had been involved in the anti-Mikoyan
demonstration. FEU President Cubela called for the expulsion of "the traitors who conspired against the University." Students burned bundles of *Trinchera* and other
anti-Communist propaganda. Dissenters, including DRE
leaders Alberto Müller and Juan Manuel Salvat, were
beaten, threatened, and bodily forced off the campus.
At the same time, Raúl Castro inaugurated a new scholar-
ship plan through his Ministry of Defense to expand opportunities in higher education for the children of workers and peasants. In the process, support for the regime
from these less privileged social sectors naturally increased.
By implementing this plan, the government was able to
swell university enrollments with loyal followers and effectively stifle student opposition.

Denied the shelter of the University, the DRE leaders
had to choose between the underground, imprisonment,
and exile. . . .

Castro had promoted loyal *Fidelistas* as FEU Presidents,
ended university autonomy, purged dissenting students
and professors, and destroyed the DRE. But he still needed
a centralized body that could control Cuba's youth and
ensure their loyalty to his regime. Early in 1960, Castro

established the Association of Young Rebels (AJR). In October 1960, the youth branches of the July 26th Movement, the PSP, and the *Directorio* (the latter still under Chomón's leadership) merged into the new association. Over the next two years, the AJR expanded until it controlled every youth group in Cuba. In the case of the FEU of the University of Havana, however, a special arrangement was made. While it too merged with the AJR, FEU maintained its existing structure and leadership. In 1962, the Association of Young Rebels changed its name to the Union of Young Communists (UJC) and organized a University Bureau in charge of political indoctrination within the University of Havana.

Two reasons can be advanced for the special treatment given FEU. First, the Federation's prestige abroad enabled Castro to influence international student movements and congresses, and provided an ideal vehicle for the penetration of Latin American universities. Second, the dissolution of FEU would have alienated many students who still revered the organization's traditional and past importance.

By 1967, the government felt it unnecessary to preserve the University Bureau of the UJC and the FEU as two distinct organizations within the University. On November 21, 1967, claiming that university students now shared the same ideology, the FEU President explained that there was no need for two parallel organizations and announced the fusion of the FEU and the UJC in a new body, to be called the University Bureau UJC-FEU. This process was repeated at the universities of Las Villas and Oriente.

.   .   .

Another challenge to Castro's authority arose early in 1966. This time it involved a full-fledged conspiracy within the armed forces led by the former President of FEU, Major Rolando Cubela, and involving the exiled MRR leader Manuel Artime. The plotters planned to assassinate Castro, land an expedition under Artime's leadership, and establish a provisional regime with Cubela and Artime sharing top posts. Castro uncovered the conspiracy in March 1966, arrested Cubela and six others, and sentenced them to long prison terms.

The Cubela affair is significant for the disillusionment it revealed in a generation of students hitherto loyal to Castro. Cubela was well known at the University of Havana and had been extremely popular there. During the trial, while the prosecution was requesting the death penalty for Cubela, students at the University demonstrated against the regime and distributed leaflets warning Castro that he would also die if Cubela were executed. The protests reached such a high pitch that Castro had to order the army to occupy the University. Many students were arrested; others were silenced by the threat of imprisonment. Perhaps aware that killing Cubela would only cause more resentment, Castro sent a letter to the prosecutor asking him not to insist on the death penalty. The tribunal obediently sentenced Cubela to twenty-five years in prison.

Today, with the Communist Party of Cuba directing student activities and the universities shorn of their autonomy and geared to socio-economic development, student involvement in politics has reached a low ebb. Fidel unquestionably enjoys student support, but its intensity and extent cannot be accurately determined. Student opposition has been contained primarily by the coercive strength of the Castro regime. Dissident students are periodically purged, strict discipline is imposed by student militias and other repressive forces, and "counterrevolutionaries" are prevented from enrolling in the universities.

Other factors can also be adduced to explain the present lack of student political opposition. First, the regime maintains the students, and for that matter the entire Cuban population, in a state of emergency and mobilization. Castro's propaganda incessantly warns that Cuba is surrounded by powerful enemies, that the future of the revolution is at stake. Students share in the continuous mass mobilizations and spend many weekends cutting sugar cane in the fields. These and other extracurricular activities required by the government exhaust the students' energy and leave little time for politics.

Castro's constant exhortations to the students to participate in these chores, and his criticism of "pampered youths who lack a revolutionary conscience and willingness to work for society" may indicate a decrease in nation-building enthusiasm. Apparently, university students still retain their elitist, middle-class attitude toward manual labor. More than the abstract goal of "working for society," what probably motivates them is ambition and a mixture of fear and hope for the future. Furthermore, the charismatic appeal exerted by Castro has probably eroded over time; today many students may have grown apathetic and immune to the regime's constant revolutionary exhortations.

A second factor is the new orientation of university education in Cuba. In the past, liberal arts studies were emphasized and the universities produced a crop of underemployed intellectuals every year. Today the emphasis is on technical and scientific studies, and the government absorbs almost all university graduates. An assured salaried job and a guaranteed social position after graduation are undoubtedly important disincentives to opposition activity. Since "good behavior" is one of the requisites for government aid, the regime's scholarships have also contributed to political conformism.

This government control over scholarships and future jobs is, however, a double-edged sword. Since the regime makes a considerable investment in educating a student, it will hesitate before stopping his career, especially in its later stages. Students realize and take advantage of their privileged position. In a December 1966 speech at the University of Havana, Castro lashed at government-supported technical students "who think they are doing society a favor." "They know," said Fidel, "that technicians are needed, and that bourgeois technicians are leaving; therefore, they think they are important."

Third, the class composition of the university student body has changed. Although statistics are not available, sons of workers and farmers probably constitute a much larger proportion of the student body today than in the past. The regime has started special preparatory course programs to qualify industrial workers for university study. Also, students from poor families receive priority attention from the government in the granting of scholarships. This assistance naturally tends to build loyalty to the regime among recipient students.

A fourth factor is the establishment of the UJC at the University of Havana. Besides its coercive influence, the UJC offers the students a legitimate channel, in addition to FEU, through which they can operate and voice their discontent directly to the Party.

These factors indicate that anti-Castro student activity of any significance in the future is extremely unlikely.

.　　.　　.

13

RICHARD FERREE SMITH

THE EXILES:
A MASS MIGRATION

*One evidence of the all-embracing nature of Fidel
Castro's revolution is seen in the flow of Cubans from
the island of Cuba to new homes in the United States
and in numerous Latin American lands. This tide,
running at 50,000 a year or more, had yet to abate
by the end of 1971.*

*Most of it by the end of the 1960s was on a legal
basis—by the daily refugee airlifts from Varadero in
Cuba to Miami in Florida. A trickle of refugees were
still coming by other means: a homemade raft, a com-
mandeered fishing boat, a plunge across the barbed
wire around the United States naval base at Guantánamo.*

*Richard Ferree Smith, a member of the board of
the United States Committee for Refugees, wrote
about the refugee flow into the United States at a
time when the airlift was just getting underway. While
his statistics are dated (there were more than 650,000
Cuban exiles in the United States by the end of 1973,
for example), the general currents in his short article
remain valid.*

Reprinted from Richard Ferree Smith, "Refugees," *The Annals*,
367 (September 1966), 48–50, by permission of the author and
The American Academy of Political and Social Science.

Two characteristics set the Cuban refugee problem apart from all other refugee groups. For the first time, the United States became a country of first asylum for a large group of refugees. Secondly, the United States government assumed a great deal of financial responsibility in assisting the Cubans to resettle. The Cuban influx began in 1959, increased in tempo during 1960, and became a flood in 1961–1962 when as many as 2,000 a week reached Miami.

The initial wave of refugees, numbering perhaps 3,000, were Batista supporters, who arrived during the winter of 1959. They were followed shortly by some well-to-do Cubans who quietly left their island with their money. One observer commented that a number of this group are still in Miami, living well and constituting no problem except that they give "the country club set" a false idea of the typical Cuban refugee.

The real refugee began to arrive in 1960. Mainly members of the growing middle class of professional and business people, they were cared for by the Cuban colony in Miami. By December 1960, over 40,000 had arrived. In 1961, additional thousands fled, with the added handicap of being allowed to bring with them only five pesos, one watch, one ring, and the clothes on their backs.

In the first year, Miami officials, with the assistance of voluntary organizations, set up emergency food, clothing, and counseling programs. They soon, however, were swamped by the magnitude of their task, and an appeal was made to Washington for assistance. A federal program, started in 1960, eased the situation. Under President Kennedy, the Department of Health, Education, and Welfare assumed administrative and financial responsibility for the Cubans. An efficient two-pronged program was developed. In Dade County those Cubans who had arrived after January 1, 1959, were eligible for federal-financed, state-administered public assistance at the monthly rate of $100 per family and $60 for an individual. At the peak, some 68,000 Cubans received this assistance. The case load has now been reduced to 13,000 persons. The main thrust, however, was to encourage the Cubans to resettle in other parts of the United States. Four voluntary agencies—National Catholic Welfare Conference (NCWC), Church World Service (CWS), International Rescue Committee (IRC), and United HIAS service—under contracts from the federal government, were responsible for the mechanics of this movement. Together they have since resettled 109,-000 Cubans.

The largest concentration of Cubans outside of southern Florida has been in northern New Jersey and in New York where some 72,000 have settled. Other concentrations have been in Chicago and southern California. Resettled Cubans are eligible for public assistance through federal grants in forty-eight states, but only 5 per cent needed to apply for it; most of these cases have been on a temporary basis. This seems to indicate a rapid economic adjustment.

The migration of 4,000 to 6,000 Cubans a month was abruptly terminated in October 1962, because of the "missile crisis." Up until the late autumn of 1965, a steady but quite small number of Cubans continued to come to Florida in small boats, chancing a dangerous two-day voyage. A few others flew to Mexico or Spain and then proceeded to the United States.

The New Influx

Since December 1, 1965, southern Florida has again been receiving a substantial number of Cubans. In accordance with President Johnson's request, arrangements were made with Cuba to airlift persons from Havana to Miami. At the current rate of four thousand a month, it will take more than sixteen years for this airlift to fly in all the Cubans that have requested to come to the United States. These air flights represent a high degree of efficiency and co-operation between the United States and Cuban officials.

The newly arrived Cubans have two alternatives. One is

to settle in Miami. Here they will be largely dependent on their relatives and friends. The second is that they may be resettled in other parts of the country, sponsored either by relatives or by organizations. It is hoped that they will become independent. About one-third of the newcomers are choosing to stay in Miami because they have relatives there, while the others elect resettlement. These are provided with free accommodations at a well-run, government-financed hostel near the airport, where they wait for completion of arrangements for their resettlement in other parts of the United States.

The Cuban experience has differed radically from other refugee resettlement programs in many ways. One is that most Cubans are not considered resident aliens or even parolees. Instead, the majority remain in the United States on an indefinite voluntary-departure status—a status that is impossible for native Cubans to adjust unless they make a trip to Canada or some other country and then return with a resident-alien visa. This is beyond the reach of most Cubans. It means that the United States now has a growing group of about 285,000 people who are prevented from becoming citizens, unless Congress passes special legislation allowing them to adjust their status. At present this does not seem to be an immediate possibility.

The United States government has made heavy financial commitments to the Cuban group. It has assisted in financing the overburdened school system in Miami, established surplus-food centers, and furnished public assistance to the earlier group of Cubans in Miami, and for any who leave there. It provides the air passage for the Havana-to-Miami trip as well as for those continuing to other parts of the United States. In addition, it covers some of the administrative resettlement costs of the voluntary agencies.

Thus, the Cuban experience has, for the first time, involved the United States government in all phases of a refugee-resettlement program. This participation has been effective due to the imaginative leadership provided by the

Cuban Refugee Assistance Program of the Department of Health, Education, and Welfare.

The heavy concentration of over 100,000 refugees in Miami has created problems. But experience has indicated that Cubans have been an economic asset to Miami. Tension, of course, has existed between the native Miamians and the Cubans; yet the city has become almost bilingual with no overt disturbance. In all, it is a tribute to the restraint and good will of both the Cubans and the Miamians.

14

ORLANDO CASTRO HIDALGO

A DEFECTOR'S TESTIMONY

*Throughout the 1960s, a steady stream of congres-
sional hearings on the Communist threat to the
United States were held in Washington. Many of
these sessions dealt specifically with Cuba. The Senate's Committee on the Judiciary, for example, argued that Cuba's revolutionary activities in Latin
America and through minority groups in the United
States were harmful to the United States.*

*Many of those who testified before the congress-
men were either defectors from the Castro government or refugees who had left the island. One of the
most fascinating testimonies was that of Orlando
Castro Hidalgo, a young Cuban who had served in
his nation's embassy in Paris for two years before
defecting. His testimony is illuminating for its description of the role of political intelligence activities
carried on by the Cuban government. It is also quite
typical of the sort of testimony that North American
congressmen heard during the 1960s.*

*Castro Hidalgo's remarks include reference to a
secret agreement between Cuba and the Soviet Union*

Excerpted from the testimony of Orlando Castro Hidalgo before
the United States Senate Committee on the Judiciary's subcommit-
tee to investigate the administration of the Internal Security Act
and other internal security laws (October 16, 1969), pp. 1423–1429.
In the testimony, Senator James O. Eastland of Mississippi served
as chairman. J. G. Sourwine, the committee's chief counsel, acted
as interrogator. The "Mr. Tarabochia" was Alfonso L. Tarabochia,
the committee's chief investigator, who acted as Castro Hidalgo's
interpreter.

supposedly signed sometime in early 1968. Although there was no other corroboration of such a pact, the agreement, if indeed it did exist, might explain Fidel Castro's support in August 1968 of the Soviet invasion of Czechoslovakia.

SENATOR EASTLAND. Will you please rise, Orlando Castro Hidalgo?

Do you solemnly swear to tell the truth, the whole truth, and nothing but the truth, so help you God?

MR. CASTRO. I do.

MR. SOURWINE. Mr. Castro, will you give us your full name?

MR. CASTRO. My name is Orlando Castro Hidalgo.

MR. SOURWINE. Where were you born?

MR. CASTRO. I was born in La Pedrera, Puerto Padre, Oriente Province, Cuba.

MR. SOURWINE. When were you born?

MR. CASTRO. June 16, 1938.

MR. SOURWINE. What is your marital status?

MR. CASTRO. I am married to Norma Esther Ramos Alonzo. We have two sons, aged 3 and 1.

MR. SOURWINE. What is your address?

MR. CASTRO. At the moment, I have no permanent address and I am not involved in political activity.

MR. SOURWINE. Mr. Castro, would you give us a brief rundown of your activities prior to your joining the General Directorate of Intelligence.

MR. CASTRO. I joined the rebel army of Fidel Castro's 26th of July movement during their campaign against the Batista regime in Cuba in 1957. Following Castro's takeover in Havana in 1959, I was assigned to a detachment of national police under the Ministry of Interior in Havana where I was charged with the responsibility of controlling juvenile delinquency. In 1965, while still in the Ministry of Interior and while attending preuniversity courses, I was recruited into the intelligence service of the General Directorate of Intelligence.

MR. SOURWINE. Were you ever a member of the Cuban Communist Party?

MR. CASTRO. Yes, I joined the Communist Party as a result of my being a DGI Officer.

MR. SOURWINE. You joined the Communist Party because you were an intelligence officer? Would you explain that further please?

MR. CASTRO. Yes. The DGI considers itself as the elite corps of the Cuban Government and has the ambition to take control of all the Cuban Government's foreign affairs. In order to get positions overseas, the DGI is in a better position to compete with other government agencies, particularly Ministry of Foreign Relations, if its officers are members of the PCC. For instance, if the DGI and Ministry of Foreign Relations both have candidates of equal ability for a diplomatic post overseas, the man who is a PCC member is the one who will get the post.

MR. SOURWINE. Then what percentage of DGI officers are also members of the PCC?

MR. CASTRO. I don't know but it is DGI policy not to send any more officers overseas unless they have joined the PCC.

MR. SOURWINE. Is the DGI having any success in its efforts to assert itself as the Cuban Government's prime instrument in foreign affairs?

MR. CASTRO. That's a very difficult question. It's difficult because I don't know how the Ministry of Foreign Relations is going to react to the DGI efforts; however, I do know of some success. Armando López Orta was the chief of the DGI center operating out of the Embassy in France and he told us that the DGI had taken over Prensa Latina and the Institute for Friendship with the Peoples (ICAP).

MR. SOURWINE. When was this?

MR. CASTRO. Lopez was called hurriedly to Havana in the winter of 1968–69 and didn't return to Paris until February 1969. When he talked to the DGI officers after his trip, he told us that the DGI had taken Prensa Latina and ICAP. Our immediate reaction was, "What about the Ministry of Foreign Relations?" He answered, "Not yet."

MR. SOURWINE. Do you mean that Prensa Latina and ICAP are now part of the DGI?

MR. CASTRO. I'm not sure exactly what López meant. I do know that the DGI now nominates and selects officers to work in Prensa Latina and ICAP and, through the control of personnel, controls the organizations.

MR. SOURWINE. In other words, any Prensa Latina representative overseas has the stamp of approval from the DGI.

MR. CASTRO. Yes, and, in addition, many, if not the majority, of Prensa Latina representatives overseas are actually DGI officers and agents under cover.

MR. SOURWINE. That's very interesting but let's return to you. Would you care to comment on why you chose to leave the DGI and Cuban Government service? Your revolutionary credentials speak for themselves, yet you quit the DGI?

MR. CASTRO. Yes, I had to. First of all, let me say many have been the times when I would have gladly given my life for the Cuban revolution. My life was nothing compared to the revolutionary tasks facing the Cuban people. I left high school to fight against Batista. But certain developments in recent years forced me to make the very difficult decision to disassociate myself from that revolution. My major reasons were two. First and foremost, the Cuban revolution has delivered itself as a colony to the Soviet Union since the Soviet invasion of Czechoslovakia and——

MR. SOURWINE. Excuse me. Could you please follow up that point now? What was the relation between the Soviet invasion of Czechoslovakia and increased Soviet influence in Cuba?

MR. CASTRO. Again, I must mention the trip of López back to Havana during the winter of 1968–69. López and all other chiefs of DGI centers were called back to Havana to have explained to them the new relationship with the Soviet Union. That was the principal reason for López's trip. I have prepared a summary in writing of that new Cuban-Soviet relationship which you might like to review.

MR. SOURWINE. Yes, thank you very much.

MR. CASTRO. It discusses some of the points of the new Soviet-Cuban agreement under which the Cuban Government is forced to cede its sovereignty in exchange for Soviet economic aid which the Soviets have applied and withdrawn as it suited their political objectives. I have chosen to write this summary because I, as an intelligence officer stationed in Paris, did not know all the terms of the agreement and I'm not sure exactly how the invasion of Czechoslovakia led to the agreement. I can say that Fidel Castro's endorsement of the Soviet invasion of Czechoslovakia played a critical role in the new agreement but, again, I was not aware of exactly how.

MR. SOURWINE. Mr. Chairman, I should like to introduce Mr. Castro's written comments on the Cuban-Soviet agreement into the record.

MR. CHAIRMAN. It will be accepted.

(The comments referred to follow:)

On his return to Havana in February 1969, Armando López said to us, "We are closer to the Soviets," and then he gave us the general information that Piñeiro had delivered to them, which is as follows: That Cuba has grown closer to the Soviets as a result of the lessening of contraditions between both countries. This is a result of the high-level secret agreements and discussions held with the Soviets (for example, discussions and agreements with the Soviet Vice Minister who visited Cuba at the beginning of 1969).

Agreements on the Part of the Soviets

To increase considerably their technical assistance through which they would send an approximate number of five thousand technicians, who would be distributed in: the Armed Forces, minerology, industrial processing and exploration of mineral deposits, atomic reactor, agriculture, fishing, DGI, etc.

In minerology the Russians are very interested in nickel, petroleum, and iron. At present the one they desire the most is nickel, which they have said is of primary importance to them for spacial conquest.

To increase their shipments of raw materials and agricultural machinery.

To increase the volume of their purchases from Cuba, etc.

Agreements on the Part of the Cubans
(Fidel)

Not to make public pronouncements against the Soviets.

To accept the historic role that the Communist Parties play in the world revolution and especially in Latin America; not to discredit these parties publicly so that there will not be anti-communist and anti-Soviet belief in Latin America, etc.

Armando emphasized that the Cuban-Soviet agreement was considered very important by both sides and very satisfactory at the same time. The Cubans believed that it was going to mean a great leap forward for the Cuban Revolution.

Personally, Armando told me that the situation between Cubans and Soviets had become quite critical and the Soviets had no scruples in rationing shipments of petroleum and other raw materials basic to certain industries. All of this provoked great indignation among Cuban leaders, and Raúl Castro found it necessary to supply 30% of the fuel of the Armed Forces so that the agricultural machinery would not have to stop work.

There were factories that stopped for lack of raw materials, which had been cut off by the Russians (for example, factories for crackers, plastics, etc.) and the workers from these plants were sent to work in the fields. And the pretext given to them was that the plants had been stopped for mechanical difficulties, so that anti-Sovietism would not be created among the working class.

Armando ended his report saying simply: "Now we are closer to the Soviets," and that this was information known to a very limited circle in Cuba; consequently it could not be given to any Cuban personnel, except by the official people, and also that none of it could be known by any of our wives.

MR. CASTRO. You will note in that summary that Fidel Castro has agreed not to make any public pronouncements against the Soviet Union. You can check but I'm sure that Fidel Castro has lived up to his part of the bargain in this respect—he has done nothing but laud the Soviet Union since the time of the invasion of Czechoslovakia and he has not attacked any pro-Soviet Communist Parties in Latin America. The Soviet economic strangulation of Cuba must be very intense for a revolutionary like Fidel Castro to have to accept Soviet direction of Cuba's foreign policy.

MR. SOURWINE. Did the DGI give any specific orders as to behavior and pronouncements to its cadres regarding the Soviet invasion of Czechoslovakia?

MR. CASTRO. In this regard, the DGI ordered all intelligence chiefs abroad to instruct the officers in their respective centers not to discuss the subject widely or deeply with agents under their supervision. They were to wait for Castro's speech and then use the text as the basis for discussion of the invasion of Czechoslovakia. A similar attitude toward the intellectuals, friendly to the Cuban revolution, was to be adopted and once they had Castro's speech in their hands to discuss it fraternally with those intellectuals who had honestly disapproved of the invasion in their confusion about the Czech problem.

MR. SOURWINE. Did that cause any problem and examination of conscience by some of the officers?

MR. CASTRO. Yes, indeed. The uncertainty and horrible weight imposed by this situation was reflected by some officers. I can speak from personal experience and I can say that at the Paris office no officer was able to say anything against the Russian invasion but as they interpreted what they read in the press, I could see in their faces the bitterness and pain that said events usually evoke. There was only one officer who dared to say, "This is going to create a lot of problems and arouse much antipathy against them."

MR. SOURWINE. Did anybody ask you about your feelings?

MR. CASTRO. Yes, the wife of an officer asked me, "What do you think of the invasion?" And I replied, "I am not yet well documented." And she remarked, "Everything seems to condemn the Russians." And, I, in turn, terminated the conversation by saying, "Well, we'll see."

MR. SOURWINE. Very interesting. I note here on your summary that the Soviet Union was to increase its technical assistance to the DGI. Can you elaborate on that, please?

MR. CASTRO. Yes, as a result of the new agreement

with the U.S.S.R. the DGI will have from five to eight Russian advisers and a course for young DGI trainees in Moscow will continue. The 1968 course was to have been the last one because of our fear that the Russians were using the course to recruit agents in the DGI but it was decided to continue the courses as a result of the agreement.

MR. SOURWINE. About how many DGI officers are in these courses?

MR. CASTRO. It is my understanding that about 25 students take the yearly course in Moscow.

MR. SOURWINE. Do you know the identities and functions of the Russian technical advisers to the DGI in Havana?

MR. CASTRO. I don't know their identities as they all use pseudonyms. Also, they work directly with the highest level officers of the DGI and do not associate with the lower and medium-level officers of the DGI. An interesting note on these advisers is that all of them had been thrown out of Cuba in early 1968 because it was feared that they were recruiting their own agents in the DGI to work for the Russians. The head of the DGI, Manuel Piñeiro, known as "Red Beard," caught his Soviet adviser talking with Aníbal Escalante, the well-known leader of the pro-Soviet microfaction, under mysterious circumstances. The Soviet adviser, whom I knew only as "Pedro," acted very guilty and this incident led directly to the removal of the Soviet advisers from the DGI. In spite of our conviction that the Russians were trying to recruit their own agents in the DGI, the so-called advisers were brought back to Cuba as a result of the agreement with the Soviet Union.

MR. SOURWINE. Do you know the identities of the trainees?

MR. CASTRO. Many of them; yes. One of them was "Arturo," the radio operator for Ernesto "Che" Guevara in Bolivia in 1967. "Arturo" told me that he received radio operator and explosives training in the Soviet Union in 1964.

MR. SOURWINE. Mr. Tarabochia, can you tell us who "Arturo" is?

MR. TARABOCHIA. "Arturo" was the pseudonym used by René Martínez Tamayo. He was killed by the Bolivian Armed Forces in combat. He was one of the DGI officers who accompanied Guevara.

MR. SOURWINE. Can you tell us some more about the "microfaction"?

MR. CASTRO. Yes. When the problem of the microfaction developed, the person who took the leadership of the operation regarding the problem was Raúl Castro. He is the one who personally gave the orders to the State Security Department on the measures to adopt against those involved. Once the operation was completed, Fidel Castro made a speech in which he said that the microfaction was a very small group made up of members of the party, the old Communist Party, who were displeased with all the revolutionary measures and laws adopted by the revolution.

MR. SOURWINE. Did this group seek support from the Soviet Union and other Socialist governments?

MR. CASTRO. Yes; not only did they seek support, but there were a number of Russian, Czech, and Polish Embassy officials involved.

MR. SOURWINE. Does that mean that they had been recruited as agents for these Socialist countries?

MR. CASTRO. Yes; the intelligence officers were convinced that they were agents, Soviet agents formerly recruited who knew what the goal to be achieved was. They knew that it was not a very small group of dissident party members who wanted Soviet support such as represented by Fidel publicly but rather a Soviet group already trained to operate as such.

MR. SOURWINE. This is interesting, indeed.

MR. CASTRO. Yes, and there was a joke making the rounds among the officers which went this way. If we lived close to the Soviet border, we would have very serious problems with the Soviet Government. They would have never allowed us to tell what we said about them publicly. But now it appears that, even living far from their borders, we cannot say publicly what we really think of them.

MR. SOURWINE. Do you have other examples of Soviet influence upon, or within, the DGI, or Soviet use of the DGI?

MR. CASTRO. Yes. During Armando López' trip to Havana, he was told that there would be a new emphasis on espionage to acquire scientific and technical information. This requirement could only have been imposed by the Soviet Union because much of the information required was not of benefit to the Cuban revolution.

MR. SOURWINE. Did you see any indication that the DGI was actively working on this type of espionage?

MR. CASTRO. Yes, I handled one agent of the DGI in Paris who was a national of a South American country. I prefer not to reveal his identity publicly because it might lead to this man's life and career being unduly damaged as a result of revealing his name. He was really just playing at the game of being a revolutionary and will probably remove himself from these activities if he hasn't already done so. I was using this man as an intermediary by letter with revolutionaries in his native country. He also was working at a French technical institute. Shortly before I left my post in Paris, I received orders from Havana to stop using the man as an intermediary and start using him to acquire espionage information from the French technical institute. I analyzed the

situation and saw clearly that the information he was
to acquire would not benefit the Cuban revolution
and the order must have come indirectly from the
U.S.S.R. As the man was shortly to return to his native country where he could contribute to the revolution in that country, I was ordered to convince the
man to stay in France to carry out his new tasks.
I refused to do so because the orders were not in the
interest of the Cuban revolution. The man returned
to his native country.

MR. SOURWINE. Do you have any other examples?

MR. CASTRO. A man came to the embassy, presented himself, and said he belonged to the Colombian Communist Party, that he had something important for the government. Since there was a problem with the party, I paid no attention to him. Later
on, I told López, "There was a Colombian here who
claimed to be a member of the party and wanted to
go to Cuba, and I thought I would pay no attention
to him." But, he said no, send a cable to Havana.
The cable was sent to Havana and Havana answered
immediately saying to send him over there. Prior to
the agreement with the Soviet Union, the man would
not have been authorized to travel to Cuba.

MR. SOURWINE. This has been a most interesting
digression. Can we now return to the reasons for your
disassociating yourself from the DGI and Cuban
Government service?

MR. CASTRO. In addition to turning Cuba into a
Soviet tool, I could not support the recent events in
the Cuban revolution. It serves the Russians and the
new elite in Cuba. The sad truth of the Cuban revolution was dramatized for me directly on a trip I
made to Havana and throughout the island in April
1968. I saw that the heroic effort and dedication of
the Cuban people was being wasted by the leaders of
the revolution. I saw that the revolution had become

self-serving and was not helping the economic situation of the average Cuban. I saw an economy floundering, only maintained by the tremendous sacrifice and long hours of labor of the average Cuban who wanted a better life for his children. I saw a people deceived, a people who thought they were working for their sons but were actually serving Soviet economic and foreign policy interests.

MR. SOURWINE. Thank you. Can you tell us the circumstances of your leaving your post in Paris? When did you formally request asylum in the United States?

MR. CASTRO. March 31, 1969, at the American Embassy in Luxembourg after, I with my family, left from Paris.

.   .   .

I I

The Economic Thrust

*

15

ROBIN BLACKBURN

THE ECONOMICS OF THE
CUBAN REVOLUTION

*More attention has been paid to the question of the
Cuban economy under Fidel Castro than to any other
aspect of the revolution. Books, scholarly journals,
magazines, and newspapers in the United States and
elsewhere have carried analyses* ad infinitum *on the
overall question of Cuba's economy.*

*The following selection, written in the late 1960s
by Robin Blackburn, is one of the most succinct analyses of the Cuban economy available in English. He
suggests that the Cuban economy under Castro despite its many problems has shown itself "to be much
more dynamic, and more egalitarian, than that which
it replaced."*

*Blackburn is a lecturer in sociology at the London
School of Economics and a member of the editorial
board of* New Left Review.

The greatest achievement of the Cuban revolution in the
economic field is that Cubans can now make their own
mistakes. Before the revolution there was, in a sense, no
such entity as a "Cuban" economy. Neither the economic

Reprinted from Robin Blackburn, "The Economics of the Cuban
Revolution" in Claudio Veliz (ed.), *Latin America and the Caribbean: A Handbook* (New York: Frederick A. Praeger, 1968), pp.
622–631, by permission of Praeger Publishers, Inc., New York, and
Anthony Blond, Ltd., London.

successes nor the economic failures of the island owed very much to the policy of Cuban governments or to the exertions of Cuban entrepreneurs. Pre-revolutionary Cuba's arrested development and her combination of wealth and poverty were the consequence of international market forces, the trade policy of the United States government and the responses of foreign investors. Emancipation from the economic embrace of the United States has not reduced Cuba's ultimate external dependence but it has decisively enlarged the government's ability to conduct its domestic economic and social policy. Together with an economy of her own Cuba has acquired a host of problems which her novice planners and economists have often aggravated. Those who dislike revolutions would be unwise to count on any lasting comfort from this entirely natural process—making their own mistakes the Cubans are at least more likely to learn from them.

Underdevelopment and Overexploitation

When Fidel Castro overthrew Batista's military regime in January 1959 Cuba was one of the richest underdeveloped countries in the world. With GNP per capita in the mid-1950s at $360 (a conservative estimate) Cuba was comfortably above the world average figure ($200 per capita) and well ahead of Japan ($254 per capita) and Spain ($240 per capita), while most of the population inhabited a world entirely different from that of the miserable peasant masses of India ($72 per capita: an average figure which, like all the others, conceals great inequalities of distribution). Despite this Cuba was essentially *underdeveloped*. Even with a heavy public works program, unemployment in the *tiempo muerto* ("idle season") of August to October 1956 ran at 20 per cent of the labor force. During the sugar harvest of February to April 1957 registered unemployment was still 9 per cent. About a quarter of Cuba's farm land was kept as a reserve in case high sugar prices warranted a sudden increase in production: in 1956 the sugar companies who owned or controlled 188,000 *caballerías*[1] of land cut only 74,000 *caballerías* of cane. Many owned land primarily for prestige reasons. One consequence of this was cattle densities on Cuban soil no greater than those on the dusty plains of Texas. Neglect of the country's natural resources occurred particularly where they could be developed only for the home market. The island's feeble agriculture and fishing industry coexisted with imports of food, drink and tobacco which averaged $168 million in 1955–7, between one-quarter and one-third of the total import bill. Cuba's mineral resources include the world's largest known deposits of nickel, a steel alloy which has enjoyed high prices and rising demand since the beginning of the second world war, yet nickel contributed only 2 per cent to the total value of exports. The United States government which controlled the nickel deposits preferred to hoard them as strategic reserves. Taking into account both unemployed labor and under-utilized resources there is little doubt that Cuba's development potential exceeded that of many countries in the underdeveloped world.

Cuba's comparatively high GNP per capita in the 1950s was a legacy of a prodigious expansion of the sugar industry that had already reached its peak in the mid-1920s. Income per capita in 1922–5 averaged $200 in current prices (perhaps $400 per capita using the prices of the mid-1950s). The intervening period of stagnation was a consequence of the fact that Cuban sugar exports had reached the saturation point of a market which was attracting rival producers. Of course the large economic surplus generated by sugar should have been used to develop other lines of production as well as to improve the productivity of the sugar industry itself. Neither of these things happened. Not only was the size of the sugar crop

[1] One *caballería* is equal to approximately 33 acres.

similar in the 1950s to what it had been thirty years earlier but so were the methods used to produce it. In the words of the 1950 *Report on Cuba* prepared by the IBRD, the Cuban sugar industry "displayed a conspicuous lack of technical progress."

The island's population doubled between the 1920s and the 1950s so that only a rise in sugar prices and an expansion of non-sugar production prevented a rapid fall in living standards. Thus between 1945 and 1958 income per capita declined at an average annual rate of 0.3 per cent. However, in this period the economy was probably faring better than it had from 1925 to 1945. Whereas population rose by 41 per cent between 1925–9 and 1945–9, consumption of rice was estimated to have risen by 22 per cent, of potatoes by 5 per cent, of electricity by 12 per cent and of cement by 5 per cent. Moreover, these long-period comparisons conceal the fact that Cuba's extreme dependence on sugar (consistently 80 per cent of exports) meant that the country's entire economy was at the mercy of the fluctuations of the sugar market. Bad years, like those of the late 1920s and most of the 1930s, were very bad indeed. The statistical information available on many aspects of the Cuban economy is open to question but the near-unanimity of the longer-period figures reliably indicates that increases in consumption rarely exceeded population growth and more usually fell below it.

The immediate explanation of Cuba's prolonged stagnation lay in the failure of those who received the economic surplus to reinvest it in the right places and in sufficient amounts. New capital formation averaged only just over 10 per cent of GNP, one of the lowest rates in the world. Cuba's sharply unequal income distribution, and extremely lenient tax system, would only have been justified in an economic sense if the Cuban rich had ploughed their money back into productive investments. Most of them preferred to spend it in luxury consumption so that more money was spent by Cuban tourists in the United States than was earned by Cuba's own tourist industry and more was spent importing fashionable foreign drinks than was earned by the export of Cuban rum. The fact that a large proportion of the Cuban economy was foreign-owned also contributed greatly to the loss of investable resources. In 1955 U.S. companies owned 40 per cent of raw sugar capacity, 90 per cent of the telephone and electric services and 50 per cent of the public service railways. Direct remittances of profits and interest to the United States totalled $378 million between 1950 and 1958. This drain of capital was indirectly increased by the practice of foreign companies establishing subsidiaries in the island to whom they then sold intermediate products at above market prices. Indeed it was an attempt by the Castro government to end a situation like this in the field of oil-refining which led to the break with the United States.

The lack of enterprise demonstrated by businessmen operating in Cuba must be explained mainly in terms of the economic structure they confronted. The Cuban domestic market was small but a sizeable middle class could, under other circumstances, have provided a spring board for economic development. It was the extreme vulnerability of this market rather than its smallness which deterred the Cuban investor: vulnerability, that is, both to the fluctuations of the sugar market and, even more important, to overwhelming competition from United States manufacturers. The trade treaties by which the United States established a sugar quota for Cuba also gave products from the United States preferential entry to the Cuban market. No Cuban businessman could hope to compete with the giant U.S. corporations and these corporations were given little incentive to establish subsidiary plants on a wide scale in a market which they could penetrate without appreciable transport or tariff costs. A report on investment in Cuba published by a U.S. Government Department in 1955 pointed out:

A high percentage of U.S. investments in manufacturing in Latin America have resulted from tariff or import restrictions which have made local manufacture or assembly practically unavoidable. Cuba has, with exceptions, followed a tariff policy which permits a considerable freedom of choice between local production and importation. It has also largely avoided non-tariff controls, such as import licensing, quota restrictions, and exchange measures.

The foreign subsidiaries which were established were concentrated in the service sector or closely linked to it (telephones, railways, petrol, tires, soft drinks).

Under the circumstances it is not surprising that Cuban investment capital was squandered, exported or left idle. Between 1950 and 1958 some $300 million seems to have been invested by Cubans abroad. The corruption of which government officials were guilty leads one to suspect that this figure understates the true position—in 1955 for example the category "errors and omissions" in the balance of payments accounts was baldly listed as minus $58 million. The island's financial system was invariably highly liquid with banks holding one-third to a half of their assets in cash. The only sector of the economy to experience an investment boom was construction, both public and private. Eighty per cent of this building took place in Havana where casinos, hotels and luxury apartment blocks did little to add to the country's productive resources or to raise the living standards of the mass of the population. A feature of an economy like Cuba's at this period, so intimately linked by trade and investment to that of another country, is that progress in one sector may easily fail to spill over into other sectors. The national character of "the Cuban economy" was revealed by the weakness of inter-sectoral integration—the multiplier effects of new public or private activity usually led to a rise in imports, not to complementary domestic production.

In summary, the features which so drastically retarded the Cuban economy before the revolution formed an intricate system, mutually reinforcing one another. The richness of the country in no way mitigated this system—indeed it was battened on by it. For example public revenue was large enough to finance a scheme of industrial development but such a scheme inevitably foundered on the hopeless corruption of all concerned—politicians, administrators, businessmen. In an economic sense this corruption could have been justified if the personal fortunes it created had been invested in the island. Corruption, as such, does not necessarily stifle economic growth, as the case of Mexico demonstrates, but it will help to do so where there is little incentive for private investment. The Cuban economy was overexploited because the chances of making money out of it greatly exceeded the attractions of reinvesting that money. Monoculture was the consequence rather than the cause of this situation. If in pre-revolutionary Cuba the government and business community had collectively decided to change the state of affairs which they maintained and profited from singly, then perhaps some development could have been achieved. After all, economies initially founded on primary production with a high incidence of foreign investment and dominated by a single market have still been able to reach take-off point (e.g. Australia). Indeed, in some ways Cuba enjoyed a more favored position than do most other underdeveloped countries today. In particular the sugar agreement with the United States came to protect Cuba to some extent from the fluctuation and deterioration of world market prices to which most primary products have been subject. Nevertheless the ability to use this advantage to develop the island's economy as a whole was quite beyond the Cuban élite. This group was mortally infected by the fatalism which history and geography naturally created in the island. Cuba's political and business leaders had never succeeded in assuming responsibility for the country's economic fortunes and even as late as 1958 there seemed to be no pressing reason why they should wish to do so.

The Creation of a Cuban Economy

Fidel Castro's immediate economic program after the revolution combined income expansion, income redistribution and structural change. The existence of unused and underused resources meant that in *economic* terms this program could be remarkably effective. However, it involved very considerable *political* problems which were in the end to halt economic success.

The first policies of the revolutionary government redistributed income from rich to poor and, as part of this, from the cities to the countryside. Castro's Rebel Army had been sustained in its struggle by the small peasantry of the Sierra Maestra so that it is not surprising that the first major act of the revolutionary regime was the Agrarian Reform promulgated in May 1959. This first reform expropriated all private estates above a certain size (in most cases 30 *caballerías*). Where the land had formerly been worked by small peasants on a tenancy or share-cropping basis it was distributed to them in the areas of large-scale cultivation; where estates had been run as a single unit, cooperatives and state farms were formed. The reform involved the abolition of rural rents which had previously run at $74 million a year, and it gave land to over a hundred thousand peasants. In the towns the Rent Reduction Act of March 1959 lowered rents by a minimum of 30 per cent and a maximum of 50 per cent; urban rents had previously amounted to $99 million a year. In both 1959 and 1960 rises in agricultural and industrial wages also added to the expansion of purchasing power. Government expenditure on social services (health, education and housing in particular) raised public expenditure from $390 million in 1959 to $1,321 million in 1961, greatly contributing to the expansion and redistribution of income.

Felipe Pazos, president of the National Bank in 1959 before he emigrated, has estimated that the sum effect of the various measures sponsored by the revolutionary regime in its first two years was to transfer about 15 per cent of the national income from property-owners to wage workers and small peasants. Moreover, in the words of the UN *Economic Survey of Latin America,* 1963: "Under the stimulus of the marked expansion of internal demand, economic activity increased at a rapid rate in 1959 and 1960." The unemployed who had numbered 627,000 in the summer of 1956 had been reduced to 376,000 by the summer of 1960. In the agricultural sector rice production rose from 167,000 tons in 1957 to 306,000 tons in 1960, and tomato production from 44,000 tons to 116,000 tons in the same period.

The counterpart to previously idle land in agriculture was surplus capacity in industry. The UN survey quoted above further reports that: "In 1959 the proportion of utilized capacity was estimated at not more—and often less—than 60 per cent in the following branches of industry: metallurgy and metal transforming, certain chemical products, rubber, textiles, foods and beverages, and certain mining products." In pre-revolutionary Cuba's narrow domestic market restrictive and monopolistic practices had flourished among both employers and unions. The great expansion of employment and demand in the first year or so of the revolution removed the economic rationale for these practices even where they were not directly abolished by the government. In the summer of 1960, before the break with the United States, the revolutionary government had already "intervened" [2] an estimated $200 million of assets for various reasons, including the island's largest textile mill, the ten firms which comprised the so-

[2] "Intervention" is a Cuban legal formula by which the state assumes control, though not ownership, of property.

called "Match Trust," the Telephone Company, the Matanzas Bus Company, four frozen fish companies and
Havana's twenty-four leather supply companies. Some of
these assets were taken over by the government on the
grounds that their owners had acquired them corruptly.
On other occasions companies were taken over because it
was felt that the owners were unsympathetic to the aims
of the revolution. Increasing government control of the
economy, and the threat of greater control, ensured that
industrial production was allowed to meet rising demand
up to the limits of installed capacity. The production of
cotton fabrics rose from 3,000 tons in 1957 to 11,000
tons in 1960. During the same period production of cement
rose from 651,000 tons to 813,000 tons.

The danger of the government's expansionary policy was
that it might stimulate imports rather than domestic production. To forestall this, import quotas and tariffs were
imposed on a wide range of consumer goods. In April
1960 the revolutionary government announced a trade
agreement with the Soviet Union under which Cuba was
to purchase Soviet oil at an estimated annual saving of
$20 million. The international oil companies refused to
allow their Cuban subsidiaries to refine this oil and, as a
result, the refineries were "intervened" by the revolutionary
government. In response the United States government cut
Cuba's sugar quota for 1960 by the outstanding amount.
In the ensuing clash the Cuban government nationalized
all foreign property in Cuba, including U.S. owned assets
worth over $1,000 million, as well as large-scale private
property owned by Cubans. The United States imposed a
complete embargo on trade with Cuba and later persuaded
many other countries to follow suit.

The Time of Troubles

The sugar harvest in 1961 was the second highest in
Cuban history—this was to be the revolution's last un-

equivocal economic success for some time. In the space of a few months Cuba had transformed the structure of ownership and management in all sectors of the economy. Simultaneously it had totally changed both its sources of supply and its export market. Moreover, these upheavals coincided with the loss of many thousands of managers and technicians. At more or less the same time the distinct threat of invasion involved the diversion of national resources to defense. Thus the typical, newly appointed Cuban manager found himself running a newly created enterprise whose machinery came from a country with which Cuba could no longer trade. The new suppliers and customers were many thousands of miles away and employed completely different trading practices. Under the circumstances it is not surprising that the boom of 1959 and 1960 was checked despite the continuing pressure of domestic demand.

The advantages of the new industrial and agricultural structure were only likely to appear in the long run. Indeed, in the short run the new control which Cuba's leaders exercised over the economy led to mistakes which worsened the economy's problems. In this period the economic policy of the government was informed by a diagnosis of the economy which corresponded closely to that which can be found in almost every major study of Cuba before the revolution. Such reports invariably concluded that vigorous government action was needed to diversify agriculture and to foster industrialization on the basis of import-substitution. As implemented in the years 1960–3 this policy led to a number of unfortunate results. Diversification of agriculture led to a severe drop in the sugar harvest just at a time when beet failures in Europe produced high international sugar prices. The expansion of non-sugar agriculture in 1959–61 had, it was thought, brought into production all the previously idle land or, at any rate, those lands which could conveniently be cultivated given existing transport facilities. As a consequence, in the course of 1962–3 about one-third of the area planted to cane was transferred to other uses. The execution of this switch seems to have been carried through with insufficient technical advice so that it was not always the least productive cane lands that were ploughed up nor those most suitable for other crops. Moreover, the expansion of non-sugar agriculture created an acute shortage of labor at the peak of the sugar harvest.

The policy of import-substitution seems to have deserved more limited application than was realized at the time. The production of light consumer products, with high domestic inputs, was certainly wise—for example, the expansion of cigarette production. Indeed one of the remarkable features of the economy during the revolution has been its ability to maintain and even increase the supply of basic goods to the population. Unfortunately even success during this early period was liable to have negative aspects—it tended to breed subjectivism and over-optimism. Available resources were spread over too many new projects with wasteful lengthening of the period of time necessary for completion. Hasty project evaluation led to the purchase of factories requiring too high a proportion of imported raw materials: about sixty complete industrial plants were purchased abroad in 1961 and 1962 alone. Failure to reach absurdly high targets (based on an excess of optimism and a paucity of reliable statistics) threw real planning out of gear.

The visiting French agronomist René Dumont in a series of critical but sympathetic studies of Cuba's economic policy expressed alarm at the "dangerous generosity" of the government, especially to the rural workers. He found the state farms far too big for effective management and feared that overcentralization of the economy was leading to "bureaucratic anarchy."[3] Clearly political as well as economic considerations accounted for some of these features of the Cuban economy. The newly established revo-

[3] See René Dumont, *"Cuba et le socialisme,"* Paris, 1964.

lution was committed to pursue a "generous" policy towards previously neglected sections of the population. Centralized control was unavoidable in a revolution which had, to a large extent, come from "above." However, the difficulties and setbacks of 1962–3 were serious enough to prompt a reorientation of policy and a more realistic assessment of the island's resources. In late 1963 the policy of diversifying at the expense of sugar was replaced by a plan which envisaged the sugar crop rising to some 10 million tons a year by 1970. In March 1964 the Soviet Union agreed to buy, at the very fair price of 6 cents a pound, 2.1 [million] tons of sugar in 1965 rising to 5 million tons by 1970. The Cubans hoped that by the late 1960s the foreign exchange earned from sugar sales could then be used for a genuine diversification of the economy. Until that time the tempo of industrialization would slow down and resources would be concentrated in those sectors which promised a quick return—fishing, cattle-raising and nickel. A second Agrarian Reform in October 1963 brought the remaining middle-sized estates into the public sector, reducing the private (small peasant) sector of agriculture to some 40 per cent of total cultivated area. Since 1963–4 there has been a partial recovery of the economy though most foods are still rationed. By June 1965 the London Economist Intelligence Unit in its *Quarterly Report* on Cuba pointed to a recovery of sugar production:

> The beginnings of mechanization coupled with a strenuous national effort by volunteers from the Premier down, overcame the chronic labor shortage in the cane fields so that production is now at the prerevolutionary level. This has been an impressive performance given the fact that regular employment in the sugar fields is far below the level of the years before 1959, and that American-made mill equipment has been without spare parts from the United States for five years so that improvization has been the rule.

In the industrial sector the 1965 position was summarized

by the *Report* as follows: "Despite the difficulties and the retrenchment, industrial production under the present government is considerably higher than it was under capitalism." Employment in the non-agricultural sector has risen rapidly—more rapidly than the rise in production. By 1963 employment in industry and construction already accounted for a labor force of 420,000 compared with 290,000 in 1956–7.

Taking the revolutionary period as a whole, the most consistently successful aspect of its policies has been the provision of social services. For a large number of Cubans, especially those in rural areas, the government's efforts in this field offset the shortages of those consumer goods and foodstuffs which were formerly imported.

The number of hospital beds in Cuba in 1958 was 22,000: by 1963 the figure had risen to 42,000. Public expenditure on education and culture was $11 per capita in 1958: by 1962 it had risen to $38 per capita. The phenomenal expansion of education included a campaign which, it was claimed, reduced illiteracy to insignificant proportions and at the same time brought the urban volunteer teachers face to face with conditions in the countryside. Technical instruction on a large scale was made available for the first time. The transformation of social and economic priorities led also to a switch from urban to rural construction. A road system was begun in the Sierra Maestra, while the building industry concentrated on factories, schools, clinics and low-cost housing rather than casinos and hotels. Formerly exclusive housing in Havana vacated by the émigrés is now used to house scholarship-holders from the countryside.

The Resilience of the Cuban Economy

What is most puzzling about the performance of the Cuban economy in the post-revolutionary period is that despite Cuban incompetence, and despite the U.S. blockade, it has kept going, nowhere failing to provide a minimum flow of goods and services and increasing this flow in some sectors.[4] Though domestic production has not quite filled the vacuum previously occupied by imported consumer goods it seems as if it might be able to do so in the near future. Aid from the Soviet Union and other communist countries partly explains this. It has been estimated that up to the end of 1964 the Soviet Union alone had extended economic aid worth $300 million to Cuba and had given trade credits worth an equivalent sum. Moreover, the Soviet Union was able to provide goods on a scale and of a type which Cuba could not have obtained elsewhere.

The resilience of the Cuban economy is also to be partially explained in terms of the suppressed productivity of the pre-revolutionary economy. A continuing theme of the post-revolutionary economy has been the mobilization of national resources for the previously neglected internal market. Whereas the "internal market" was almost confined to Havana before the revolution, it now embraces even the most remote mountain settlement. An especially critical feature of the new economy is suggested by Martin Bronfenbrenner. His central contention is that the public "confiscation" of privately owned productive resources in underdeveloped countries would make possible "economic development without sacrifice to the scale of living of the mass of the people . . . by shifting income to developmental investment from capitalists' consumption, from transfer abroad, and from unproductive 'investment' like luxury housing." As we have seen, property income was largely eliminated in Cuba by confiscation.[5] Whereas new capital formation averaged just over 10 per cent of GNP

[4] Visiting experts from both West and East are continually surprised, even perhaps shocked, to discover that Cuban mistakes do not seem to bring upon them proportionate failures.

[5] Where compensation was paid, valuation was usually based on tax declarations in which the owners had invariably attempted to evade taxation by grossly understating the value of their property.

before the revolution it subsequently rose to about 18 per cent in 1961–3. This "Bronfenbrenner effect" will continue to operate in the future when the path of Cuba's development is compared with that of any country where those who receive the national economic surplus do not reinvest it in the national economy.

As Bronfenbrenner takes pains to demonstrate, even quite large-scale government incompetence is unlikely to dissipate the positive advantages of confiscation. In the case of Cuba it can be seen that the effect of expropriation goes beyond a switch of resources towards developmental investment. It forces the economic decision-makers to start formulating, as a matter of urgency, a strategy of development for the economy as a whole. Moreover, they now possess a formidable ability to mobilize the resources of the economy to this end. A revolution tends to make the whole population intensely concerned with economic affairs. At first fatalism is likely to be replaced by voluntarism, but at least the underdevelopment of the economy is henceforth experienced as a challenge rather than as a destiny. For this reason it is not surprising that vigorous debate took place in Cuba in 1963–5 concerning the nature of the new economic order. The experience of 1961–3 had led to the abandonment of over-hasty diversification, to a slower pace of industrialization and to a concentration on directly productive investment. The debate which followed did not focus so much on specific policies of this sort as on the criteria to be used for deciding between rival policies and on the means for implementing them.

In the debate one school of thought, represented mainly by Alberto Mora, the then minister of foreign trade, advocated the use of a market mechanism for pricing policy and project evaluation. Material incentives and a measure of decentralized autonomy were to be used to raise the productivity of the existing labor force. The other tendency, represented primarily by Ernesto Che Guevara, then minister of industry, emphasized the primacy of nonmarket criteria for an underdeveloped country aiming at a socialist form of society. The economy should be run as if it were one great enterprise with firm central budgetary control. Guevara also believed that "moral" or social incentives could play a large part in a post-revolutionary society where identification with the aims of the revolution was widespread. He feared that the use of material incentives would corrode revolutionary consciousness by reawakening the competitive and possessive individualism of a market society. The French economist Charles Bettelheim also intervened in the dispute with the publication of an article in *Cuba socialista*. Though sympathetic to Guevara's proposals he suggested that Cuba did not have the resources (administrators, technicians, statisticians, etc.) to implement effectively the central control which he envisaged. Until Cuba had reached a more advanced stage of development Guevara's ideas would tend to encourage the proliferation of bureaucracy as the absence of real administrative control was illusorily corrected by multiplying regulatory measures. At the Trade Union Congress of August 1966 Fidel Castro came out in favor of Che Guevara's ideas and since then they have informed government policy. At the same time a vigorous campaign against "bureaucracy" has been launched: not only have the ministries and other central organs been severely reduced in size but they have also been stripped of their special powers and privileges. Castro himself constantly tours the countryside with a team of economists and technicians tackling problems at the grass roots level. For the moment this style of leadership helps to minimize the dangers pointed out by Bettelheim though in the long run it may produce problems of its own as it inhibits the development of long-range planning. The full consequences of the economic debate have yet to be worked out but it is already evident that, unlike discussions in the past, this one is being directly related to policy implementation.

Conclusions

In the future Cuba will be facing many of the same problems as all small developing countries. The prospects for sugar are if anything worse than for other primary products. A small internal market provides too narrow a base for industrial exports. Moreover, Cuba will probably have the continued disadvantage of geographical isolation.

In January 1967 the Economist Intelligence Unit arrived at the following balance sheet: "On the credit side of the ledger are the facts that the average Cuban today is better fed, better housed and better educated than he ever was before. On the debit side are the mistakes and misguided experiments that led to an overambitious industrialization plan which had to be scrapped at the cost of millions of dollars of scarce foreign exchange used to buy plant and equipment that now lie idle."

Living standards should rise with investments in fishing and cattle-raising. The expansion of nickel mining should earn valuable foreign exchange. Mechanization should greatly increase the productivity of the sugar industry and the new flow of technicians will raise standards throughout the economy. The scarcity of managerial and administrative skills is likely to remain a more difficult bottleneck to remove. Lastly, the level of future Soviet aid and trade will condition many of the possibilities of the Cuban economy. While it would seem that Cuba's sub-tropical agriculture complements Soviet needs, there will always be the possibility of cheaper alternative suppliers on the world market. Though many of Cuba's economic problems cannot be solved in isolation from those which afflict the developing world as a whole, her new economic system has at least already shown itself to be much more dynamic, and more egalitarian, than that which it replaced.

16

ERNESTO CHE GUEVARA

THE CUBAN ECONOMY

Rural Cuba underwent radical transformation as Premier Fidel Castro expanded state control over land ownership after 1959 and departed from the individual ownership patterns that his early supporters had expected of land reform.

Ernesto Che Guevara, the Argentine-born close associate of Premier Castro, was deeply involved in all phases of Cuba's economic life during the early years of the revolution. In a 1964 article for the respected British quarterly International Affairs, *Guevara explains the transformation from private to public ownership and takes a broad look at the Cuban economy in general, pointing to successes as well as failures in the years of the revolution.*

The article is generally regarded as one of the key documents on the Cuban revolution appearing in the English language.

The Paris Peace Treaty of 1898 and the Platt Amendment of 1901 were the signs under which our new Republic was born. In the first, the settlement of accounts after the war between two Powers led to the withdrawal of Spain and the intervention of the United States. On the island, which had suffered years of cruel struggle, the Cubans were only observers; they had no part in the negotiations.

Reprinted from Ernesto Che Guevara, "The Cuban Economy: Its Past and Its Present Importance," *International Affairs*, 40, 4 (October 1964), 589–598, by permission of the publisher.

The second, the Platt Amendment, established the right of the United States to intervene in Cuba whenever her interests demanded it.

In May 1902 the political-military oppression of the United States was formally ended, but her monopolistic power remained. Cuba became an economic colony of the United States and this remained its main characteristic for half a century.

In a country generally laid waste the imperialists found an interesting phenomenon: a sugar industry in full capitalistic expansion.

The sugar cane has been part of the Cuban picture since the 16th century. It was brought to the island only a few years after the discovery of America; however, the slave system of exploitation kept the cultivation on a subsistence level. Only with the technological innovations which converted the sugar mill into a factory, with the introduction of the railway and the abolition of slavery, did the production of sugar begin to show a considerable growth, and one which assumed extraordinary proportions under Yankee auspices.

The natural advantages of the cultivation of sugar in Cuba are obvious; but the predominant fact is that Cuba was developed as a sugar factory of the United States.

The American banks and capitalists soon controlled the commercial exploitation of sugar and, furthermore, a good share of the industrial output and of the land. In this way, a monopolistic control was established by U.S. interests in all aspects of a sugar production which soon became the predominant factor in our foreign trade, due to the rapidly developing monoproductive characteristics of the country.

Cuba became the sugar producing and exporting country *par excellence,* and if she did not develop even further in this respect, the reason is to be found in the capitalist contradictions which put a limit to a continuous expansion of the Cuban sugar industry, which depended almost entirely on American capital.

The American Government used the quota system on imports of Cuban sugar, not only to protect her own sugar industry, as demanded by her own producers, but also to make possible the unrestricted introduction into our country of American manufactured goods. The preferential treaties of the beginning of the century gave American products imported into Cuba a tariff advantage of 20 per cent over the most favored of the nations with whom Cuba might sign trade agreements. Under these conditions of competition, and in view of the proximity of the United States, it became almost impossible for any foreign country to compete with American manufactured goods.

The U.S. quota system meant stagnation for our sugar production; during the last years the full Cuban productive capacity was rarely utilized to the full; but the preferential treatment given to Cuban sugar by the quota also meant that no other export crops could compete with it on an economic basis.

Consequently, the only two activities of our agriculture were cultivation of sugar cane and the breeding of low-quality cattle on pastures which at the same time served as reserve areas for the sugar plantation owners.

Unemployment became a constant feature of life in rural areas, resulting in the migration of agricultural workers to the cities. But industry did not develop either; only some public service undertakings under Yankee auspices (transportation, communications, electrical energy).

The lack of industry and the great part played by sugar in the economy resulted in the development of a very considerable foreign trade which bore all the characteristic marks of colonialism: primary products to the metropolis, manufactured goods to the colony. The Spanish empire had followed the same pattern, but with less ability.

Other exports were also primary products, but their proportion only reached 20 per cent of Cuba's total exports. They were: tobacco, principally in leaves; coffee—only occasionally, due to the small production; raw copper and manganese; and, during later years, semi-processed nickel.

Such was the picture of the Cuban economy: in effect, a monoproductive country (sugar) with one particular export and import market (the United States), and vitally dependent on its foreign trade.

Under these conditions a *bourgeoisie* dependent on imports came into being and grew to be one of the greatest obstacles to the industrialization of the country. Only in later years did the *bourgeoisie* ally itself with American manufacturing interests, creating industries which used American equipment, raw materials, technology and a cheap native labor force. The profits of those industries went to the country of the monopolies, either to the parent companies or to the American banks which the native capitalists considered the safest place for deposits.

This twisted development brought with it great unemployment, great poverty, great parasitic strata, and the division of the working class through the appearance of a labor aristocracy made up of the workers of the imperialist enterprises, whose wages were much higher than those of the workers who sold their labor to the small native capitalists, and, naturally, infinitely higher than those of the part-time employed and totally unemployed.

The "American way of life" came to our defenseless society through the penetration of the monopolies; and the importation of luxury articles accounted for a great percentage of our trade while the sugar market stagnated and with it the possibility of acquiring precious foreign exchange. The deficit in our balance of payments became yearly greater, consuming the reserves accumulated during the Second World War.

With the exception of the two years 1950 and 1957, during which sugar prices jumped temporarily due to the war in Korea and the tense military situation in the Near East, our terms of trade showed a constant decrease during the decade following 1948. (A sad fate; only war could give the people of Cuba relative well-being.)

In that decade the flow of our exports had become stagnant and the terms of trade downward; the Cuban standard of living was bound to decline if remedial measures were not taken. And they were "taken," chiefly in the shape of budgetary increases for public works and the creation of state credit organizations to encourage private investment in industry.

Never have the state stabilization measures recommended by the Keynesian economists been so openly employed to conceal embezzlement of public funds and the illegal enrichment of politicians and their allies. The national debt rose considerably. Expensive roads and highways were built, as well as tunnels and enormous hotels in Havana and the great towns; but none of these works was of any real economic utility nor did any of them constitute the most appropriate action to be taken in an underdeveloped country.

A number of industries were created which by their characteristics could be divided into two groups: the first consisted of factories of relatively high technical standard, the property of American enterprises which used the few credit resources of a poor and economically very underdeveloped country to increase their foreign assets; the other, of a number of factories with obsolete equipment and uneconomic methods, which from the very beginning required state protection and subsidies. It was this group that served as a means of enrichment for politicians and their capitalistic associates; they made enormous commissions on the purchases of equipment.

In 1958, Cuba had a population of 6.5 m. with a *per capita* income of about $350 (calculating the national income according to capitalist methods); the labor force comprised one third of the total population, and one fourth of it was virtually unemployed.

Although great areas of fertile land were lying waste, and rural labor was far from being fully utilized, imported foodstuffs and textile fibers of agricultural origin amounted to 28 per cent of the country's total imports. Cuba had a coefficient of 0.75 head of cattle per inhabitant, a figure exceeded only by the great cattle-breeding countries. Nevertheless, the exploitation of this great number of cattle was so inefficient that it was necessary to import cattle products.

In 1948, imports amounted to 32 per cent of the national income; 10 years later the figure had risen to 35 per cent. Exports provided 90 per cent of the total income of foreign currencies. On the other hand, profits on foreign capital transferred abroad absorbed up to 9 per cent of the foreign currency income on the trade balance.

Due to the constant deterioration of the terms of trade and the transfer of profits abroad, the Cuban trade balance showed a total deficit of $600 m. for the period 1950–58, the effect of which was to reduce the available foreign currency reserves to $70 m. This reserve represented 10 per cent of the average annual imports during the last three years.

The two main economic problems of the Cuban Revolution during its first months were unemployment and a shortage of foreign currencies. The first was an acute political problem, but the second was more dangerous, given the enormous dependence of Cuba on foreign trade.

The Revolutionary Government's economic policy was directed primarily towards solving these two problems. It is therefore appropriate to make a short analysis of the actions taken and the errors made during the first months.

The Agrarian Reform implied such a profound institutional change that it became immediately possible to make an effort towards the elimination of the obstacles that had prevented the utilization of human and natural resources in the past.

Because of the predominant part which had been played by the *latifundia* in agricultural production, and the enormous size of the sugar cane plantations organized along capitalistic lines, it was relatively easy to convert this type of rural property into state farms and co-operatives of considerable size. Cuba thus avoided the slow-moving development characteristic of other agrarian revolutions: the division of land into a fantastic number of small farms, followed by the grouping of such small units to enable more modern techniques, feasible only on certain levels of production, to be applied.

What was the economic policy followed in agriculture after the transfer of the large estates? As a natural part of this process, rural unemployment disappeared and the main efforts were directed towards self-sufficiency as regards the greater part of foodstuffs and raw materials of vegetable or animal origin. The trend in the development of agriculture can be defined in one word: diversification. In its agricultural policy the Revolution represented the antithesis of what had existed during the years of dependence on imperialism and of exploitation by the land-owning class. Diversification versus monoculture; full employment versus idle hands; these were the major transformations in the rural areas during those years.

It is well known that, nevertheless, serious agricultural problems immediately arose, and these have only begun to be solved during recent months. How can we explain the relative scarcity of some agricultural products, and particularly the decline in sugar production, when the Revolution began by incorporating all the idle rural productive factors in the agricultural process, thus greatly increasing its potentialities? We believe we committed two principal errors.

Our first error was the way in which we carried out diversification. Instead of embarking on diversification by degrees we attempted too much at once. The sugar cane areas were reduced and the land thus made available was used for cultivation of new crops. But this meant a general decline in agricultural production. The entire economic history of Cuba had demonstrated that no other agricultural activity would give such returns as those yielded by the cultivation of the sugar cane. At the outset of the Revolution many of us were not aware of this basic economic fact, because a fetishistic idea connected sugar with our dependence on imperialism and with the misery in the rural areas, without analyzing the real causes: the relation to the uneven trade balance.

Unfortunately, whatever measures are taken in agriculture, the results do not become apparent until months, sometimes years, afterwards. This is particularly true as regards sugar cane production. That is why the reduction of the sugar cane areas made between the middle of 1960 and the end of 1961—and, let us not forget the two years of drought—has resulted in lower sugar cane harvests during 1962 and 1963.

Diversification on a smaller scale could have been achieved by utilizing the reserves of productivity existing in the resources assigned to the various traditional types of cultivation. This would have permitted the partial use of idle resources for a small number of new products. At the same time, we could have taken measures to introduce more modern and complex techniques requiring a longer period of assimilation. After these new technical methods had begun to bear fruit in the traditional fields, particularly in those related to exports, it would have been practicable to transfer resources from these fields to the areas of diversification without prejudice to the former.

The second mistake made was, in our opinion, that of dispersing our resources over a great number of agricultural products, all in the name of diversification. This dispersal was made, not only on a national scale but also within each of the agricultural productive units.

The change made from monoculture to the development of a great number of agricultural products implied a drastic transformation within relatively few months. Only a very solid productive organization could have resisted such rapid change. In an underdeveloped country, in particular, the structure of agriculture remains very inflexible and its organization rests on extremely weak and subjective foundations. Consequently, the change in the agricultural structure and diversification, coming simultaneously, produced a greater weakness in the agricultural productive organization.

Now that the years have passed, conditions have changed and the pressure of the class struggle has lessened, and so it is fairly easy to make a critical assessment of the analysis made during those months and years. It is for history to judge how much was our fault and how much was caused by circumstances.

At any rate, hard facts have shown us both the errors and the road towards their correction, which is the road the Cuban Revolution is at present following in the agricultural sector. Sugar now has first priority in the distribution of resources, and in the assessment of those factors which contribute to the most efficient use of those resources. The other sectors of agricultural production and their development have not been abandoned, but adequate methods have been sought to prevent a dispersal of resources of which the effect would be to hinder the obtaining of maximum yields.

In the industrial sector our policy is directed towards the same two objectives: the solution of the two problems of unemployment and scarcity of foreign exchange. The Agrarian Reform, the revolutionary measures as regards redistribution of income, and the increase in employment observed in other sectors of the economy and in industry itself, extended the national market considerably. This market was further strengthened by the establishment of a government monopoly of foreign trade, and by the introduction of a protectionist policy as regards the importation of goods which, without any disadvantage to the national consumer, can be manufactured in Cuba.

What industry there was in Cuba only worked to a fraction of its capacity, due to the competition of American goods, many of which entered the country practically duty free, and also to the fact that national demand was limited by the concentration among the parasitic classes of a large part of the national income.

Immediately after the Revolution the explosive increase of demand permitted a higher degree of utilization of our industrial capacity, and nationally-produced articles accounted for a greater share of total consumption. This industrial growth, however, aggravated the problem of the balance of payments, for an extraordinarily high percentage of the costs of our industry—which was nationally integrated only to a small degree—was represented by the importation of fuel, raw materials, spare parts and equipment for replacement.

The problem of the balance of payments, and that of urban unemployment, made us follow a policy aimed at an industrial development which would eliminate these defects. Here, too, we both achieved successes and committed errors. Already during the first years of the Revolution we ensured the country's supply of electric power, acquiring from the socialist countries new plant-capacities which will meet our needs until 1970. New industries have been created, and many small and medium-sized production units in the mechanical field have been re-equipped. One result of these measures was that our industry could be kept running when the American embargo on spare parts hit us hardest. Some textile factories, some extractive and chemical installations and a new and vigorous search for fresh mineral resources have all contributed to successes in the more efficient use of native natural resources and raw materials.

I have spoken of certain achievements in the industrial field during the first years, but it is only just that I should also mention the errors made. Fundamentally, these were caused by a lack of precise understanding of the technological and economic elements necessary in the new industries installed during those years. Influenced by existing unemployment and by the pressure exerted by the problems in our foreign trade, we acquired a great number of factories with the dual purpose of substituting imports and providing employment for an appreciable number of urban workers. Later we found that in many of these plants the technical efficiency was insufficient when measured by international standards, and that the net result of the substitution of imports was very limited, because the necessary raw materials were not nationally produced.

We have rectified this type of error in the industrial sector. In planning new industries we are evaluating the maximum advantages which they may bring to our foreign trade through use of the most modern technical equipment at present obtainable, taking into consideration the particular conditions of our country.

So far the industrial development achieved can be described as satisfactory, if we take into account the problems caused by the American blockade and the radical changes which have occurred in only three years as regards our foreign sources of supply. Last year our sugar production fell from 4.8 m. metric tons to 3.8 m., but this was offset by an increase, in general terms, of 6 per cent in the rest of industry. This year, 1964, given the greater strength of our internal productive organization and our greater experience in commercial relations with our new sources of supply, the industrial advance should be still greater.

The transformations so far made in the Cuban economy have produced great changes in the structure of our foreign trade. As regards exports the changes have been limited chiefly to the opening up of new markets, with sugar continuing to be the main export article. On the other hand, the composition of our imports has changed completely during these five years. Imports of consumer goods, particularly durables, have decreased substantially in favor of capital equipment, while a small decrease can be noted in the import of intermediate goods. The policy of substitution of imports is showing slow but tangible results.

The economic policy of the Revolution having attained a certain integral strength, it is clear that imports of durable consumer goods will once more increase, to satisfy the growing needs of modern life. The plans being made for the future provide for both an absolute and a relative increase in the importation of these articles, taking into account the social changes which have occurred. It will be unnecessary, for example, to import Cadillacs and other luxury cars, which in former years were paid for to a great extent with the profits derived from the labor of the Cuban sugar worker.

This is only one aspect of the problems connected with the future development of Cuba which are at present being studied. The policy we shall follow in years to come will largely depend on the flexibility of our foreign trade, and on the extent to which it will permit us to take full advantage of opportunities which may present themselves. We expect the Cuban economy to develop along three principal lines between now and 1970.

Sugar will continue to be our main earner of foreign exchange. Future development implies an increase of 50 per cent in present productive capacity. Simultaneously a qualitative advance will take place in the sugar sector, consisting of a substantial increase in the yield per unit of land under cultivation, and an improvement in technology and equipment. That improvement will tend to make up for the ground lost through inefficiency during the last 10–15 years. During that period the complete lack of expansion of our market led to technological stagnation.

With the new possibilities which have opened up in the socialist countries, the panorama is changing rapidly.

One of the main bases for the development of our sugar industry, as well as for the development of the country as a whole, is the agreement recently signed between the U.S.S.R. and Cuba. This guarantees to us future sales of enormous quantities of sugar at prices much above the average of those paid in the American and world markets during the last 20 years. Apart from this and other favorable economic implications, the Agreement signed with the U.S.S.R. is of political importance inasmuch as it provides an example of the relationship that can exist between an underdeveloped and a developed country when both belong to the socialist camp, in contrast to the commercial relations between the underdeveloped countries exporting raw materials and the industrialized capitalist countries—in which the permanent tendency is to make the balance of trade unfavorable to the poor nations.

The second line of industrial development will be nickel. The deposits in north-eastern Cuba offer great possibilities for making this part of the island the future center of the metallurgical industry. The capacity of the nickel smelting works will be increased, making Cuba the second or third largest producer in the world of this strategic metal.

The third line of this future development will be the cattle industry. The large number of cattle, great indeed in proportion to the size of the population, offers rich possibilities for the future. We estimate that within about 10 years our cattle industry will be equaled in importance only by the sugar industry.

As I have indicated, the role played by foreign trade in the Cuban economy will continue to be of basic importance, but there will be a qualitative change in its future development. None of the three principal lines of development will imply an effort to substitute imports, with the exception of the cattle industry, during the first years. After these first years the character of our new economic development will be fully reflected in our exports, and although the policy of substitution of imports will not be abandoned, it will be balanced by exports. For the decade following 1970 we are planning a more accelerated process of substitution of imports. This can only be achieved on the basis of an industrialization program of great scope. We shall create the necessary conditions for such a program, making full use of the opportunities offered to an underdeveloped economy by our external trade.

Has the indisputable political importance in the world achieved by Cuba any economic counterpart? If so, should that importance lead to the contemplation of more serious economic relations with other countries, materializing in trade? In such an event, how would we build up this trade which has been greatly reduced due to the American blockade?

In considering these questions I leave aside reasons of a utilitarian nature which might lead me to make an apology for international trade, for it is evident that Cuba is interested in an active, regular and sustained interchange of trade with all countries of the world. What I am trying to do is to present an exact picture of the present situation. The American Government is obsessed by Cuba, and not only because of its abnormal colonialist mentality. There is something more. Cuba represents, in the first place, a clear example of the failure of the American policy of aggression on the very doorstep of the continent. Further, Cuba provides an example for the future socialist countries of Latin America and so an unmistakable warning of the inevitable reduction of the field of action of U.S. finance capital.

American imperialism is weaker than it seems; it is a giant with feet of clay. Although its present great potentialities are not seriously affected by violent internal class struggles leading to the destruction of the capitalist system, as foreseen by Marx, those potentialities are fundamentally based on a monopolistic extra-territorial power exercised by means of an unequal interchange of goods and by the political subjection of extensive territories. On these fall the full weight of the contradictions.

As the dependent countries of America and other regions of the world cast off the monopolistic chains, and establish more equitable systems and more just relations with all the countries of the world, the heavy contributions made by them to the living standard of the imperialist Powers will cease, and of all the capitalist countries the United States will then be the most seriously affected. This will not be the only outcome of an historical process; displaced finance capital will be forced to seek new horizons to make good its losses and, in this struggle, the most wounded, the most powerful and the most aggressive of all the capitalist Powers, the United States, will employ her full strength in a ruthless competition with the others, adopting, perhaps, unexpected methods of violence in her dealings with her "allies" of today.

Thus the existence of Cuba represents not only the hope of a better future for the peoples of America but also the prospect of a dangerous future for the seemingly unshakable monopolistic structure of the United States. The American attempt to strangle Cuba implies a desire to stop history; but if, in spite of all kinds of aggression, the Cuban state remains safe, its economy becoming increasingly strong and its foreign trade more important, then the failure of this policy will be complete and the move towards peaceful co-existence will become more rapid.

New relations based on mutual interests will be established. These will benefit the socialist bloc and the countries now liberating themselves. Yet the great capitalist countries, including England, facing serious economic problems and limitations of markets, could have the opportunity to lead this new interchange, as France has already tried to do to a certain extent.

To such countries the Cuban market, although not unimportant may not be worth a break with the United States, but Latin America as a whole is a gigantic potential market of 200 million people. It is useless to close one's eyes to the reality that this continent will continue its struggle for liberation, and that it will ultimately, if gradually, establish either groups or a bloc of countries free of imperialism and with internal systems related to socialism. Therefore, the capitalist countries should decide whether it is worthwhile to use Cuba as a means of testing a situation which may prove to be of great advantage even if it represents a danger to the future of the capitalistic system.

The alternatives are clear, and in our opinion they imply the need for serious decisions: one can be an ally of the United States until the collapse of a policy of oppression and aggression and then fall victim to the same internal and external problems as will afflict the United States when that moment arrives; or one can break that alliance, which in any case is already beginning to crack in relation to Cuba, in order to help—by means of trade—the rapid development of the countries which are liberating themselves, thus not only giving greater hopes to those peoples still fighting for liberation, but simultaneously creating conditions which will bring closer the disappearance of capitalism.

We think this is the great dilemma now facing countries like England. Cuba is part of that dilemma in her role as a catalyzing agent of the revolutionary ideas of a continent, and as the pioneer of these ideas.

It is not for us to say what final decision should be taken. We simply state the alternatives.

17

ROBERT S. WALTERS

SOVIET ECONOMIC AID
TO CUBA

*Soviet financial and technical assistance began flow-
ing to Cuba in 1960, presaging the heavy dependence
of Cuba upon Soviet aid that developed later during
the decade.*

*Robert S. Walters, a professor at the University of
Michigan, specializing in Soviet economic affairs, analyzed the Soviet-Cuban economic relationship in the
early 1960s in an article from which the following
material is excerpted. While subsequent Soviet-Cuban
agreements have extended the total amount of aid
and trade between the two nations, the general patterns of economic relationship between the Soviet
Union and Cuba were set in the period studied by
Professor Walters.*

Soviet-Cuban economic relations essentially began in early
1960, amid circumstances and fanfare characteristic of the
Soviet economic offensive in developing nations all over
the world. On February 5, 1960, a Soviet scientific, cultural and technical exhibition was opened in Havana by
Mikoyan; and on the same day the Soviet Government
cabled an order for 345,000 tons of sugar, which was an-

Reprinted from Robert S. Walters, "Soviet Economic Aid to Cuba:
1959–1964," *International Affairs*, 42, 1 (January 1966), 74, 76–81,
by permission of the author and the publisher.

nounced in the introduction of Mikoyan to the Cubans attending the grand opening of the exhibition. On February 13, a commercial agreement was signed by Mikoyan and Castro, under which the Soviet Union would buy 425,000 tons of sugar in 1960, and 1m. tons of sugar each of the subsequent four years. The U.S.S.R. would pay the world market price (three cents a pound), with 20 per cent of the purchase price being in U.S. dollars and the remainder applying against Cuban purchases in Russia.[1] Simultaneously there was announced a Soviet credit to Cuba of $100m. which could be used for equipment, machinery, materials and technical assistance from the U.S.S.R. over the next five years. The credit carried the standard terms of 2.5 per cent interest, repayable in traditional exports over a period of 12 years. In May, Cuba and the U.S.S.R. re-established diplomatic relations at the embassy level.

．　　．　　．

The Soviet Union, since its first trade agreement with Castro's Cuba, has responded time and again to the emergency needs of the Cuban economy. After the United States cut the remaining 700,000 tons of the Cuban sugar quota in July 1960, the U.S.S.R. quickly stepped in to purchase this quantity of sugar in addition to already existing agreements. The terms of this purchase were identical to those advanced in February of the same year, with

[1] Since both Cuba and the Soviet Union, as well as the other Socialist countries, have controlled information media, it is difficult to acquire data regarding the quality and problems of implementation of aid in general and for specific projects; consequently, evaluation of economic assistance to Cuba since 1959 must necessarily be qualified by this fact. Also, as the Soviet Union and Cuba express their agreements in dollars and then convert these amounts into their respective currencies at the official exchange rates, and since comparison of various trade and aid figures is more meaningful if expressed in a common currency unit, figures throughout this paper will be given in U.S. dollars. When changing rubles to dollars the official exchange rate for the year in question was used—this was 1 r = $0.25 until January 1961, and 1 r = $1.11 since that time. Cuban *pesos* were converted to U.S. dollars at the official exchange rate of one Cuban *peso* per dollar.

20 per cent of the price being paid in United States dollars and the remainder being applied to purchases from the U.S.S.R. The price paid for the sugar under this agreement was 3.25 cents a pound—the price which Cuba asked for her sugar after the United States cut the quota.

Under the multilateral trade agreement [between Cuba, the East European countries (except Albania and Yugoslavia), the U.S.S.R. and Mongolia] . . . , signatories of the bloc contracted to buy over 4m. tons of Cuban sugar a year. Of this amount the U.S.S.R. agreed to take 3.5m. tons (at four cents a pound), which had been the quantity planned for Cuban sugar exports to the Soviet Union over the period between 1961 and 1963. As we shall see below, the amount of the deliveries was subsequently reduced to accommodate Cuban requests.

An examination of Soviet-Cuban trade statistics between 1959 and 1963 is particularly interesting in terms of the trade balances of the Soviet Union with Cuba. From 1959 to 1961 there was a small Soviet import surplus ($65.3m. over the entire three-year period) which was significant only as a reflection of the rapidly increased commitment by the U.S.S.R. to support Cuba economically through huge purchases of sugar. As we have noted, it was in 1960 that the Soviets not only agreed to long term purchases of sugar from Cuba, but also stepped forward to fill the gap in Cuba's exports opened by the elimination of the sugar quota by the United States. The year 1961 witnessed permanent replacement by the U.S.S.R. of the American share of Cuban sugar exports, as measured by volume. The harvest in that year was 6,767,000 metric tons—the second largest in Cuban history—of which the Soviet Union purchased 3.3m. tons.

In 1962–63, however, the trade balance reveals a substantial export surplus from the U.S.S.R. to Cuba ($136.6m. in 1962 and $235.1m. in 1963). In large part, this export surplus was the reflection in foreign trade of the domestic economic problems in Cuba as Soviet exports to Cuba continued at increasing levels, while her imports from Cuba fell drastically. This was a result of the decrease in Cuban sugar production to the extent that she could not meet her delivery schedules with the U.S.S.R. during these years.

Soviet exports to Cuba over the period 1959–63 were dominated by machinery and equipment, fuel, mineral raw materials, metals, and food products which in 1963 accounted for almost 75 per cent of total Soviet exports to Cuba. It is interesting to note that there was a sharp increase in the export of foodstuffs to Cuba after 1962 when agricultural production, and particularly the sugar crop, fell drastically owing to domestic economic dislocations accompanying Castro's sweeping economic and institutional reforms. This is one of many instances since 1959 in which the domestic economic ills of Cuba were mitigated by exports from the U.S.S.R.

This summary of Soviet-Cuban trade should conclude with developments which have taken place more recently and which, therefore, cannot be seen in the figures quoted. When the Cuban economic experiment broke down in 1962 and 1963, as manifested by the necessity to ration food and consumer goods, by the decline in sugar production, by the decline in Cuban exports to the U.S.S.R., and by the increased imports of food from the U.S.S.R. in those two years, conditions became so chronic that in August 1963 Castro declared that the program of economic diversification and industrialization would have to be postponed for several years, and that sugar would have to be the focus of the Cuban economy for some years to come.

Virtually all Cuba's domestic economic problems show up in Soviet-Cuban trade; this was no exception. In January 1964, it was announced that a new long-term trade agreement between the U.S.S.R. and Cuba for 1965–70 would replace the 1960 agreements, which had hitherto been the foundation of Cuban-Soviet trade. This new agreement reflects the Cuban emphasis on sugar as the mainstay of its economy. It provides that the Soviet Union will purchase over 24m. tons of sugar between 1965 and 1970, with imports of 2.1m. tons in 1965, 3m. tons in 1966, 4m. tons in 1967, and 5m. tons in each of the following three years. Six cents a pound will be paid during this period, with the expectation that the agreement will create stable prices and a firm basis for future planning in the Cuban economy. It should be noted that planned deliveries of sugar in 1966 will be less than the 3.5 million-ton delivery schedule of 1961; this indicates a realistic assessment of Cuba's more recent economic capacity, and the bail-out operation implicit in this trade agreement is obviously tailored to meet Cuban needs and capabilities.

.　　　.　　　.

The February 1960 credit for $100m., which has already been described, marked the beginning of the Soviet economic offensive. Under this credit the Soviet Union has provided technical assistance and equipment necessary for geological prospecting for iron ore, chromites, petroleum, and other minerals. In addition, the credit was used to finance the construction of two thermal power plants, with a combined capacity of 300,000 kw.; the reconstruction of three existing metallurgical plants, expanding their capacity from 110,000 tons to 350,000 tons annually; the construction of a file factory; and the construction of a modern machinery plant to produce annually 4,000 tons of spare parts for machinery and equipment.

This credit was surrounded by much fanfare and is repeatedly referred to in Soviet publications. It is particularly interesting to observe that in Soviet discussions of their economic assistance to Cuba this credit is often the only one in which the actual amount is referred to in concrete terms. This is true in spite of the fact that at least two more credits for economic development of identical magnitude and terms subsequently have been offered to Cuba. Such a practice might indicate that the economic burden imposed by Cuba on the U.S.S.R. is of a size to render the

Soviet leadership reluctant to reveal plainly the amount of economic aid going to Cuba.

A second credit of $100m. was extended in mid-1961 for the development of Cuba's nickel and cobalt industries. The bulk of this amount was to go into construction of a new nickel plant, for which Cuba and the U.S.S.R. will together invest some $200m.

In mid-1962 another 100 million-dollar credit was given by the U.S.S.R. to help Cuba build 20 factories and to develop her chemical industry. The agreement provided for the construction of a nitrogen fertilizer plant with an annual capacity of 110,000–120,000 tons, and a plant for the manufacture of superphosphates with a yearly capacity of 150,000–200,000 tons. Also included were plans for prospecting for salt, phosphate raw materials, and sulphur to extend the domestic resource base for the chemical industry. This credit, unlike the first two which were to be utilized through 1965, was to be used between 1964 and 1967. The terms of the 1961 and 1962 credits were not explicitly stated by the Soviets; but with no evidence to the contrary, it is assumed that the standard 2.5 per cent interest and 12-year amortization period applied in each case.

The Soviet-Cuban trade protocol for 1963 included a credit, of an undisclosed amount, for the purpose of financing a large export surplus from the U.S.S.R. to Cuba during the year. On the basis of the actual export surplus in 1963, and the size of a similar credit for 1964 trade, it would seem reasonable to estimate the size of the 1963 credit to be $100–150m. The 1964 credit for the same purpose as the one the year before was $159m.

It should be emphasized that these last two credits were not for the purpose of economic development, but rather were to finance trade during the years in question. Thus, they were fully utilized during the years in which they were offered.

The estimated total of Soviet economic assistance offered to Cuba at the end of 1964 is, therefore, $559–609m., of which 300m. was in the form of credits for economic development, and the remainder for financing trade at a level which Cuba could not otherwise sustain. This is separate and distinct from the $157m. in credits offered by East Europe and China over the same period.

Accompanying economic assistance for development, the U.S.S.R. has extended much technical assistance in the form of Soviet technicians sent to Cuba to work on projects and to instruct Cubans, as well as in the form of training Cubans in the Soviet Union. By the end of 1963 some 3,000 Cubans had completed studies on agricultural mechanization in the Soviet Union, and about 900 Cubans were trained as engineers and technicians in Soviet universities, institutes, and trade schools.

18

CARMEN VELASCO, *ET AL.*

ECONOMIC REGIONALIZATION OF CUBA

In 1965 a team of Cuban and Soviet geographers, under the research supervision of Professor B. N. Semevskiy of the Institute of Geography and Geology of the Cuban Academy of Sciences, proposed a scheme of economic regionalization of Cuba along Soviet-Marxist principles. Their work was typical of research efforts by joint Cuban-Soviet teams in a variety of economic fields.

The geographers set up a six-region system for Cuba: a Western region, embracing Pinar del Río province; a Havana-Matanzas region, covering those two provinces; a region for Las Villas province; another for Camagüey province; and two regions for Oriente province, a northern and a southern. Much of their regional breakdown is on the basis of energy supply and clearly defined economic centers. The boundary lines for the regions correspond somewhat, but do not always follow the provincial boundary lines.

The regionalization proposal was outlined in an article for a Soviet geographical journal.

Reprinted from Carmen Velasco, Francisco Iglesias, Pedro Cañez Abril, Juan Pérez de la Riva, Angel Recio, Roberto Santana, Juan Torrente, and Yaniz and B. N. Semevskiy, "A Preliminary Scheme for the Economic Regionalization of Cuba," *Izvestiya Akademii Nauk SSSR, seriya geograficheskaya,* 3 (1965), 110–119, translated in *Soviet Geography: Review and Translation,* VI, 8 (October 1965), 26–39, by permission of the American Geographical Society.

A well-founded economic regionalization of a country requires thorough economic-geographic research, the collection and processing of much statistical material, taking account of the prospects of economic development and its regional characteristics, and much other work, and cannot be completed in a short time. However, socialist construction requires economic planning not only by sectors of the economy, but by regions, and management of the economic life of a country must take account not only of general laws of development but of regional characteristics. This confronts the research agencies of Cuba with the task of working out at least a preliminary scheme of economic regionalization that could serve temporarily until more thorough research makes it possible to determine fully the objectively existing and most suitable network of economic regions.

In accordance with Marxist theory and the practice of economic regionalization in socialist countries, there are economic regions of various orders and gradations, i.e., a system of regionalization units, each of which corresponds to a certain level of state planning. This is the result not of some arbitrary delimitation of the "most convenient" system of regions, but of the fact that both economic planning in a socialist country and the formation of economic regions derive from the effect of the same economic law, the law of planned, proportional development of the national economy.

If we consider economic regions of the largest scale (first order), of the type of the basic economic regions of the USSR (the Center, Urals, West Siberia, Far East, etc.), all Cuba would probably have to be considered an economic region on such a scale.

The essence and basis of each such large-scale region are the existence of a specific key economic problem which combines all facts and phenomena inherent in the given region into a single complex. The problem reflects the interdependences and interactions that combine diversified activities into a single productive whole (or complex) and reveals the internal and external "metabolism" that takes place in the process of production. Solution of the problem insures the most rational development, deepening, and strengthening of the productive specialization of a region.

In the case of Cuba, the key economic problem is that of sugar, which combines all aspects of the economic life of the country. Agriculture not only produces sugar cane, but receives from the sugar mills livestock feed, fertilizers, and fuel; at the same time it supplies food to cane growers and sugar mill workers.

A sugar mill produces not only sugar, but also raw materials for other branches of the economy, including the chemical industry. The future of the Cuban chemical industry is related to a large extent to comprehensive use of by-products of sugar production. Even such seemingly unconnected industries as metalworking and machine building are part of the complex by involving the repair of sugar-mill equipment, the supply of spare parts, and the repair of trucks and farm machines used in the production and transportation of sugar cane.

The sugar problem includes not only agriculture and industry, but also transportation. Many rail lines were built especially to serve only sugar mills; cane and refined sugar occupy a leading position in the freight traffic on all forms of transport. Finally, sugar is the main export item and thus enables the importation of raw materials, supplies, and finished goods needed by other branches of the national economy.

The sugar problem is thus really a wide-ranging national economic problem, forming an economic region of the largest scale, and one of international significance within the world system of socialism.

Is there another national economic problem in Cuba that plays a similar role in tying together all branches of the economy and is of similar region-forming significance? Evidently not.

This makes it possible to consider Cuba as a single economic region of the first order, encompassing all parts of the country and linking them into a single territorial-production complex.

Not all parts of the country play an equally important role in the solution of the key national economic problem. In some parts the main industry is combined with one activity, in other parts with another. Because of the importance of livestock in Cuba, there are areas in which livestock raising is not only combined with sugar production but sometimes even assumes a dominant position. There are areas in Cuba where mining and primary processing of ore are the dominant activities. There are also small coffee and cocoa-growing areas, larger acreages of tobacco, and even henequen-producing areas (around Mariel and Cárdenas).

In other words, in addition to the key sugar problem, involving almost all branches of the economy and all regions of Cuba, there are also local economic problems that determine the role, the place, and the functions of the given region within the national economy of the country.

In the course of the planned solution of all these problems, there takes place a process of formation of second-order regions, i.e., regions that participate in the solution of the key sugar problem and, at the same time, are concerned with a specific local problem. The economic regions discussed below are economic-territorial complexes of the second order (the first order being the country as a whole) in which the economy will be centrally planned.

The present article is devoted to a preliminary (so far quite arbitrary) delimitation of these second-order regions. They are the largest units of economic regionalization within Cuba. They are economic regions that have arisen objectively in the process of development of the revolution and have become national planning units.

Each economic region can include subregions as its specialized parts (a region is a complex, and a subregion its specialized part). Within each economic region, there are also economic microregions. But these minor units have not been considered in the present scheme and have been left for future investigation.

The theoretical basis for the proposed regionalization scheme of Cuba is the methodology of economic regionalization of socialist countries worked out in the USSR in the first years of the Soviet regime under the supervision of V. I. Lenin and later developed by Soviet economic geographers, and for specific application to Cuban conditions, the statements of Fidel Castro and other leaders on the prospects of economic development of the country and its problems.

An economic region is an objective category. It is formed independently of the will of man under the influence of the laws of social development. However, under socialist conditions, the state plays an active role in forming economic regions. By relying on its perception of the laws of social development and by using them in the interest of man, the socialist state is able to intensify the tendencies and processes favorable to the development of society, to create favorable conditions for their operation, and, at the same time, to oppose and slow tendencies operating in the opposite direction. The socialist state thus plays an active role in the development and formation of the territorial division of labor, and, consequently, of economic regions. In the economic regionalization of Cuba, we can thus speak not only of uncovering (identifying) objectively developing economic regions, but also of a desirable influence on that process.

Of great importance in the economic regionalization of Cuba is the long-range factor, which determines the direction of the planned development of economic regions and changes in the structure of the territorial division of labor and economic relations.

This is especially characteristic in the case of Cuba in view of the nature of its economic development; in many large areas industry is still underdeveloped, the degree of territorial division of labor is low, and the process of regional formation is not clearly evident. In these areas, the availability of raw materials and energy plays a relatively minor role in the process of regional formation; more important are factors like manpower, soils, etc. This provides a somewhat wider range of choice in economic planning, in forming a territorial division of labor, locating productive forces, and using local conditions.

While such Cuban industries as mining, ore concentration, sugar, and a few others gravitate toward raw material sources, various locations are possible in the case of chemical plants and many other branches of industry. One can thus give various directions to the formation of individual economic regions. Economic planning has a wide freedom of choice (within the framework of many laws and operating forces). Planning thus plays an important region-forming role.

In any socialist country, there is a certain fundamental unity (but not identity) of economic regionalization and the administrative-territorial divisions. However, Cuba still retains administrative divisions that were formed under different historical conditions and never reflected the real economic characteristics of the country. Consequently those divisions do not reflect the existing structure of the territorial division of labor, and the boundaries of provinces and even municipios sometimes split areas that constitute a single whole from the point of view of economic relations of the present and of the future. The eastern part of Pinar del Río, for example, is closely tied to Havana and is part of the Western power system; even the sugar produced by the centrals of eastern Pinar del Río and other farm products of the area are shipped through the port of Havana. The Mariel-Artemisa area has no economic ties with the town of Pinar del Río or with the western and central parts of the province in general, and is not expected to have any in the future. The present administrative divisions of Cuba, therefore, cannot serve as a reliable basis for economic regionalization.

Under these conditions, the economic regionalization proposed in the present article can be regarded only as a preliminary approximation, as the first draft of an economic regionalization scheme for Cuba. This work should be continued to provide a thorough basis for regionalization and to change the political-administrative structure of the country accordingly.

This first draft is based mainly on economic ties between territories, proposed future changes in such relations, and the suitability of joint development. Much attention was also paid to the fact that individual regions may have a certain specialization, and, at the same time, be diversified economic units (if not now, in the future), or at least possess the prerequisites for such integrated development.

Also taken into account were transport conditions and expected future changes, and the existence in each region of developed or developing urban centers fulfilling the role of central organizing places.

One of the characteristics of Cuba that had to be taken into account is the peculiar centralization of its domestic trade, most of which moves between Havana and the other regions. There is little trade between outlying regions. Transit freight movements also pass to a large extent through Havana. This extreme gravitation toward Havana makes it difficult to delimit boundaries between the Havana region and the others. Trade between outlying regions is often negligible and relations with local municipal and even provincial centers are sometimes less developed than with Havana, which also makes it difficult to draw regional boundaries.

Further work in this area should be concerned with a thorough study of Cuba's economic regions, determination of the economic structure of each, identification of the existing division of labor between regions and of regional productive relations, and the participation of each region in the national and even international division of labor.

On the basis of the above-mentioned principles, the Institute of Geography and Geology of the Cuban Academy of Sciences and the School of Geography of Havana University (research supervisor: Prof. B. N. Semevskiy; Professors Pedro Cañez Abril, Roberto Santana, Juan Torrente, Francisco Iglesias, Juan Pérez de la Riva, Yaniz, Angel Recio, and Carmen Velasco) compiled a preliminary scheme of economic regionalization of Cuba.

.   .   .

19

RICHARD R. AND
PATRICIA N. FAGEN

REVOLUTION FOR CUBA'S
LOBSTER INDUSTRY

*As a part of the change in Cuba's economic structure
under the Castro government, fishing activities were
elevated to a role of major importance. The fishing
industry is a growing factor in the economy, based on
a serious commitment by the Castro government to
allocate large sums for expansion of the industry and
to give fishing a top priority in overall economic planning. These large-scale efforts are directed by a co-
ordinated central agency in Havana. Fish products
are much more common on Cuban tables today than
they were in pre-Castro times, but the adaptation of
the Cuban diet to seafood is proving a slow process.
Much of the fish production is exported.*

*One aspect of this new emphasis on fish products
is the growth of the lobster industry. Political scientist Richard R. Fagen and his wife, surveying the extent of change in the lobster industry and the fishing
industry as a whole, conclude in an article written in
1970 that the "entire fishing industry" has been transformed "economically, technically, and socially."*

Fagen is professor of political science and com-

Reprinted from Richard R. and Patricia N. Fagen, "Revolution for
Cuba's Lobster Industry," *The Geographical Magazine*, XLII, 12
(September 1970), 867, 870–872, 874–875, by permission of the
publisher.

*munication at Stanford University, while his wife is
an assistant professor at San Jose State College in
California.*

Fish and shell-fish of all kinds swarm in the warm seas
around the island of Cuba. So long as the Cuban economy
was tied to the United States, however, the fishing industry
was of minor economic importance. Cubans in general ate
relatively small amounts of fish, and except for a modest
traffic to Miami, there was little exportation. Much of the
production of rock lobster, shrimp and luxury fish found
its way on to the tables of the restaurants catering for the
tens of thousands of tourists who flocked to pre-revolutionary Cuba during the season. Fishermen remained
among the poorest and most neglected groups in the country, living in villages scattered along the coasts, and fishing
from skiffs and small boats of local design and construction.

Anxious to earn as much as possible from middle-men
who came to the villages and bought their catches for re-
sale at much higher prices in the urban markets, and not
able to bargain effectively with the buyers because of the
rapid spoilage of their catch in the tropical sun, fishermen
exploited the lobster banks ruthlessly in the quest for their
meager share of the profits. Working with tridents, traps,
and even by hand when the lobster were "running" across
the shallow banks, they scooped up all the *langosta* available. In the process, the undersized and the egg-bearing
females were caught and sold along with the others. It was
not a system conducive to the rational use and conserva-
tion of one of Cuba's most valuable marine resources.

One effect of the Cuban Revolution has been to transform the entire fishing industry, economically, technically,
and socially. Starting in the early 1960s, the regime gave
high priority to the development and modernization of the
fishing fleet and the improvement of the lives of the fisher-

men. As far as deep sea and gulf fishing were concerned, this meant in effect the creation of an entirely new industry. The government invested in new boats, expanded ship-building facilities, and created schools for the preparation and technical training of personnel for the enlarged fleet. With the help of the Soviet Union, a massive deep-water fishing port was built near Havana. For lobstermen and other coastal fishermen, the changes were equally dramatic, although of a different order. For them, cooperatives were organized, ice houses, storage sheds, and local schools were constructed, in some cases whole fishing villages of neat concrete homes were built to replace the former thatched huts, and new varieties of boats, traps, and nets were designed and distributed. At the same time, an intensive campaign to control the kind of lobsters taken and the methods of taking them was instituted.

The reasons for these controls are based on the essential fragility of the lobster population. *Panulirus Argus,* the Cuban variety of rock lobster, begins life as an egg, and then hatches into a larva which floats for six to eight months as part of the current-borne plankton of the tropical seas. In the post-larval stage, the lobster molts numerous times as it grows, attaining about 35 millimeters of length by its first birthday, 75 millimeters by its second, 144 millimeters by its third, and 214 by its fourth, the normal time of sexual maturity. Of the quarter to three-quarters of a million eggs laid by an adult female, it is estimated that only about seventeen survive to reach the post-larval stage, and only three of these eventually reach adulthood. Given these rates of natural attrition and the relatively long maturation period, it is easy to see why indiscriminate and intensive fishing can irreversibly deplete the lobster banks. Furthermore, because of this reproductive calendar and the many months the larvae spend floating with the oceanic currents, it is not commercially feasible to attempt the artificial cultivation of langosta.

Thus, the revolutionary government undertook the regulation of the lobster industry.

During the reproductive months of April and May fishing is now prohibited in most areas, but the key to the preservation of lobstering in Cuba is the rule that lobsters must be taken alive. This allows the under sized and the egg-bearing females to be returned to the water. It has the additional advantage of allowing the major part of the catch to be brought to processing centers alive so that the meat is fresher and the amount of spoilage less. Although the ruling that lobsters must be taken alive—and kept alive until processed if possible—might seem easy to implement, such was not the case. Not only was it contrary to the long-standing use of the trident by Cuban fishermen, but it required the development and distribution of several new kinds of equipment. Traditionally, whether they took lobsters alive or speared them, Cuban fishermen operating from their small boats immediately ripped off the valuable meaty tails, put them on ice, and threw the rest of the lobster away. Enforcement of the new policy meant, therefore, that boats incorporating wet-holds would have to be built so that live lobsters could be retained in good condition until deposited in a collection center. Additionally, fishermen accustomed to using the trident would have to be given nets and traps in sufficient quantity to maintain their productivity, and would also have to be convinced of the efficiency and correctness of using them instead of the trident.

The organization of the fishermen into cooperatives made the necessary changes possible. Although they are called cooperatives, the thirty or so coastal fishing centers do not, in fact, have the organizational form of true cooperatives. They are state fishing enterprises in which some fishermen continue to own their boats, buying their supplies at fixed prices from the enterprise and selling their catch back. What profits they earn, they keep, although because they usually have older and less well-equipped boats, their productivity is generally not high enough for them to earn more than the salaried fishermen in the state sector of the cooperatives. These workers have their boats and supplies given to them by the enterprise, and records of their catches are kept for purposes of planning and management only, not for remuneration. Gradually, as new boats are built and the older ones taken out of service, the state sector grows at the expense of the private sector, for the new boats are put exclusively in the hands of salaried crews.

The boats that are being built in Cuba to replace the aging, traditional lobstermen are called *Cayo Largos*. It is said that their basic design resulted directly from conversations between Fidel Castro and several fishermen which took place near the southern island of Cayo Largo. Constructed of native woods, powered by a large diesel, beamy and functional, they are slightly more than eighteen meters long. Amidships they have a massive *vivero* or wet-hold for live lobsters, and a dry-hold capable of carrying as much as 10,000 lb. of ice. Accommodation for the crew of as many as ten is spartan; wooden bunks slung under a shelter aft, food cooked over an open-air charcoal stove. With a range of hundreds of kilometers, the Cayo Largos often stay on the coastal banks for twenty or more days, depositing their catch periodically in collection centers scattered throughout the area. These centers are complexes of piers and pens built directly on the shallow coastal shelf. At the centers, the hauls of live lobsters are weighed and then dumped into underwater pens, there to await the launch that will take them to processing plants on the mainland.

To observe the arts of lobstering at sea, we traveled almost due south from Havana through the fertile Cuban countryside to the port of Batabanó. The cooperative of Batabanó is one of the two largest lobstering cooperatives in the country, and is centrally located on the shore of the shallow gulf from which 70 per cent of Cuba's rock lobsters come. The Gulf of Batabanó, ringed by islands and covering hundreds of square kilometers on the western end of Cuba's south coast, seldom exceeds nine meters in depth. In these warm and sheltered waters live one of the world's great concentrations of rock lobster.

The cooperative which has replaced the pre-revolutionary fishing village at Batabanó is impressive in its size and facilities. It has more than 200 boats, a small but complete shipyard, docks strung out along a perfectly protected lagoon, a large ice house, a well-equipped and provisioned warehouse, a neat row of administration buildings, a modern factory for the processing and quick-freezing of both whole lobsters and lobster tails, and a small factory for the processing of natural sponges. The morning scene is one of considerable activity. In the provisioning warehouse, ships' cooks are collecting supplies of food for several weeks on the Gulf. In addition to domestic products, there are canned fruits from Albania, peppers from Bulgaria, rice and canned pork from China, and stewed beef from the Soviet Union. At the docks, crews are hoisting 400 lb. blocks of ice into the holds; children and wives are down to see the boats set sail.

Following the traditional patterns of fishing, each boat has its own area with its own line of traps and *jaulas,* or cages. . . .

Over the past half-dozen years, the Center of Fishing Studies has conducted extensive research on the relative efficiency and durability of different traps, and there has been a strong movement toward standardization. The favored model is an "S"-shaped construction of galvanized wire, about one meter across at its widest point and half a meter deep. . . .

When the live lobsters arrive at Batabanó, they go immediately to the freezing plant. Although in other areas most lobsters are canned, here, in an attempt to capture a major share of European and Canadian luxury markets, extremely modern quick-freezing equipment has been installed. While still alive, the lobsters are sorted by size and plunged for about twenty minutes into cold brine. . . . Later, they are placed in a pressure oven to cook for about fifteen minutes. They emerge from the oven a rosy orange, steaming on large tins. White gowned and capped ladies give the freshly cooked lobsters a good scrubbing and then place them in transparent plastic bags emblazoned with the Cuban trademark, "Caribbean Queen Rock Lobster." After being quick-frozen, they await shipment to those world markets where whole lobsters command top prices, even though only the tail contains meat in any quantity.

The demand, both from restaurants and individuals, for whole rock lobster is so great that the Cubans are even sending them alive to France. Once a week, conditions permitting, a cargo plane lifts off from Havana International Airport. Loaded aboard are three tons of spiny rock lobster, packed 22 lb. to a box in a nest of wet, natural sponges. . . . It is doubtful that those who so enjoy the fruits of the Cuban sea appreciate either the fragility of the lobster population or the care which the Cubans are taking to insure its continuance. [But in dozens of small ports around the island, Cuban fishermen are operating under a code and with equipment designed to protect the ecological balance on which their industry depends. To have achieved this while at the same time greatly improving the life styles of the fishermen and their families is one of the small but nevertheless significant triumphs of the revolutionary government.]

20

ERICH H. JACOBY

THE WINNER: CUBA'S AGRICULTURAL WORKER

Erich H. Jacoby, a former official of the Food and Agriculture Organization of the United Nations, provided a generally favorable look at the Cuban economy following a visit to the island early in 1969, just ten years after Fidel Castro came to power. "The actual winner of the Cuban revolution," he concluded, "is the countryside, and more specifically the agricultural worker."

Erich H. Jacoby is a research professor at the Institute for International Economic Studies of the University of Stockholm in his native Sweden. His article is interesting not only for his conclusions, but also for his description of the methods he used in surveying the Cuban economy during his visit to the island.

When I recently visited Cuba, I found a society and an economic system which are alive and ready to take risks —often perhaps too large ones; most people seem energetic and there is a great deal of true enthusiasm, especially among the youth. But, no doubt, the country suffers

Reprinted from Erich H. Jacoby, "Cuba: The Real Winner Is the Agricultural Worker," *Ceres*, 2, 4 (July–August 1969), 29–30, 32–33, by permission of the Food and Agriculture Organization of the United Nations.

from growing pains, a considerable part of which are probably self-inflicted because even ten years after the revolution the leaders are still inclined to think in terms of guerrilla warfare without any regard for the capacity of the people to suffer and take risks.

Cuba has become an ambitious country and today it displays the one fundamental characteristic which distinguishes it from most other underdeveloped countries: it has no unemployment problem; on the contrary, it has a painful labor shortage. How was this possible? I put the question over and over again to my Cuban hosts.

The most plausible explanation was given to me by Carlos Rafael Rodríguez, formerly president of the National Institute of Agrarian Reform (INRA) and now a member of the Central Committee of the Party (PCC). He gave the following reasons for this surprising success in the fight against unemployment: (1) abolition of child labor through compulsory education; (2) the more or less general introduction of the 8-hour working day even during peak seasons both in agriculture and industry; (3) the considerable expansion of the agricultural area combined with a diversification of agriculture, particularly through the introduction of labor-intensive crops such as coffee and citrus fruits; (4) the increased industrialization; and (5) the building of roads and dams, reforestation, house construction, etc.

The army too absorbs a considerable part of the labor force, which it makes available for harvesting, reforestation and construction works.

It was my impression that the Cuban government was sincerely determined to promote the human factor in agriculture and that this had contributed very considerably to solve the employment problem and at the same [time] improve the quality of labor. The gradual abolition of unemployment and underemployment has been the constant feature during the various stages of development, which ranged from the rigorous reduction of agricultural production and hasty industrialization to the diversification of agriculture and the simultaneous expansion of the sugar-cane production.

This unorthodox approach to problems of agriculture and industrial development was matched by an equally independent labor market policy. Cuba is the only socialist country, in fact, which permitted the free movement of labor after the revolution, with the result that hundreds of thousands of agricultural workers left their rural distressed areas and poverty for the glamor of Havana and other cities. I was told by an official of the Planning Commission that this exodus from the countryside to a considerable extent forced the government to hasten industrialization during the first years of the revolution even beyond the original plans. Yet, any other approach to the labor market, any compulsory limitation of the freedom of the agricultural worker, would have been in contradiction to the proclaimed humanitarian policy of the Cuban revolution: another characteristic unnoticed in other socialist countries. Perhaps this labor policy was not simply humanitarianism, but combined with a shrewd political calculation based on the facts of Latin American life—with its unique capacity for evasion practices—and on the rational understanding that the pressure of an excess population in the rural areas would force the hand of the government to distribute land to agricultural workers. This in turn would force it to dissolve the highly efficient sugar estates of the foreign companies.

This lack of regard for orthodox socialist tenets is a basic feature of the Cuban revolution and perhaps the reason for its success. The Cubans did not control the labor market, probably a mistake from an economic point of view, but preserved instead the large sugar estates as economic entities and thus skipped the first stage of all socialist revolutions: the redistribution of land to the landless.

This, of course, was not too difficult since Cuba is largely a country without peasant tradition, particularly in the sugarcane cultivated areas. Thus the Cuban revolution could immediately establish state farms instead of collective farms (the latter only appeared briefly at the very beginning in the sugar areas). This fundamental decision greatly facilitated the implementation of agricultural development programs and helped to avoid black market operations.

On the other hand, tenancy was abolished and peasant farming became recognized—at some cost to efficiency—on 30 percent of the agricultural area involving 40 percent of the agricultural population. This type of tenure is particularly common in the tobacco areas, notably in the province of Pinar del Río, and the tobacco farmers represent to a certain extent a rural middle class with farms of about 50 acres on the average and never exceeding 165 acres, with an income considerably above that of the agricultural workers. Yet, from a political and economic point of view these peasants are neutralized since there are no free market operations in the island. The government and public agencies are the only purchasers of the produce for which they pay stable prices that do not reflect world market trends; and they alone can hire labor, and provide credit. Thus, the government, through price fixation and the volume of credit, determines the way of life of the individual farming families.

I had the opportunity to talk with the leader of the national peasant organization and with some tobacco growers about the economic position of the peasant farmers in Cuba. My impression is that to some extent the older generation still has a conservative outlook and, particularly in the Havana region, cherishes the memories of booming prices for vegetables and other agricultural produce. But the dynamics of Cuban society have taken a firm hold on the sons and daughters of these farmers and the new educational institutions and voluntary working groups are gradually isolating the older people. I was told that in many cases the children declined to succeed their fathers, with the result that upon the death of the owner the farm is acquired by the government. On a private tobacco farm in the province of Pinar del Río I saw the laborers who were employed and paid by the co-operative working with the planter on an equal footing and addressing him with the term "compañero" (comrade). Since the Cuban revolution has conquered the young generation and is gradually narrowing the income gap between agricultural workers and peasant farmers, the landowning peasant class in Cuba will probably disappear within the lifetime of one generation.

. . .

The actual winner of the Cuban revolution is the countryside, and more specifically the agricultural worker who for the first time in the history of Cuba is experiencing security and increasing real wages. Formerly he had to carry the burden of unemployment and of an extremely unfair distribution system, but today he reaps the benefits of the large-scale irrigation dams—as for instance the recently completed Carlos Manuel Céspedes dam in the province of Oriente which irrigates 125,000 acres for the cultivation of sugar and rice—and is favored by the administration of the rationing system. In addition, he has the satisfaction that the urban people, students, intellectuals and officials on all levels, go to the countryside in order to help him harvest the sugarcane.

In Cuba the problem of incentives is very delicate, since according to the ideology of the revolution the "hombre nuevo" shall be motivated by collective progress and not by individual advantage. No doubt, the Cuban government has succeeded in arousing the enthusiasm of the young generation for collective objectives but the critical observer cannot help noticing the existence of a reward system which functions as a sort of substitute for incentives. Furthermore, the agricultural workers expect higher wages for hard work and the private tobacco farmer has the incentive to improve the quality of his crop since prices are fixed according to a detailed grading which recognizes 52 different qualities of tobacco. The prices paid to the farmer, in fact, even include a certain element of a land rent since some of the better paid grades of tobacco depend upon the quality of the soil.

Regarding the present shortages in Cuba we have to remember that, before the revolution, 95 percent of all agricultural produce was shipped to the Mercado Unido in Havana where it was sold by middlemen at the highest prices in the country. These "good old days" are over. The meat supply is very limited but nevertheless the rations are distributed over the whole country in the same quantities for all, and 70 percent of the people live better than they ever did before. There is neither poverty nor misery in the countryside; instead there are more schools and hospitals.

The pressure of economic difficulties has affected the distribution system and there are, in fact, different distribution levels: the people working in the fields, in the factories, in offices, universities and schools get their food at cheap prices or even free of charge, while the official prices for the rations are considerably higher. Undoubtedly, this multiple distribution system contains elements of unfairness but it does give the government a possibility to support the rural areas which have been neglected for centuries, and thereby discouraging any further migration to the towns.

.   .   .

It is true that production declined considerably during the first five years after the revolution but recently, as I was told, there have been some considerable increases particularly in the production of rice, poultry and eggs. A very favorable development seems to be the expansion of cattle-raising concentrated in the so-called genetic enterprises which promises a multiplied meat production in the next 5–6 years. Altogether I got the impression of a large expansion of agriculture which is closely associated with the completion of irrigation works and the improvement of infrastructures. On the other hand, some of the diversification efforts seem rather doubtful. The planting of millions of coffee trees exposed to the sun seems a risky enterprise, although Cuban experts assure that this particular variety does not need any shade. It is one of the romantic though dangerous qualities of the Cuban economy that the government has to take chances because it has no time to wait for the final results of thorough experiments with new varieties.

Finally I observed some experimentation in the field of agrarian organization. It seems that the trend is changing once more from decentralization to centralization, this time on the highest level. . . . There are some indications that Cuba is on the way to establish a new type of socialist organization which is based on regional economic planning units. From the standpoint of the land distribution pattern, such regional planning units represent a kind of land consolidation on the land utilization level. If this new type of organization is developed to its logical conclusion, the state farms will disappear at least in the rice and sugar areas. Under conditions of a permanent labor shortage, the difficulties of agricultural planning have jeopardized the original principle of a high measure of autonomy for the state farms.

From this point of view it was only natural that with its flair for improvisation and its admirable flexibility Cuba would try to change to a system of organization which allows rapid adjustments in the field of labor distribution and, at the same time, economizes with staff resources. However, in introducing such a system, the government takes the risk that the workers might lose their identification with a specific enterprise, and it will have to accept all the hazards involved in central planning and investment.

.   .   .

There is a considerable shortage of consumer goods. The

Western visitor accustomed to the affluence of picturesque markets in underdeveloped countries will be disappointed in Cuba. He has no possibility to spend his money except on movies, stamps and in night clubs. If one were to think only in terms of a consumer economy, the report from Havana would be pessimistic, telling about long queues in front of the stores, rationing and shortages.

I was very much aware in Cuba of three possibilities for reporting conditions in a country: (1) from the static point of view; (2) from a retrospective point of view; and (3) from the point of view of appraising planning for the future. All three reports would be true though they would have very different dimensions. Personally I used the excellent report of the World Bank Mission to Cuba from the early 1950s as guidebook, and in the light of the factual findings of this report I was able to appraise the progress, see the shortcomings and evaluate the plans for the future. In my view, only this approach provides the proper perspective for the judgment of political and social realities in terms of income distribution, investments, and employment.

21

CARMELO MESA-LAGO

UNPAID LABOR IN CUBA

*One of the most interesting economic aspects of
Cuba's socialist economy is the question of unpaid
labor. The Castro government uses various types of
such labor, but because of insufficient data, the
studies of the subject are in their infancy. Carmelo
Mesa-Lago, a professor of economics at the University of Pittsburgh, has done pioneering research in the
field. Some of his very technical findings are included
in the following excerpt.*

*Professor Mesa-Lago concludes in this 1969 study
that the total product of unpaid labor is greater than
the operational costs of such labor—and that Cuba
can be expected to continue the practice. Unpaid
labor in Cuba in the late 1960s involved otherwise
employed persons working on their own time; unemployed women; students; politico-administrative
prisoners, as part of a rehabilitation effort; and soldiers fulfilling compulsory military service.*

. . . Cuba is a new socialist country which has relied
heavily on the use of various types of unpaid labor. This
experience has unusual validity because the Cuban revolu-

tion is a source of inspiration to several other developing countries.

At the end of 1966, UNESCO held in Havana its first International Seminar on Leisure Time and Recreation. In his opening address to the seminar Antonio Núñez Jiménez, chairman of the Cuban Academy of Sciences, stated:

> In Cuba, since the Revolution took place, leisure time is a social value used in the national reconstruction, both in the economic and ideological fields. . . . In our effort to raise production and productivity, hundreds of thousands of persons have been mobilized to perform numerous [unpaid] tasks, such as the arduous jobs of cutting cane or picking coffee. All these tasks have been fulfilled during the leisure time of the people.

.   .   .

Five types of unpaid labor may be distinguished in Cuba: (1) work performed by employed workers outside of regular working time, (2) work done by unemployed women, (3) work performed by students as a method of socialist education, (4) work accomplished by politico-administrative prisoners as a means of "social rehabilitation," and (5) work included as part of the compulsory military service.

.   .   .

Unpaid labor performed by employed male and female workers is usually called "voluntary work." It is performed beyond the regular working hours, whether at the work site or any other place, in behalf of the state and commonly without pay. Voluntary work may be accomplished in four different ways: as overtime hours subsequent to the regular workday; on weekends, especially on Sundays; during the annual paid-vacation time; or for a continuous period of several months, during leave of absence from a regular job. The last is generally known as "long-term" voluntary work; workers abandon their regular jobs from one to six months to work mainly in agriculture. Because such workers use a leave of absence, they are paid their regular (i.e., industrial) wages. Their companions who remain on the urban job site must maintain production levels by carrying out the duties of those mobilized.

Fragmentary information suggests that the number of voluntary workers (measured in man-years) rose from 15,000 in 1962 to 70,000 in 1967, and that the number continues to grow. The tasks performed by the voluntary work force are varied: planting and cutting sugar cane; picking coffee, cotton, vegetables and fruits; harvesting rice; planting trees; weeding and fertilizing fields; repairing damage caused by hurricanes; building construction; and almost any kind of industrial and service work.

With the exception of those on leave of absence, voluntary workers receive neither wages nor other kinds of pay. Long-term voluntary workers are provided with lodging and board as well as tools. Since 1963, voluntary workers suffering occupational accidents have been credited, for benefit purposes, with the time spent performing unpaid labor. Long-term voluntary workers on leave of absence are also credited with this time of service for retirement pensions.

Early in the revolution, unpaid labor was donated on a spontaneous basis, but since 1962 voluntary workers have been recruited because of pressure from trade unions and the managers of state enterprises and have been organized in battalions and brigades under Communist party guidance. The state has regulated the performance of unpaid labor by introducing several measures: criticism among voluntary workers, annual contracts binding the workers to achieve a determined number of unpaid hours of labor, management and trade union checks on the amount and quality of the labor done, weekly reports by the battalions on their own performance and that of others, inspection teams to keep discipline and discover flaws, and penalties for disciplinary violations of the state regulations.

Since the Federation of Cuban Women (FMC) was

formed in 1960, tens of thousands of Cuban females, particularly those doing housework, have been recruited by that organization as unpaid laborers in the cane, cotton, rice, and coffee fields. There are no accurate data on the number of women annually donating unpaid work, but a 1967 estimate, based on scattered information, of from 5,000 to 10,000 man-years seems reasonable. Women do not receive wages, and because they often perform their agricultural tasks close to their homes, lodging and board facilities are reduced to a minimum.

In mid-1962, students began to perform unpaid labor during vacation time, in coffee, cotton, and rice plantations. Recruitment was mainly done through exhortations by the student unions, the Communist Youth League (UJC) and the school boards. In mid-1964, the system was made compulsory by a decree of the Ministry of Education. Subject to the legislation are youngsters from six to fifteen years of age, enrolled in elementary and secondary schools, between first and ninth grades. One type of unpaid labor (titled "productive") is performed by from 150,000 to 180,000 secondary-school students on state farms and factories, on weekends and during school vacations. In the case of agricultural work, students generally remain at the work site for a period of from one to six weeks. Another type of unpaid labor (titled "socially useful") involves 1,280,000 primary-school children and is aimed to suppress differences between physical and intellectual work as well as to inculcate in the children a sense of obligation to society. Toward the end of 1965, the Ministry of Education also ordered university students to participate in unpaid labor for a period of from three to six weeks a year. Students performing unpaid labor are provided food and shelter when mobilized away from their homes.

Unpaid labor is used as a punishment for two classes of convicted persons: state employees and functionaries guilty of errors or transgressions committed during the performance of their functions; and political prisoners, i.e., people imprisoned for opposing the government. In both cases, forced labor has two goals: "rehabilitation" or "reeducation" of those convicted and the performance of a productive task. Political crimes are judged by the revolutionary courts while administrative faults are under the jurisdiction of the Administrative Disciplinary Commission (CODIAD). The management of labor camps is entrusted to the Ministry of the Interior. According to Prime Minister Castro, in 1964–1965, there were from 15,000 to 20,000 political prisoners in Cuba, although other sources give figures ranging from 50,000 to 75,000. The number of convicted state officials is unknown but is presumed to be small. Tasks to be performed by those convicted include cultivation of rice, planting trees, extraction of minerals, etc. Prisoners receive food, shelter, and clothing.

The desire to bring a large number of "vagrants" (i.e., idle youngsters, jobless bourgeoisie, etc.) into production was allegedly a main reason for establishing compulsory military service in 1963. Included are males between the ages of sixteen and forty-five, who are obligated to serve a period of three years. Recruits are divided into two categories, i.e., those "not politically integrated" and those "free of suspicion." Those in the former group enter the so-called Military Units to Aid Production (UMAP) and are employed in agricultural work throughout their service period. Recruits free of suspicion are under a training regime which combines military instruction and productive work.

The number of recruits is unknown. The Minister of the Armed Forces (FAR), charged with the administration of the military service, said in 1963 that 1.5 million persons were covered although only a selection of youngsters between seventeen and twenty-two years old would be drafted initially. The author has estimated, based on official data released in 1963, that 84,000 persons were enrolled in military service at the end of 1966. In 1968, however, the Prime Minister asserted that the compulsory military system embraced practically every young man within the military age bracket. Hence, the previous estimate seems conservative. Recruits receive food, shelter, and clothing, plus a monthly allowance of seven pesos ($7).

When unpaid workers are totaled, it appears that by 1967 from 200,000 to 300,000 man-years of unpaid labor were employed in the Cuban economy. These figures may be measured against the 1967 labor force of some 2.5 million workers. Unpaid labor thus represented from 8 to 12 percent of the regular labor force. The man-year contribution from the several types of unpaid labor was as follows: 60,000 to 70,000 from employed workers; 5,000 to 10,000 from women; 18,000 to 23,000 from secondary-school students; 84,000 to 120,000 from military recruits; and 20,000 to 75,000 from prisoners. . . .

Unpaid labor may serve educational and sociological objectives, i.e., it may build up "the communist man" by reducing discriminatory practices allegedly produced by capitalism and based on location, sex, and type of work. Despite its potential value as an ideological tool, two economic factors seem to have stimulated the initiation of the system in Cuba. The most important factor is the artificial labor shortage in agriculture caused by migration to the cities of part of the rural unemployed and by the reduction of the full potential of effort and the consequent low productivity of the remaining agricultural workers, due to poor economic incentives. Optimal solutions to the artificial labor shortage include mechanizing agriculture, increasing the productivity of the employed rural labor force, or training the existing urban surplus and pointing it toward agricultural employment. But these are complex, long-term types of solutions while unpaid labor has provided an easy, expedient way to cope with the labor shortage.

Another factor influencing the utilization of unpaid labor has been the desire to reduce current inflation through wage savings—filling the labor vacuum with unpaid workers. During 1962–1967 the total wages saved through unpaid labor exceeded 300 million pesos, an annual average of more than 50 million pesos. The latter figure represents approximately 1.4 percent of the estimated annual average of the Cuban national income for this period.

Despite their economic value as manpower-supply and wage-saving devices, some kinds of unpaid labor have had negative effects on sugar production and other sectors of the economy. This is due to the low productivity of unskilled, unpaid laborers, their high operative costs, and the economic dislocation and waste caused by their utilization. Nevertheless, the total product contributed by Cuba's unpaid labor seems to be greater than its operational costs plus its alternative costs, therefore resulting in net product. This conclusion should be analyzed in more detail.

The premise is that net product always occurs when the total product resulting from the use of unpaid labor is greater than the real costs involved in its utilization. Net product may result in each of the following three cases:

1. When unpaid workers are already fully or partially employed and unpaid labor is done at the work site, net product always results from overtime, weekend work, and vacation work because there are neither operational costs involved (i.e., maintenance, transportation) nor damage inflicted on production. This is the typical case of unpaid labor done by employed workers at the job site. In this case net product is always equal to total product.

2. When unpaid workers are not already employed, net product results if the output created by them is greater than their operational costs. This is the case of military recruits, prisoners, females, and students whose output must be balanced with their transportation and maintenance expenses, plus the potential damage which they may inflict on the production process because of their lack of skills. Despite some contradictory reports, the overall trend seems to be that the use of these kinds of unpaid labor is beneficial to the Cuban economy. The best reason support-

ing this assumption is their continued utilization by the state.

3. When unpaid workers are already employed, either fully or partially, and unpaid labor is of a different nature than their regular job, net product results if the total output created by them, at the new place of work, is greater than their operational costs plus the potential costs induced by their absence from their original job. This is the case of unpaid workers, often underemployed at the work site, who are recruited to perform agricultural work. Another way to approach the problem is to check whether net product generated by these workers at the unpaid job is greater than their former net product at the work site.

Alternative opportunity costs in the latter case appear to be almost negligible for two reasons: the relatively small contribution of this excess labor to the sectors from which they departed, and the extra unpaid labor required from the remaining employees at the work site to offset the deficit of labor experienced by these sectors. With regard to operational costs, the situation is not as clear, but the continuing use of long-term unpaid workers suggests that costs incurred by them are smaller than total product generated by them. In any event, the government is trying to reduce such operational costs through the following measures: selection of unpaid workers according to their previous unpaid-labor performance, organization of training courses for the heads of brigades, training of special brigades to do a given type of job, and strict regulation of unpaid labor including the imposition of output standards. Even more significant is the fact that as time passes, formal organization of unpaid labor—akin to military organization—is emerging, and the long-term types of unpaid labor are gaining in use over the short-term type. Through such a process the state seeks to eliminate the negative effects of some kinds of unpaid labor, thereby strengthening the net contribution of unpaid labor to the Cuban economy.

The final conclusion is that the total product created by

all kinds of unpaid labor is greater than its operational and alternative costs, therefore resulting in net product. Improved organization seems to have resulted in a rising net product. Lack of data, due to Cuban secrecy on the subject, impedes quantification of this net product, but the author hopes that in the future better statistical information will permit further research.

III

The Cultural Thrust

*

22

GERALD H. READ

THE REVOLUTIONARY OFFENSIVE IN EDUCATION

Even Fidel Castro's severest critics acknowledge the educational accomplishments of his revolution. A new educational system has come about since 1959 and a degree of administrative organization has resulted. The Cuban revolution has imposed styles of education that contrast to those that existed in Cuba for several centuries prior to the revolution.

The grand design in Cuban revolutionary education, as gradually evolved by Castro and his education planners, seeks to universalize schooling, imposes a Marxist orientation on education, relates theory to practice, and incorporates the working masses in the nation's educational structure.

Gerald H. Read, professor of comparative education at Kent State University, takes a broad look at education in Cuba since 1959 in the following article.

The "grand design" of Cuban revolutionary education can best be described in terms of four major goals which are being pursued simultaneously.

1. Making education universal from nursery school through the university, so that knowledge, science, and technology will be made available to all.

Reprinted from Gerald H. Read, "The Cuban Revolutionary Offensive in Education," *Comparative Education Review*, XIV, 2 (June 1970), 131–143, by permission of the author and the publisher.

2. Developing a Marxist orientation in education.
3. Combining education with technological principles, productive work, and research.
4. Incorporating the working masses into education.

The most significant achievement of the Castro regime in its first ten years of existence has been the establishment of genuinely free co-education of all types of schools and on all levels, by eliminating registration fees and tuition, and by providing free text books, school supplies, scholarships, and economic aid for thousands of young people, peasants, and workers who otherwise would never have had the opportunity to secure an education. The principle of universality of education through state control and management has been put into effect for the first time in the history of Cuba in order to meet the social, economic, and cultural needs of its children and adults, as well as the needs of a technologically developing nation.

This indeed is a huge undertaking for a newly established revolutionary government and involves a great investment of human resources and money for a nation that is still industrially underdeveloped, but it is a necessary investment if a successful and widespread transformation to a socialist state is to be achieved.

The Minister of Education, José Llanusa, has repeatedly said "the proposed draft of the Law for Compulsory Secondary Education will soon be discussed," but no date has ever been set. In January 1969, however, he filled in a few more details of the proposed law relative to measures for enforcement. "The responsibility for compliance with the law will fall on the parents, and the law will also include measures to be taken in case of non-compliance. Discussions will be held with all the people concerning this law. Their opinions will be taken into consideration, block by block, work center by work center."

The new program forecasts a huge demand for secondary school teachers. Many young people will have to be enrolled in the pedagogical institutes of the three universities or in a special center in Camagüey for a five-year course after having graduated from the new technological institutes. An organized effort is already being made to direct into the pedagogical institutes those who have served as monitors.

Castro gave little personal attention to the ideological mission of the schools in the early years of the 1960s. Slow and laborious spadework to this end, however, was undertaken by cadres from the Trade Union of Education and Scientific Workers (SNTEC). In advance of the thoroughgoing reformulation of objectives, revision of course content, reorientation of teaching procedures, and a reconstruction of teacher education, the Trade Union conducted a series of conferences for the purpose of ideological orientation. At one of these meetings, on December 13–15, 1961, Gaspar Jorge García Galló, the Secretary-General, made very clear the source and inspiration of the new pedagogical theory and practice.

> Those who are going to study in the primary school during these years will become adults in a society different from that of today; let there be no doubt about it. The society in which the children will live, for whom we are working in these programs, will be Communist when they are adults. Communist! I suppose that you have studied the program approved by the 22nd Congress of the Communist Party of the Soviet Union. [October 17–18, 1961]. If some have not studied it, note here that one ought to study it and he who has only read it, note that he ought to study it.

Later in this same meeting, Secretary García made the point that the schools could not be refashioned in a short time but that a long-range plan was contemplated.

> What is proposed is to train active and conscientious builders of the communist society. But this cannot be achieved immediately by means of simple decrees and administrative orders of the new revolu-

tionary authority. It is not enough to meet here and agree to modify all the plans of study. This will require a longer time and it will be achieved to the degree that the old educators are reeducated and a new mentality is created, a new socialist mentality.

The real revolution in education got underway after October 1965 when the July 26th movement was converted into an organized Communist Party of Cuba. In June, 1965, the Minister of Education, Armando Hart Dávalos, proclaimed the start of a new phase in educational development which would be marked by an aggressive effort to secure an ideological transformation in the moral and social consciousness of every citizen. He resigned his post as Minister shortly thereafter to become the Organizing Secretary of the Communist Party of Cuba. A hundred-member central committee, a six-man secretaryship, and an eight-man political bureau assumed responsibility for coordinating the Party's ideological pronouncements and programs, which for the most part emanated from the office of the First Secretary, Fidel Castro.

Castro gradually succeeded in putting together what can be called a system of attitudes, beliefs, values, assumptions, ideals, and goals—in short, an ideology. He used this, in August 1968, as a whip for chastizing Czechoslovak socialists who, he claimed, were sacrificing glorious ideals for the illusory immediate material gains that would come from commercial ties with the imperialist powers of the West. What were the glorious ideals which the Prime Minister had come to hold so dear, even to the point of supporting the invasion of a socialist country?

> . . . those beautiful aspirations that constitute the communist ideal of a classless society, a society free from selfishness, a society in which man is no longer a miserable slave to money, in which society no longer works for personal gain, and all society begins to work for the satisfaction of all needs and for the establishment among men of the rule of justice, fraternity, and equality.

These are the stated aspirations and ideals that now guide and direct Castro's educational visions and revolutionary endeavors.

.　　.　　.

The theoretical framework of Cuban education . . . is a peculiar mix of Marxism and Castroism. Leninism is almost never mentioned. The nationalism and independence of Castro is so great that Marx is seldom directly quoted. It is best, perhaps, to identify the conceptual guidelines as Castroism while recognizing that the sources are to a large extent those of Marxism and socialist humanism. Educational structures and practices, on the other hand, are much less dependent upon imported sources, although even here borrowings from the socialist countries of Eastern Europe may be observed.

Although Castro is still committed to socialist humanism and has kept it in a rather fluid state with varying interpretations, all evidence points to the beginnings of a more systematic ideology, perhaps even a dogmatism. On September 28, 1968, he asserted with great confidence: "We can state that it has taken years for revolutionary conscientiousness to triumph in our masses . . . and I believe that it has actually been during this past year that the triumph of the Revolution has become most evident in the consciousness of the masses of our capital."

.　　.　　.

[Minister of Education José] Llanusa has been a close collaborator of the Prime Minister since the guerrilla days in the Sierra Maestra mountains. No one in Cuba today is more devoted to the task of furthering the ideological orientation of the entire educational establishment. On August 18, 1968, he addressed the Makarenko Pedagogical Institute in Havana, where he directed this challenge to the graduating class: "You must help develop your students as Communists, representatives of generations that will be better than yours—which, in turn, will doubtless be better than ours. That is the revolutionary pledge you are making today to the Revolution. You must be concerned about the conduct of students . . . the ideological formation of those students."

On January 24, 1969, "creating a new conscience" was the theme for the Minister of Education's address to the activists who were responsible in the Party for indoctrination in all educational, scientific, and cultural institutions. The aspiration of the new revolutionary pedagogy, he emphasized, was "the creation of a new scale of values in which man and his complete development are the fundamental considerations." What should be the relation of the individual to the collective? The Minister took great care to say: "This means a complete development of his individuality for the benefit of collective interest, based on the revolutionary and international principles our leaders have taught us." The "New Cuban Man" which this pedagogy is to create must be one "for whom work is enjoyment and not obligation, and for whom study is a permanent process. A man of culture, science and technology."

To achieve these ends, the Minister of Education has conceived a strategy called the "Mass Line." The leaders of the Revolution patiently and repeatedly describe and explain in their major addresses the grand design of the new education and all the difficulties being encountered in putting it into operation. They elaborate upon the plans and strategies they have proposed, tried out, or hope to put into action to meet the operational problems. All of the mass organizations, government agencies, and party branches are then called upon to cooperate in getting the educational program moving forward. Llanusa has said that the "Mass Line" is not simply a theoretical postulate; it is a revolutionary reality, a style of work. To be more specific, he declared: "Revolutionary pedagogy must be everyone's concern, a consistent application of the anti-bureaucratic methods which Fidel teaches us . . . Everyone teaching, everyone learning, everyone working, everyone devoted to national defense, everyone creating for the revolution."

A similar line was taken at the Seventh National Assembly of the People's Organizations in Education. "We need teachers whose motivation is to form new men . . . True revolutionary teachers who will replace the turncoat teachers who deserted their country."

. . .

[A] polytechnical program [was] started on May 25, 1964, under a law which proclaimed that the new concept of education would run the entire span of the educational system from the first grade through the university. The ideological aim is to develop a new attitude toward life, work and the working class, and to overcome the tendency of students to develop a bookish outlook on life.

The then Minister of Education, Armando Hart, went to the U.S.S.R. in 1961 to study its educational system and methods. The Trade Union of Educational and Scientific Workers of Cuba, modeled after that of the U.S.S.R., conducted seminars throughout the island on the theoretical and operational meaning of polytechnical education. Ivan Grivkov of the U.S.S.R., Lu Ting-Yi of China, and Alfred Wilke of the German Democratic Republic contributed descriptions of the operation of polytechnic education in their countries to a Trade Union publication. Later *Tres Experiencias Sobre La Politecnización* illustrated how three Cuban schools had interpreted and applied polytechnical education.

Another step toward a more utilitarian education was taken in 1968 when the Plan for Technological Instruction converted all the Agricultural-Cattle Raising Technological Institutes into military centers. There are now 23 institutions in this program, under the direction of the Office of Military Centers for Intermediate Education, in the Ministry of the Armed Forces. The technical and teaching portions of the programs are supervised by the Ministry of Education. Students live under strict military discipline at boarding institutions and complete their military draft obligations while they study.

Major Belarmino Castilla Mas, deputy minister for tech-

nological military training, directs all intermediate level
technological training, sets priorities, and developed the
strategy for the change-over to the new system. He has
asserted: "It is our job to determine where and how this
army of technicians is to be trained, where we are to
employ these human resources and in which direction the
efforts must be aimed." The major will also have full responsibility for determining "the rational use of the teaching personnel."

Fidel was candid in giving another reason for combining
secondary education with military training:

> ". . . nothing makes a military commander hap-
> pier than to have a technological school assigned to
> one of his units. Indisputably, any youth with one or
> two years of senior high or technological education
> finds it easier to learn military techniques and is much
> more capable of learning the handling of complex
> military equipment in a short time. Military units
> have a hard time training personnel composed of
> young people with only a second-, third-, or fourth-
> grade education."

.　　　.　　　.

Will this military training be similar to the ROTC arrangement found in American universities? What will be
the status of the regular armed forces? Some hint as to
what Fidel has in mind appeared in an article recognizing
the fifth anniversary of the promulgation of the Military
Service Law: "At the present time tens of thousands of
young students drawn from our technological and high
schools make up our military units." This article then went
on to distinguish between the Revolutionary Armed Forces,
as an organization of cadres-on-call, and the regular troops
which are the students on active duty at each of the institutes. Moreover, the schools of the future will not only
be in the army but will also be in the country. This was
made clear in an address by Fidel on December 8, 1968.
". . . it will no longer be today's '45-Days School Goes
to the Countryside'; by then it will be the 'School in the

Countryside.' " On March 13, 1969, he was even more certain that this would be the case. "In the future we will have the Schools in the Countryside . . . The first of these will soon be under construction."

. . .

The National Office of Worker-Farmer Education, in the Ministry of Education's elementary school division, seeks to up-grade the meager knowledge of the peasants and workers which was acquired during the literacy campaign or after a few years of schooling. Improvement courses are given for adults (14 years of age, and above) to advance them to the third-grade, sixth-grade, and through the basic secondary levels. Classes are held in work and farm centers, usually in the evenings or before the work shift begins. More than 15 million textbooks, technical pamphlets, workbooks, magazines, and newspapers have been printed by the Ministry of Education and distributed without charge to participants in these programs.

Completion of the basic secondary course opens the way to further education in the upper secondary classes, the Worker-Farmer Preparatory Faculties of the universities, or special technical and vocational courses for adults. The Worker-Farmer Faculties, created in 1964 with branches in many cities and towns, undertake crash courses to prepare adults for entrance into various schools and the universities. In order to enroll in one of these faculties one must be a member of the trade union, Armed Forces, Ministry of Education, or mass organizations. The time schedule is co-ordinated with work-shifts; classes are usually held at the place of work. Experience derived from these courses has led Castro to predict that: "In the future, practically every plant, agricultural zone, hospital, and school will become a university."

Adult education also includes the Women's Educational Advancement Program. This program brings thousands of farm girls and women from the Sierra Maestra mountains and other remote places to boarding schools which prepare them politically and educationally to return to their own areas to expand the Party's influence and to teach. The Ana Betancourt School for Farm Girls is one of these institutions. Founded in 1961 at the suggestion of Fidel Castro, it has an enrollment of more than 10,000 and is under the direction of the Federation of Cuban Women. It is housed in more than 300 mansions where the wealthy elite formerly lived.

Study and work-camps are maintained for delinquent youth between 14 and 17 years of age who for various reasons have not completed the sixth grade. This is a very active program designed to bring these youth back into the mainstream of society. The principle is: "Work should be the great teacher of youth."

Over 460,000 adults were enrolled in courses in 1968; from 1962 to 1967, 365,720 persons completed the sixth-grade and 578,444 the secondary courses. This program of adult education is exceptionally important in view of the massive exodus of the educated classes from Cuba during the past ten years. It is still common to find people with a sixth-grade education in charge of state farms, factories, and other important work centers. Some have served adequately, but the pressing need is for better educated administrators and supervisors.

Since 1959, schools have increasingly reflected Castro's attempt at total control of everyday life and activities, thoughts and attitudes, although one wonders if regimentation can ever be achieved and maintained to the degree reached by the socialist countries of Eastern Europe. The island at the present time can be characterized as a vast reformatory, or, more charitably, a comprehensive school, with the Party showing no sign of discouragement in its mission to inculcate revolutionary enthusiasm, commitment, and morale. The leadership has given top priority to rural development and a regeneration of the masses through education in the spirit of the July 26th movement and ideological evangelism. The Revolutionary Offensive has demonstrated above all else that the appetite for education is insatiable, is still growing, and will continue to grow faster than the national production. If present projections become a reality, the teaching profession will absorb more than half the graduates of higher and secondary institutions.

If Cuba is to resist the domination of the great powers, she must develop her agriculture and industry. Serious problems arise, however, when the educational system must be geared to meeting pressing societal needs and their required fulfillment outweighs all other ends, including even human freedom. The utopian and commendable dreams of Fidel Castro, which flow from his belief in the possibility of a better life for all Cubans, are in danger of being reduced to purely economic strategies.

Cuban education is increasingly becoming a victim of economic planning and systematization, in spite of everything Castro has done and said in efforts to prevent it. On the other hand, it may be that this is what the revolution is all about and to reverse the process is to deny the revolution. The supreme sacrifice that José Martí preached was to die for Cuba. He was strongly opposed to placing personal rights above the national welfare, for only *patria* mattered. Martí proclaimed: "He who loves the fatherland cannot think of himself."

Whatever the final judgment may be, Cuba in the past decade has witnessed a political, social, and pedagogical revolution. Cubans who have lived and are living through it will never be the same, and the future of Cuba will surely be different if Castro achieves his educational goals. "All soldiers, all students, all workers. An army of the people advancing along the three fundamental paths toward progress: educational development, defense of the country, and productive work."

23

LUDINI BARZINI

BREAKING EDUCATIONAL BARRIERS

One of the basic goals of Cuban education under the revolution has been the effort to bring schooling to all children—not only in the cities, but also in the countryside. This effort, in turn, is seen by Cuban educational planners as a way of breaking down the barriers between the city and the country.

In the course of a visit to Cuba, Ludini Barzini, Italian journalist, examined a number of rural schools around the island and concluded these schools have an additional advantage: that of helping alleviate agricultural problems resulting from labor shortages. Miss Barzini, United States correspondent for the Italian magazine L'Espresso, *wrote the following report for* The New York Times.

Three miles south of Guayabal on a narrow dusty road there is a sign that reads, "The Path Up From Underdevelopment Is Education." A couple of miles east of here, standing on the main road to Tarara amid bushy green coffee plants, another sign says, "The School Plan Is Your Responsibility."

Reprinted from Ludini Barzini, "In City and Country, Cuba Invests Big Effort in Schools," *The New York Times* (April 3, 1971), p. 6, by permission of the publisher. © 1971 by The New York Times Company.

Such slogans and colorful billboards reflect the serious business of education in Cuba, where one of the main goals now is to break down the barriers between city and country by taking modern education to the children of the mountains and forgotten villages and to teach city children not just how to read and write but also how to work with their hands—pick coffee beans, nurse citrus trees, grow pineapples, bananas and mangos.

The program, under which three boarding schools have been set up in rural areas and 15 more are planned, has an additional advantage: It has helped to alleviate agricultural problems arising in part from labor shortages.

One such school encountered on a short visit to Cuba recently is a smooth 25-mile drive from Havana. On a narrow paved road to the school of Plan Ceiba, the visitor passes through the "cordón" or "green belt" (the agricultural strip encircling the city), then through villages where oxcarts stand in line beside railway tracks waiting to pick up fertilizer; past the little gray houses built by campesinos of wood and palm-tree leaves.

At the school the children get up with an untidy rhythm as a visitor enters a classroom; some stand on one foot, others lean slightly on the desk without a sign of rigidity.

The teacher in the physics class, who at age 18 is almost as young as the students, is still a student himself. The massive enrollment in Cuban schools in recent years (over two million children, or 25 per cent of the population), has resulted in a shortage of teachers, and the country cannot afford to wait for all the teachers to graduate from college before going to work. Teacher training starts in the seventh grade. The students were shy in discussing any but the most general subjects although the principal encouraged encounters and conversations with the visitor.

At one point a 17-year-old boy asked the visitor where she lived. "What are American students doing?" he asked. "They seem very quiet. Is this true?"

A question about the life of the students in Cuba prompted this reply from a blond 15-year-old girl with her hair in a pony tail: "We go home on Saturday at noon to our families and come back to school on Sunday evenings, and I am happy to come back. I enjoy it here very much."

There are 35 teachers, most of them in their early twenties, and 500 students, half of them girls, studying from the 7th to the 10th grade.

The 24-year-old principal, Ebelio Enrique Campos, said: "We should also have 61 employes for the kitchen and the cleaning, but we have only 32, so the students help keep the classes clean."

In the dormitories, red for the boys and yellow for the girls, there are bunk beds and each has a cupboard for his clothes.

"The closets are without doors to discourage disorder," the principal said as he showed his visitor around.

There was little to get out of order: two hangers of clothes, one or two pairs of shoes, a roll of pink toilet paper and a few books in a neat pile.

The girls' dormitories were lively with chatter. Some were ironing their uniforms (beige blouses and brown skirts) and some were combing their hair or putting on curlers before going to work in the fields.

The initial attempt to break down the barrier between city and country was the establishment of what are known as escuelas al campo or schools to the countryside, of which like that at Plan Ceiba, known as an escuelas en el campo, are the direct descendents.

All secondary schools in and around the cities move students and teachers to the country by bus for 45-day stays. The youngsters work in the fields, do some homework, play games and sports and conduct political discussions.

Since the urban schools have to take turns going to the countryside, the timing is not always perfect. Elsa Ro-

dríguez, a young professor of economic geography who
is the principal of a school to the countryside 10 miles
from the provincial capital of Camagüey, commented on
this in an interview with *Granma*, the only Cuban daily
newspaper.

"It would be better that the period the students spend
in the escuela al campo be either at the beginning or at
the end of the term and not in the middle," she said, "so
as not to interrupt their studies, because I understand that
the children could forget part or all of what they learned
before coming here."

The four white prefabricated buildings of the experimental school at Plan Ceiba, built in 1968, stand on the
flat reddish-brown farmland as a red skyscraper would in
a white desert though they are only three stories tall.
Lined up one behind the other, they make the compound
look impressive.

The classrooms are large, with 40 students, and full of
light. The traditional brown wooden desks, with no scrib-
bling or hearts carved on them, are lined up neatly.

In the physics class the young instructor was explaining
an experiment in an informal atmosphere, but it was clear
that he dominated.

Around noon the 250 morning farmers come back from
the fields in their brown fatigues covered with earth and
run to their showers. The leaders of the groups must
gather to write their reports. The second shift goes to
work after lunch.

On the job they are coached by agriculture experts.

In this "year of productivity," as Premier Castro has
termed it, the emphasis is not only on cutting sugar cane,
although that is of vital importance to the economy, but
also on building schools and encouraging the young to
become teachers.

24

RICHARD R. FAGEN

THE POLITICAL CONTENT
OF ADULT EDUCATION

Richard Fagen's monograph, from which the following selection is taken, makes clear that education early became a major item in Fidel Castro's revolutionary tool chest. The political content of education was evident almost from the start of the revolution. Fagen notes, for example, Castro's well-known dictum that "the most important education is the political education of the people." He also quotes a less well-known comment that "revolution and education are the same thing."

Richard Fagen is a professor of political science and communication at Stanford University.

On September 26, 1960, Fidel Castro stood before the General Assembly of the United Nations and announced:

> Next year our people propose to launch an all-out-offensive against illiteracy, with the ambitious goal of teaching every illiterate person to read and write. Organizations of teachers, students and workers—the entire people—are preparing themselves for an intensive campaign and within a few months Cuba

Reprinted from Richard R. Fagen, *Cuba: The Political Content of Adult Education*, pp. 9–15, by permission of Hoover Institution Press. Copyright © 1964 by the Board of Trustees of the Leland Stanford Junior University.

will be the first country in the Americas to be able to claim that it has not a single illiterate inhabitant.

Although the ideological and organizational roots of what came to be called the "Year of Education" predate Castro's U.N. performance, this speech is an important historical benchmark for two reasons. It was here that Castro first told an international audience that a massive campaign against illiteracy would be launched and here that he first directly articulated to such an audience his perceptions of the intimate linkages between United States policies, the domestic problems of Cuba, and the conduct of the Cuban revolution. These themes were subsequently echoed and amplified during the literacy campaign. It seems fitting—and not entirely coincidental—that both the themes and the announcement of the campaign were closely juxtaposed in the same major international address.

The official opening of the campaign came three months later. On New Year's Eve, 1960, Castro addressed more than ten thousand teachers and dignitaries at Ciudad Libertad in Havana. He reminded his listeners that illiteracy and imperialism were inextricably linked, and he announced that "Just as we have organized the National Militia, so shall we organize the Army of Education."

Actually, the organization of the "Army of Education" can be traced back as far as 1959, when the Ministry of Education created the first Literacy Commission (*Comisión de Alfabetización*). The massive effort which was mounted in 1961, however, more properly dates from the establishment of the National Literacy Commission (*Comisión Nacional de Alfabetización*) late in 1960. Participating in the commission were representatives of the Ministry of Education, the Ministry of the Armed Forces, and the mass organizations of teachers, workers, women, young persons, and others. Below the commission were municipal councils, established on a territorial basis and responsible for both planning and execution at the local level.

But at the operational heart of the campaign were the

literacy workers, the "foot soldiers" of the "Army of Education." They were of four types:

1. Conrado Benítez Brigadistas.[1] These were primarily young volunteers, recruited from school and trained quickly to serve as teachers for the duration of the campaign. They lived and taught in the more rural areas of the country.
2. Popular Alphabetizers (*Alfabetizadores Populares*).[2] This group was composed primarily of adults who volunteered to teach (often in their spare time) in the cities and towns.
3. "Fatherland or Death" Worker Brigadistas (*Brigadistas Obreros "Patria o Muerte"*). These were urban workers who served as teachers in more remote areas under an arrangement whereby their fellow workers filled in for them on the job. The scheme was designed to augment the teaching force from the urban work force without substantially weakening the latter.
4. Schoolteacher Brigadistas (*Maestros y Profesores Brigadistas*). These were professional schoolteachers who served primarily in technical and organizational positions during the campaign. Most participated full-time after April 1961, when —because technicians were needed for the campaign— the primary schools throughout Cuba were closed for the remainder of the year.

[1] Conrado Benítez was a young Negro literacy worker who allegedly was murdered by anti-Castro forces in January 1961 while teaching in the mountains of Las Villas. For a poem in honor of Benítez see Richard Jolly, "The Literacy Campaign and Adult Education," in Dudley Seers, ed., *Cuba: The Economic and Social Revolution* (Chapel Hill: University of North Carolina Press, 1964), p. 200, presents data on the school background, province of origin, province of assignment, age, race, and place of residence of the Conrado Benítez Brigadistas.

[2] There is no easy translation for the Spanish verb *alfabetizar* and its derivative forms. Literally, of course, it means "to alphabetize," but it also means "to make literate."

Something of the scope of the literacy campaign is suggested by the following official statistics:

Total population of Cuba 6,933,253
Illiterates at the beginning of 1961 979,207
Illiterates taught to read and write during
   1961 707,000
Literacy workers (breakdown below) 271,000

   Conrado Benítez Brigadistas 100,000
   Popular Alphabetizers 121,000
   "Fatherland or Death" Brigadistas 15,000
   Schoolteacher Brigadistas 35,000

Thus, counting only the literacy workers and the illiterates actually taught during the campaign, almost one million Cubans were directly participant as either teachers or students during 1961. Although we may call into question the Cuban definition of what constitutes a functional literate, there can be no doubt that the island was blanketed with eager and active literacy workers. Probably never before in the history of any country had so large a fraction of the annual budget and energy gone into a mass literacy effort.

Our primary concern, however, is not with the literacy aspect of the campaign, but rather with its political dimensions. Basically, the Year of Education and the follow-up efforts launched in 1962 had two major purposes. Using the most neutral categories possible, we can call the first purpose "skill training" and the second purpose "civic training." Under the first category the most important skills to be taught were reading and writing, although subjects such as arithmetic were subsequently added. No attempt will be made here to evaluate the success of the skill-training aspects of the campaign.

Instead, we shall concern ourselves entirely with the second purpose of the campaign, civic training. Within the context of the campaign there were two primary methods of such training. The first involved furnishing or refurnishing the minds of the students with the historical, ideological, and political images which the regime felt were appropriate to the new social order. This was attempted within the formal framework of the teacher-student relationship. The crucial point is that citizenship was taught as a subject matter just as reading and writing were taught. This method of civic training will be referred to as "political education."

The second method of training involved the interactive aspects of the recruitment, publicity, and teaching processes themselves. Here *participation* rather than substance was the key element in the training. At least two types of participation were important. The first type—direct participation—involved the literacy worker and the students in interaction; each was to learn from the other. The second type—indirect participation—involved (at least potentially) the entire population. The citizenry in general was to be imbued with national consciousness and be mobilized, made aware, made proud, and made productive by associating itself with the campaign against illiteracy and all the related symbolism. The mass media and the mass organizations supplied the crucial linkages between the leadership and the populace for civic training through indirect participation.

The importance that the Cubans themselves attached to both types of training by participation, the direct and the indirect, are so well highlighted in the following statement that it is worth quoting at length:

> Our Campaign . . . has put the youth of Cuba in direct contact, on a daily and prolonged basis (almost a year), with the peasants and mountain folk, the poorest and most isolated people on the island. Thus, almost 100,000 scholars and students, aided by more than 170,000 adult volunteers, produced a very real growth of national fusion. *This extensive ex-*

perience in communal life cannot but greatly increase
understanding among the classes and strata of the
population. But in our view *there is something more;*
[during the campaign] the entire populace could participate in the tasks of the Revolution. The Revolution no longer was a phenomenon reserved for a
small group, zealous and active; *it was converted into*
a true mass movement.

It should be apparent by now that we are dealing with
a type of civic training that differs both quantitatively and
qualitatively from the type of training which occurs in
developed democracies. The most important differences relate to organization, scope, and content. Thus, in Cuba
we have a classic example of a revolutionary regime taking positive and massive action for the express purpose of
creating the type of citizenry which the leadership feels
is necessary for the functioning of the system. New institutions were created not simply to socialize the young and
the isolated within the existing political culture, but rather
to aid in developing a wholly *new* political culture. Because directed change in the political culture is a primary
concern of the regime, there is continuing pressure toward
more comprehensive planning, control, and coverage. The
Cuban not linked to national institutions, not participating
in revolutionary activity, and thus not learning about the
new Cuba, is an anathema to the regime.

With this in mind, the historical and sociological importance of the Year of Education becomes clearer. This
effort was the testing and recruiting ground for many of
the ideas and persons that continue to sustain socio-
political change in Cuba. It was during 1961 that much
of the institutional and ideological framework that gives
such a special cast to Cuban politics was first tried out
in a program of national scope. There have been important
changes since that time, most notably the full and official
acceptance of a Marxist-Leninist world view and the related efforts to build a functioning Communist party. But

the Year of Education remains an important watershed of Cuban thought and action.

. . . one final point should be made. At least in 1960 and 1961, there were striking similarities between Cuban social and political thought and the thought of radical nationalist leaders in Africa and Asia. Few if any of the Africans or Asians could match Castro's institutional and organizational apparatus for civic training, but clearly many were thinking along the same lines. As one careful student of Afro-Asian ideologies of change and development has suggested:

> The "socialism" of the new nations is thus fed by anti-foreign feelings, by a passion for social equality, and by a desire for rapid economic development. It is influenced by the Marxist analysis of capitalism and the Leninist description of imperialism, but it does not accept the entire Marxist-Leninist theory as the basis of action.

With few changes, these words could have been written in summary of the materials presented herein.

The past two and a half years and the full and open adherence to communism on the part of the Cuban government have, of course, brought important changes in the content and processes of civic training. But these changes are deeply rooted in the experience of the Year of Education. Early in the revolution, Castro said that "the most important education is the political education of the people," and that "revolution and education are the same thing." He would say the same today.

25

FIDEL CASTRO

1868 TO 1968:
A CONTINUOUS THREAD

One of the favorite themes of Fidel Castro is Cuba's past, with particular focus on early struggles for independence. This theme appears in many of his speeches, and Castro obviously is very much preoccupied with the history of Cuba and with his own place in that history.

In an important 1968 speech, Castro spelled out his concept of Cuban history in considerable detail. The following excerpt from that speech illustrates his view that the early struggles for Cuban independence from Spain, dating back one hundred years to 1868, are linked to his own revolution in a continuous thread. The 1968 speech, detached from the language of Marxism-Leninism, is sharply nationalist in tone.

. . . What does October 10, 1868, signify for our people? What does this glorious date mean for the revolutionaries of our nation? It simply signifies the beginning of one hundred years of struggle, the beginning of the Revolution in Cuba because in Cuba there has been one revolution: that which was begun by Carlos Manuel de Céspedes on October 10, 1868, the revolution which our people are still carrying forward.

Reprinted from *Granma,* Weekly Review in English, 3, 41 (October 13, 1968), 2–5.

There is, of course, no doubt that Céspedes symbolized the spirit of the Cubans of that time. He symbolized the dignity and rebelliousness of a people—still heterogeneous in nature—which began to take shape as a nation in the course of history. It was, without doubt, Céspedes who, among the conspirators of 1868, was the firmest in his determination to rise up in arms. . . .

This commemoration today is like a meeting of the people with its own history. It is a seeking out by the people of its own history. It is a seeking out by the present generation of its own roots. Nothing could better teach us how to understand what a revolution is, nothing could better teach us to understand what the term "revolution" means, than an analysis of the history of our country, a study of the history of our people, of our people's revolutionary roots.

Perhaps there are some who have regarded the nation and the homeland as just a natural development. Perhaps many think of the Cuban nation and of awareness of nationality as things that have always existed. And perhaps many persons have seldom taken time out to think about just how the Cuban nation was born, how our awareness came into being.

One hundred years ago, this awareness did not exist. One hundred years ago, Cuban nationality did not exist. One hundred years ago, a nation, in the sense of a people with common interests and a common destiny, did not actually exist. A century ago, our people were simply a motley mass, made up in the first place of citizens of the Spanish colonial power dominating us; there was also a mass of citizens born in this country, many direct descendants of Spaniards, others more distantly related—of whom some favored colonial rule, while others were allergic to that rule; and a large mass of slaves, criminally brought to our country to be pitilessly exploited after the exploiters had already actually annihilated the primitive Indian people here. . . .

In the first decades of the last century, when the rest of Latin America had already won its independence from Spain, Spanish power still rested on a very firm basis in our country, which they called the last and the most precious jewel in the Spanish crown.

The emancipation of Latin America had very little real influence on our nation. . . .

26

BOHUMIL BAD'URA

CUBA'S RESOURCES
IN HISTORY

*Cuban scholarly activities have received varying sup-
port from the revolution. In some cases, as the following excerpt illustrates, significant advances in scholarly work have been made. But the overall picture
is mixed, as indeed the excerpt shows in the case of
historical research.*

*Bohumil Bad'ura, a leading Czechoslovakian his-
torian, who spent much of 1966 and 1967 in Cuba,
wrote the article, from which the following excerpt
is taken, for the scholarly* Ibero-Americana Pragensia, *an annual review on Latin American topics
published by the historic Charles (Karlova) University of Prague. The article and the annual review
serve as good examples of the growing European
interest in Latin America and in Cuba.*

The most profound change that the revolution caused
among historical institutions and in the organization of
historical research is evident in the creation of the *National Commission of the Academy of Sciences* [Comisión
Nacional de la Academia de Ciencias]. The Commission
set up a new institution which replaced and restructured

Reprinted from Bohumil Bad'ura, "Algunas Informes Sobre la
Organización y las Condiciones de Investigación Histórica en Cuba,"
Ibero-Americana Pragensia, II (1968), 209–211, 212–213, 218–220,
227–228.

older organizations. According to resolution No. 5 of May 14, 1962, the *Academy of History* [Academia de Historia] was dissolved; resolutions 6 and 7 of the same date created the *Institute of History* [Instituto de Historia], whose direction was entrusted to the well known Cuban historian Julio Le Riverend Brusone. . . . Later, the *National Archives* [Archivo Nacional] was put under the control of the *Institute of History* . . . ; the same was done with the *Office of the City Historian* [Oficina del Historiador de la Ciudad]. At the newly created Institute a group of young men, students at the School of History of the University of Havana, began to work along with well experienced researchers such as José Luciano Franco. It was Julio Le Riverend who took advantage of the opportunity for young people to begin the tasks of research, organizing a special "seminar" in which they learned to work together. The first result of their work was a two-volume history of [Fulgencio] Batista's government.

The new scientific orientation and character of the Institute of History which distinguishes it from the Academy of History is seen in their completely different objectives. While the Academy was an honorary organization, the Institute has been created as a center of research in which each investigator is assigned a task which is paid for when completed.

The fact that the Academy of Sciences had entered into various agreements with similar institutions in the Socialist countries, enables the Institute of History to maintain regular international ties offering foreign researchers the opportunity to do research in Cuba, giving them necessary help. Professional ties have been developed especially with German historians, including Professor Jürgen Kuczynski and his pupils from Humboldt University in Berlin. The founding of the Institute of History of the *Cuban-German Group*, dating from 1966, headed by Julio Le Riverend and Jürgen Kuczynski, shows the extent of Cuban-German collaboration in the study of history. At the present time, the group is dedicated exclusively to the study of North American monopolies in Cuba.

The Institute of History together with the National Archives provide a library equipped with works essential to the study of Cuban history. It also maintains a good collection of North American, Spanish and Latin American historical reviews. During recent years, funds for the library have shown a steady increase, thanks, above all, to the interchange of publications and also to the fact that the Academy of Science and the Institute of History publish works. . . .

The Academy of Science created the *Institute of Ethnology and Folklore* [Instituto de Etnología y Folklore] (directed by Argeliers León Pérez) and the *Scientific Department of Anthropology* [Departamento Científico de Antropología] (directed by Ernesto Tabía). With these new centers, the old *National Board of Archeology and Ethnography* [Junta Nacional de Arqueología y Etnografía] lost its reason for existence. The *Economic Society of Friends of the Country* [Sociedad Económica de Amigos del País] also ceased to exist, its library being incorporated into the *Literature and Linguistic Institute* [Instituto de Literatura y Lingüística] which works under the direction of the eminent Cuban intellectual José Antonio Portuondo. We should also mention among institutes of the Academy of Sciences, the *Working Group on Philosophy* [Grupo de Trabajo de Filosofía] which took as part of its program the task of preparing and processing a course on Cuban history and philosophy (concentrating more on the history of the teaching of philosophy). Luis Arce was appointed to direct the course. He has now been studying such subjects for the past twenty years. The Academy of Sciences also administers *The Historical Museum of Medical Sciences "Carlos J. Finlay"* [Museo Histórico de las Ciencias Médicas "Carlos J. Finlay"] which publishes its own magazine, "Finlay." The Academy's director, José López Sánchez, is the author of various historical publications among which the biography of Tomás Romay stands out.

The National Library [Biblioteca Nacional] (which is now named after José Martí) has increased its cultural services considerably. Thanks to these increased services the historian can appreciate more than ever the library's effort to offer valuable material for the investigation of bibliographies and also in reprinting many of the historical sources (from its collections of manuscripts). The *Cuban Collection Department* [Departamento de Colección Cubana], which is staffed by competent personnel devoted to the bibliographical and historical studies, is materially assisting the development of Cuban historiography. The director of this department is Juan Pérez de la Riva, "spiritus movens" of a great many activities and director of the *National Library Magazine* [Revista de la Biblioteca Nacional].

When I mentioned that the National Library "José Martí" has improved its services, I do not want to imply that it has already reached its maximum possibilities. The library's card indexes show many blanks, due to the fact that more than half of the titles are still to be catalogued. . . .

The change that came about in education at the university level in the field of history during the revolution consisted, mainly, in organizing the teaching system—beginning with history schools, followed by the Schools of Methodology and Techniques of Historical Research, and ending with changes in curricula. At the present time there are similar branches of study at the University of Havana and at the University of Oriente. Nevertheless, judging from a European point of view, it is easy to discover faults in the work being done at the new university centers. The most serious one is based upon insufficient instruction regarding sources and also upon the prevailing empiricism which lacks deeper explanation of the races which exist in the country. This kind of empiricism is a characteristic feature of Cuba's historiography . . . For example, many works have been written on genealogy, but the following question arises: Why has no one undertaken a detailed study of parochial books or other genealogic sources? In these conditions, if a teacher wants to furnish his students with this kind of information, he must prepare for his classes by studying in the archives himself. . . . New professors appear conscious of this fact and credit should be given them because the old techniques are giving way to valuable instruction to students regarding bibliography and the value of documents as sources of historic research. . . . During the school year of 1966–1967, the students of the school of history at the University of Oriente took, for the first time, a course dedicated to the methods of historical research.

The efforts to transform universities into centers of scientific activity in collaboration with faculty direction have not been too fruitful an experience. However, the students did prepare a few compilations which helped them in their learning but these, on the whole, can be judged only as promising.[1] The majority of the professors and instructors were satisfied with their teaching activities but they have not reported their results. On the other hand, the university faculties and the history schools have participated with greater decisiveness in projects of research prepared by the government. . . .

At the third most important university in Cuba, the Uni-

[1] In the school of history of the University of Havana, the students did research on the Cuban labor movement from 1899 to 1924. Each pupil was assigned a different year. In the school of history of the University of Oriente, the students undertook a study (based on protocol and legal documents) regarding the prices of slaves in Santiago de Cuba during the Hundred Years War. For the time being, only the first part is finished—that is, the compilation of data. Andrés Cue Bada is well along in a biographical study of Vicente García, while other works (regarding the history of public health, the sugar mills in Santiago de Cuba during the eighteenth century, and so on) which were begun by the students are yet to be completed.

versidad Central de Las Villas, history is not studied at the
upper graduate level; nevertheless, its School of Humanities has prepared plans for historical research. Here, the
study of the labor movement of different regions of the
province is already taking place and the recently created
university *Commission for Latin American Studies* [Comi-
sión de Estudios Latinoamericanos] proposes to "study the
problems of Latin American countries, their economic picture and historical background, present political and social
events and artistic creation." Following Rostock University's example, a working group from the Universidad Central has decided to study the way in which [Alexander Von]
Humboldt influenced the Spanish-American countries, so
that Humboldt's second centennial which was celebrated in
1969 will not be forgotten.

It is too early to guarantee that all the projects begun
by Cuban universities will accomplish the desired results,
but the future of historiography in Cuba will undoubtedly
depend largely on the level of knowledge that the future
historians achieve in their present studies. . . .

The National Archives has been enriching itself in numerous areas from different sources. What is more, it has
founded regional historical archives in Matanzas, Santiago de Cuba, and Camagüey, which are dependent on the
national center. These regional branches not only assemble
the archives of other organizations, but also are in charge
of protecting, arranging and making them accessible to
researchers. Their creation shows that the modern concept
of archives has spread to the provinces. It is obvious that
this decision is significant. The local authorities will turn
over unnecessary papers to the archives where they will be
classified and made available to the public. Unfortunately,
the desirable material has not yet been made available.
The archives had been faced with a series of obstacles, the
most serious being the lack of a building or adequate
quarters. For this reason, up to the time I left Cuba (July
1967), the Regional Historical Archives of Camagüey ex-

isted only in theory and in the Matanzas branch, which keeps valuable sources piled up in unsuitable premises, research is virtually impossible. It was not until August that it received adequate quarters to which these materials could be transported. The only branch which was able to set up a usable collection of valuable documents was the facility in Santiago de Cuba, situated in the library edifice at the University of Oriente. Nevertheless, this branch is also faced with a lack of space, since its university quarters are full.

Apart from the National Archives and its branches, there exists another series of archives which store documents for organizations connected with these archives. More often than not, they are depositories for paper and not for archival material. That these archives are disorderly and that they do not even provide the minimum of assistance which would facilitate the location of material, is the conclusion I reached during my tour in the Province of Oriente in the company of Professor Francisco Ibarra Martín. The object of the tour was to assemble informative material to help students of the School of History at the University of Oriente to select subjects for their theses. Owing to this conclusion the results were minimal, seeing that to list the different material in relation to the years involved and their topics would take weeks and months. . . . Sometimes documents, only a century old, are so moth-eaten and so stuck together that to unstick them would require the same amount of time that would be needed to ascertain what they deal with. Taking into account that at the present time there is no single study dealing with the condition of Cuban archives, and bearing in mind the proverb that a little is better than nothing, I would like to tell my readers about my experiences in Santiago de Cuba, Baracoa, Manzanillo, Jiguaní, Victoria de las Tunas, Holguín, Puerto Padre, Gíbara, Banes and Antilla, in the Province of Oriente, in Cienfuegos and Trinidad.

The majority of these places (and not only these because I think that my observations are good for nearly all the island) have their own archives of regional or municipal administration (the old municipal archives), *parroquiales,* notary materials, court records and those of the recorder of deeds. Those cities with a port also have a customs archive.

In the Province of Oriente there is a main body of documents of customs archives, most of them from the present century. It is evident that these have practically no value in the study of commercial history before the twentieth century since a serious historical study can hardly be accomplished utilizing the very few that have been preserved from the nineteenth century. A great number of documents have been purposelessly lost during the past years (in Santiago de Cuba, Manzanillo, Gíbara and Baracoa; they have been destroyed by natural calamities (as in Puerto Padre where the archives suffered great damage during the hurricane of 1965). Undoubtedly, the most significant and deplorable loss involving customs archives was that of Santiago de Cuba in 1966 in which a tile building collapsed. Nevertheless, no one was in a position to say what had really been lost since there had never been a classification of these documents, nor was the condition of the documents known. . . .

Summing up the observations stated in this report, I would like to point out that at the present time there arises in Cuba a controversy between the effort to broaden historical research and the lack of qualified personnel, between the tendency to upgrade the teaching of history and the possibilities of basing this teaching on the country's documentary resources and, finally, between the growing interest for historical research and the condition in which the archives are found. Regarding the latter observation, it is evident that it is only with great effort that many of the archives can be made use of in a desirable way. Much time is required for the study of sources and the results are not always profitable. The researcher who travels to Cuba or even Cuban researchers must bare these facts in mind. There still exists a big difference between the capital of the country and the majority of the provincial cities. Sometimes the foreigner who always goes to Havana first can rely on better conditions than the Cuban who works in the provinces. If the researcher is studying problems related to the colonial period, it would be almost utopian to think that he could do without the National Archives. Here he will find material essential for the study of local history. For example, how could one study in detail the history of Santiago de Cuba without paying attention to the documents of political affairs, The Audencia of Santiago de Cuba, the Court of Commerce, Civil Court, and other material in the National Archives? This is not only true for Santiago de Cuba but for all of the other cities. In Cuba, contrary to Czechoslovakia, there is no exchange of material among different archives . . . In Cuba, the only way to study the sources of other places is to ask for a microfilm copy. But unfortunately, even up to the present time, provincial libraries and archives (except for universities) do not possess the necessary equipment to read the microfilm copies. This does not affect the provinces so much, since, for the time being, there are few researchers. Nevertheless, the matter requires a quick solution. . . .

The purpose of this article has been to present an approximate study of the changes and difficulties in historical research in Cuba. At the end of these observations, I consider it appropriate to warn . . . that the ideas expressed in this work constitute a limited insight into a transitory period. I am convinced that this paper will not be of any substantial value when the results are in from future investigation into historical sources of Cuba and with the creation of all the necessary conditions for its development which we hope will come about soon.

27

KEITH ELLIS

CUBAN LITERATURE AND
THE REVOLUTION

*From its outset, the Cuban revolution encouraged a
certain degree of independence of thought on the part
of writers. Fidel Castro, taking a special interest in
literature, argued that he had little to fear from such
independence. He could have added, however, that
social protest and commitment have a long tradition
in Cuban writing and that this tradition has been
bolstered by the literary production of the Castro era.*

*Writing a decade after Castro came to power but
before the Padilla affair (see page 249) fully came
to light, Keith Ellis, Canadian commentator, saw significant diversity of theme and subject matter in
Cuban literature of the revolutionary years. While
the preference among state-run publishing houses was
for literature emphasizing social responsibility, his
survey suggests this "does not preclude the admissibility of other attitudes."*

*Ellis, who teaches at the University of Toronto,
however, concludes that the revolution has yet to
yield up truly important literary works. Moreover,
the best of contemporary literature in his opinion
comes from a handful of novelists and poets whose
pens were active in pre-Castro times as well. Yet he
does see promise in the works of a half dozen*

Reprinted from Keith Ellis, "Cuban Literature and the Revolution,"
Canadian Forum, XLVIII, 576 (January 1969), 224–226, by permission of the author and the publisher.

*younger poets who, he feels, "have managed with
greater success than the novelists to write of how
it is to live in the revolution."*

An examination of the Cuban revolution's impact on Cuban literary history may well be guided by some of the frequently asked questions: What is the attitude of the government towards literature? Have certain political orientations been imposed on writers? Has a new literature come out of the revolution?

In its attitude to art and artists the Cuban revolutionary government has from its incipient days shown a degree of tolerance unsurpassed by other socialist regimes. The government's policy has been to allow the various tendencies and schools of art to find their own way to the revolution and to allow them complete freedom of self-determination in their field. 'Our mortal enemies," Fidel Castro has said, "are not the Cuban writers and artists, but the North American imperialists"; and whereas Marxist theoreticians have in the past prescribed the role of the writer in terms of the doctrine of "social realism," the Cuban regime has not been tempted to regard socially uncommitted writing as being inimical to Cuban cultural advancement. But at the same time it must be stated that social commitment has always been, especially in the novel, a strong characteristic of Cuban and, indeed, all Latin American literature.

The first significant Cuban novel, *Sab* (1839), took a firm stance against slavery; and later, through figures like José Martí, social, political and economic criticism through literature became more comprehensive. This tendency was strengthened in Cuba, as in the rest of Latin America, in the late nineteenth and early twentieth centuries, with literary theorists like José Antonio Portuondo and Juan Marinello, as well as other leading writers, emphasizing this aspect of literature in the nineteen forties and fifties. Fidel Castro and Che Guevara often read Latin American poetry to their comrades between battles of the revolution;

and Castro's broad literary interests are revealed by the many allusions in his speeches to Dante and other writers. It would seem, then, that given the traditional tendency of Cuban literature, the government has not found it necessary to concern itself with reorienting the social attitudes of Cuban writers. Attitudes that lie outside the main stream are tolerated for their contribution to culture and are not considered dangerous because, as Sartre, himself an advocate of committed literature, has recently said, literature cannot by itself change people. It would also seem that the writers are sympathetic to and do not feel constrained by the revolution. By greatly expanding the facilities for book publication and working earnestly at making the whole population literate, the government has pleased the writers in two fundamental ways: their works are more easily published and more widely read—both inside and, because of interest in the revolution, outside of Cuba—than they were before. By and large they seem to be in favor of the revolution and, without any sense of irony, communicate to people outside Cuba the sense of satisfaction they feel in participating for two months each year in such communal tasks as cane cutting.

Although a special interest has been shown in republishing works by foreign and Cuban pre-revolutionary writers which reflect most accurately the socialist principles of the revolution, writers not primarily so identified are also published. Thus on the one hand numerous editions of Martí's prolific writings with their emphasis on liberty, independence and anti-imperialism have been printed; and on the other hand the complete works of Julián del Casal, a Cuban poet of more private artistic concerns, were recently published in celebration of his centenary. Similarly, the works of socially concerned foreign writers like Sarmiento, Neruda, Benedetti and Zapata Olivella have repeatedly occupied the national presses; while the centenary of Rubén Darío, a Nicaraguan poet, often criticized in Latin America for his lack of social involvement, was elab-

orately celebrated in Havana in 1967. With foreign and
Cuban pre-revolutionary writings then, as with contemporary Cuban writers, the preference for clear social responsibility does not preclude the admissibility of other
attitudes. It is, of course, taken for granted by the regime
and by the writers that "social responsibility" means a positive attitude toward the revolution and that "other attitudes" do not include literature that is hostile to the government and, consequently, in revolutionary terms, to the
people.

What is the relationship between the works themselves
and the revolution? To what extent and how is the revolution reflected in the literary works? It would seem best to
attempt to answer these questions through a brief examination of the principal genres: the novel, poetry, and
theater.

The two outstanding Cuban novels since the revolution
are Alejo Carpentier's *El siglo de las luces* (*The Century
of Lights*), 1962 and José Lezama Lima's *Paradiso,* 1966.
The novelists were born in 1904 and 1910 respectively,
and their literary reputations were well established before
the revolution. Carpentier's novel deals with the unsuccessful attempt of a Jacobin, Victor Hugues, to apply in
Guadeloupe certain ideals of the French Revolution; and
Lezama Lima's traces the biography of a middle class Cuban from his childhood in the late Spanish colonial period
to the 1930s. While it is true that history is employed in
these works, . . . not as background but as revealing significant changes in social and political consciousness, the
relationship of these novels to the revolution itself is
oblique. Also, they are difficult novels in which some of
the most sophisticated techniques of the contemporary
novel are employed and, especially in *Paradiso,* obscure
concepts are explored in complex metaphorical language.
"Our Cuban realism is surrealist," Lezama Lima has said.

The younger novelists, not following this trend, are writing in a more direct style. They tend for the most part to
concentrate on events of the bad days of Batista, while

only indirectly mentioning the good days of the revolution. Humberto Arenal's *El sol a plomo* (*The Oppressive Sun*), 1959; Hilda Pereda Soto's *Mañana es 26* (*Tomorrow is the 26th*), 1960; Lisandro Otero's *La situación,* 1963; and Guillermo Cabrera Infante's *Tres tristes tigres* (*Three Sad Tigers*), 1967 are a few examples of this tendency in the novel.

Attempts to represent the conflicts and joys within the experience of the revolution have been made by novelists such as Edmundo Desnoes in *El cataclismo,* 1965 and *Memorias del subdesarrollo* (*Memories of Underdevelopment*), 1965, as well as José Soler Puig in *En el año de enero* (*In the Year of January*), 1963 and *El derrumbe* (*The Fall*), 1964. It may be said, however, that the documentary approach predominant in these works has not yet produced the novel capable of showing the continuing "revolution within the revolution."

The figure of Nicolás Guillén dominates contemporary Cuban poetry. Since the thirties he has been a poet of social commitment; and the grievances in his poetry became the grievances of the revolution. The predominance of satire in his persistent condemnation of racism, imperialism and economic exploitation had caused some to wonder whether his writing would be affected when the social change he had always desired became reality. It would seem that he has adapted well. Since 1959 he has shown his ability to write gentle poems of contentment with the Cuban scene while his old style is kept in practice by his attention to Puerto Rico, Panama, Guatemala, Bolivia, Jamaica, etc.

In Cuba as in many Latin American countries, journals are often created to serve as vehicles for particular schools of poetry. In the late 1920s, for instance, the *Revista de Avance* represented decorative, formalist poetry. In the forties and fifties, the journal *Orígenes* favored mystical, Catholic themes. An anthology, *Poesie cubaine 1959–1966* (1967), containing poetry concerning the revolution, includes the work of almost all the leading representatives of earlier tendencies in Cuban poetry. Established poets like Manuel Navarro Luna, Félix Pita Rodríguez and Lezama Lima, without feeling, as do many younger poets, a need to change their concept of poetry have expressed sentiments inspired by the revolution and have paid homage to its significant events. Roberto Fernández Retamar (1930) and Fayad Jamís (1930) have tended to be more embracing in their commitment. They have stated that their aim is to "humanize" poetry, "to have it serve the needs of man, removing it as much as is possible from formal . . . or hermetic adventures." They add that poetry should "penetrate into daily life, nourishing it as it is nourished by it." They advocate "prosy writing, a conversational tone, violence, sentimental effusion, social and political preoccupation—although not in a mechanical or demagogic way." These poets, as well as Heberto Padilla[1] and Pablo Armando Fernández, Antón Arrufat, Miguel Barnet, Nancy Morejón, to name a few, have managed with greater success than the novelists to write of how it is to live in the revolution. They have not, however, limited their production to this theme.

Virgilio Piñero and his realistic theater remains the senior voice in Cuban drama; but in this genre, more markedly than in the others, young people—between twenty and thirty years old—are in the ascendancy. They carry on all kinds of experimentation, exploring various aspects of Cuban life and have many theaters at their disposal—several movie houses were converted to theaters after the revolution—and a large new, spontaneous public to whom to play.

In the same way that it took two decades for the Mexican revolution to yield important manifestations in the fields of painting and literature, it may be expected that with the Cuban revolution, young as it is after only ten years, major literary and other artistic works rooted in it are forthcoming.

[1] See Selection 28 [—J.N.G.].

28

HERBERTO PADILLA

MY CONFESSION

*Cuban poet Heberto Padilla was arrested in March
1971 for alleged counterrevolutionary activities
against the Castro government. Specifically, he was
accused of having talked against the revolution in
conversations with a number of European writers, including René Dumont and K. S. Karol, both of
whom have written articles and books critical of
many of Fidel Castro's economic and social experiments.[1] Padilla was also accused of writing antirevolutionary poetry and of other "subversive crimes."*

*Padilla subsequently was released after confessing
his wrongdoing and wrongthinking. In a lengthy confession, he admitted the counterrevolutionary activities and asked for an opportunity to expose and discuss his conduct publicly. Part of his confession
appears in the following selection.*

*The whole Padilla affair prompted a storm of inter-
national protest against the Castro regime for its treatment of Padilla. Some sixty European and American
intellectuals signed a letter to Premier Castro ex-
pressing their shame and anger at the Cuban action.
Many of those signing had in earlier years lent considerable support to the Cuban revolution.*

I have meditated profoundly before deciding to write this
letter. I am not doing so through fear of the inevitable and
just consequences of my contemptible, well-known, and

---

[1] See Selections 36 and 37 [—J.N.G.].

demonstrated attitudes—demonstrated far beyond what I myself could ever have imagined possible. I am moved by a sincere desire to make amends, to compensate the revolution for the harm I may have occasioned and to compensate myself spiritually. I may prevent others from losing themselves stupidly.

But, above all, I desperately want to be believed and my action not to be taken for cowardice, although I myself am overcome with shame at my own actions.

For many days I struggled with myself to make the decision to tell the truth. I did not even want my truth to be as it really was. I preferred my disguise, my appearances, my justifications, my evasions. I had become accustomed to living in a deceitful and subtle game. I did not dare to confess how ignoble, how unjust, how unworthy my position was: I really lacked courage to do so.

Under the disguise of the writer in revolt within a socialist society I hid my opposition to the revolution; behind the ostentations of the critical poet who paraded his sickly irony, the only thing I really sought was to maintain my counterrevolutionary hostility. . . Among both Cubans and foreigners, I discredited every one of the initiatives of the revolution, striving to look like an intellectual who was an expert in problems about which I had neither information nor knowledge and following this course, I committed grave faults against the true intellectual's moral code and, what is worse, against the revolution itself.

What I wanted was to call attention to myself, to profit from the scandal. I wanted to be the only writer with a political mind in Cuba, the only writer capable of confronting the revolutionary process, and to impose my ideas. Hypocritically and contemptuously, I repeated the old theory that politics is too serious a matter to leave to the politicians.

I who had not achieved anything either before or after the revolution wanted fame and looked for it along a road that could only lead to counterrevolution

My egocentrism was growing by leaps and bounds. The BBC of London did a long interview with me in color for a program dedicated to Cuban education and culture. A Canadian radio station sought me out for more interviews.

Because my vanity then had no limits I carried my disaffected political positions to heights I never should have scaled: right up to poetry. I was convinced that a poem which would represent a supposed criticism of the revolution would awaken the interest of certain international circles: those of skepticism and hatred toward revolutions. That is how I came to write insidious and provocative poems which, . . . due to the problems and demands of history, expressed nothing other than the temperament of the unbeliever, the cynic, a verse-maker trapped by his own moral and intellectual limitations.

I have been tremendously ungrateful, unjust with Fidel, and the deep repentance I feel for having acted that way motivates me to make amends for my cowardly and counterrevolutionary virulence.

When I have mentally reviewed the fragments I wrote, parts of the novel, I have felt extraordinary shame. It seems to me incredible that I could have thought that this sickly bundle of papers—containing all my bitterness—could have had some intellectual and human worth. Not only were they politically negative and deformed, not only did they reflect my ideological and counterrevolutionary vacillations, but also they expressed a profound disenchantment with life, with hope, and with the poetry of life. The man who wrote those pages was a man who was headed toward his own moral and physical destruction.

Only the vanity and petulance of considering myself worthy of all honors could lure me into such a plan—one that as always was linked to the outside world, to the purpose of giving my prestige a boost in the foreign periodicals, in editorials, and among the public. And among my most serious mistakes is precisely this one: to think that I, a Cuban, could live a double life—on the one hand to vegetate like a parasite in the shadow of the revolution, while on the other to cultivate my literary popularity abroad at the cost of the revolution and thereby to help its enemies.

I V

The International Thrust

*

29

BORIS GOLDENBERG

CASTRO AND THE AMERICAS

Fidel Castro's appeal throughout the Americas was evident even before he had finally ousted the Batista dictatorship. The appeal was part romantic, part idealistic, part practical. The enthusiasm for the Cuban revolution spread throughout the cities and into the countryside, and, within a year of his coming to power, the name "Fidel Castro" became something of a household word in Latin America.

The extent of this appeal is suggested by Boris Goldenberg in the following excerpt. Goldenberg, a European who was naturalized a Cuban before Castro came to power, observes that "Fidelism" became a mass movement in Latin America "and the more it was attacked by the United States the stronger its influence grew."

The Castro revolution was an autochthonous product of the Continent. It had not been imported from outside. Here, and here alone, was a Latin American David who dared to defy the northern Goliath. The enthusiasm which he had aroused in his own people spread to other Latin American countries.

The Chilean Socialist leader and former presidential candidate, Senator [Salvador] Allende, wrote in 1960: "Cuba's

Reprinted from Boris Goldenberg, *The Cuban Revolution and Latin America* (New York: Frederick A. Praeger, 1965), pp. 311–317, by permission of Praeger Publishers, Inc., New York, and George Allen & Unwin, Ltd. © George Allen and Unwin, Ltd.

fate resembles that of all Latin American countries. They
are all underdeveloped—producers of raw materials and
importers of industrial products. In all these countries imperialism has deformed the economy, made big profits and
established its political influence. The Cuban revolution is
a national revolution, but it is also a revolution of the
whole of Latin America. It has shown the way for the liberation of all our peoples."

The Mexican intellectual, Noyola, who had worked in
Cuba with Boti, made a speech at Mexico University on
January 4, 1961, which was warmly welcomed by the economic journal *Trimestro Económico*. "The Cuban revolution," he said, "is the common heritage of all Latin American nations. At the present moment it is our most valuable
heritage."

In the towns there was universal enthusiasm: it spread
from the intellectuals to the workers and employees. The
new gospel soon penetrated to the most distant parts: "At
peasant meetings in the Andes, a new shout: 'A la Cu-
bana' (the Cuban way) is heard echoing through the chill
mountain night."

In Mexico, it seemed that the stationary revolution might
begin to move again:

> Under President Miguel Alemán, Mexico was pa-
> tiently transformed into a country after the U.S. im-
> age, in which businessmen and the profit motive be-
> came dominant forces. At the same time, in a rather
> empty gesture of respect for the revolutionary tradi-
> tions of Mexico, politicians continued to talk as
> though they were carrying on a permanent revolu-
> tion. This make-believe was suddenly shaken by the
> hard reality of the Cuban revolution. Mexican poli-
> ticians were confronted with the simple question:
> "Did they believe in revolutions or didn't they?"

Members of parliament, artists, students and workers
demonstrated their sympathy for Cuba, and a pro-Castro

movement with its own organ, the journal *Política*—which was apparently financed by Cuba—grew up round ex-President Cárdenas. In 1961 these activities culminated in the foundation of the *Movimiento de Liberación Nacional.* In March of that year a big international Congress for National Sovereignty and Peace assembled in Mexico. It was attended by delegations from many countries and much attention was devoted to the Cuban revolution. (The Chinese delegate, particularly, stressed the central importance of this revolution, whereas the Russian delegation confined itself to general expressions of sympathy.)

President López Mateos found it necessary to emphasize that he was "on the extreme left inside the Constitution." His government became one of Castro's most energetic protectors and introduced revolutionary measures of its own. Foreign companies, for example the electricity company, were nationalized, and the government pushed ahead with the distribution of land: in the first three years of López Mateos' Presidency, 16.8 million acres were confiscated and given to peasants. This was about 5.7 million a year, as compared with an average of about 1.48 million a year for the period 1948–1958.

In Venezuela, Castro's influence strengthened the opposition against Betancourt's reformist, anti-revolutionary government. In the summer of 1960, after Betancourt turned against Castro, his foreign minister . . . had refused to sign the declaration of San José and had to be replaced. The *Acción Democrática* split, a large number of Castro-sympathizers were expelled and, together with others who had left the party in April, formed a new organization, the Movement of the Revolutionary Left (MIR) which was to become the main spearhead of Castroist influence and the organizer of terrorism and guerrilla warfare. The leader of the URD [a Venezuelan political party], Jovito Villalba, protested against the signing of the San José Declaration which he denounced as an imperialist maneuver directed against the sovereignty of Latin American nations. Two ministers belonging to his party left the government and in November 1960 the coalition was ended. From now on, the URD found itself in a common front with MIR and the Communists. Violent street demonstrations, terrorist acts and clashes between revolutionaries and government forces became common.

It was of little use to Betancourt that he seemed to have the support of the peasantry, as was shown by a mass demonstration in September 1960. In the towns the left appeared to predominate, while the extreme right attacked Betancourt as a revolutionary and supported disaffected groups in the army. In a period of serious economic difficulties the President thus found himself between two lines of fire. Time and again he found it necessary to declare a state of emergency and suspend the constitution.

In Brazil, the fast-growing peasants' leagues in the northeast expressed enthusiastic sympathy for Cuba. Castro's picture hung in their central office above the head of their leader, the socialist deputy Francisco Julião. Most students, many trade union leaders, and members of parliament of different parties came out in support of Cuba. The anti-*Yanqui* mood grew. The new President, Quadros, who had visited Cuba as presidential candidate in order to increase his prestige, took a firm stand against all anti-Cuban suggestions by the Americans. His action in conferring the highest Brazilian decoration on Guevara contributed to the crisis which led to his resignation. Civil war threatened and the army was divided. A compromise was found which enabled Vice-President Goulart to become Quadros' successor. Goulart had more than once firmly expressed his sympathies for Castro. His brother-in-law, Brizzola, governor of Rio Grande do Sul, formed a "National Liberation front" with Julião and others, which, supported by the semi-legal communists, many union leaders, politicians of the Workers' Party (Goulart's own party) and many intellectuals, seemed to be developing into the bastion of Castroism.

Of particular importance were the changes which occurred inside the Brazilian trade union movement. It had
previously been dominated by government appointed and
controlled leaders who were closely linked with ORIT
(Inter-American Regional Organization of Workers) to
which the most important Brazilian trade union confeder-
ations belonged, and which was strongly influenced by its
most important member, the AFL-CIO of the U.S.A. Under
Quadros and Goulart changes took place which became
apparent at the Workers Congress in August 1960. The old
leaders were expelled and a left group composed of *Tra-
balhistas,* socialists and communists took charge. The most
important trade union organizations, especially the Con-
federation of Industrial Workers (CNTI) became standard-
bearers of anti-imperialism, pro-communism and Castroism.

In Argentina the aged Socialist leader, Palacios, was
elected a senator for the first time, primarily because he
had supported the Cuban revolution. When in summer
1961, he changed his mind there was a split in the Socialist
party in which the pro-Castro wing retained the majority.
President Frondizi's brother formed a pro-Castro "revolutionary left." A united front of Castroists, Peronists, communists and left-wing Socialists began to develop, and in
July 1960 the bourgeois, anti-Castro *Unión Cívica Radical
del Pueblo* made public its view that Castroism was having
a favorable effect on the Latin American policy of the
United States. In this situation President Frondizi had no
choice but to adopt a policy of benevolent neutrality in the
quarrel between the United States and Castro. In spite of
increasing pressure from the right, particularly the army,
he refused to take any action against revolutionary Cuba.

In Uruguay the Castroists controlled the university and
managed to gain a foothold in the unions. Their influence
was particularly strong in the large party of the *Colorados,*
which was in the government and managed to frustrate the
anti-Castro intentions of their *Blanco* colleagues. In July

1960 the congress of Socialist and Popular Parties of Latin America, which took place in Uruguay, had expressed itself in favor of protecting the Cuban revolution. In 1961 when anti-Castro feeling increased there were demonstrations and bloody clashes in Montevideo.

In Chile Castro became a symbol for the entire left in its struggle against President Alessandri's stabilization program. Until late 1960 the important Christian Democratic Party also viewed Fidelism sympathetically. The most important trade union organization, CUTCH, controlled by communists and socialists and led at the time by an ardent Castroist, Clotario Blest, became the champion of the Cuban revolution. Pressure from below was so great that the government—consisting of conservatives, liberals and radicals—which normally pursued a right-wing policy, opposed the anti-Castro policy of the United States.

In Bolivia the Cuban revolution aroused enthusiasm among the masses and sympathy among the government. In July 1960 the powerful trade union organization, COB, which monopolized the workers and peasant movement, sent a telegram to the United Nations protesting against the threat to Cuba and saying that Latin America would not permit a repetition of the Guatemalan affair. The Communists represented only a small minority, and Bolivia was dependent on economic assistance from the United States, but both houses of parliament adopted almost unanimous resolutions in the summer of 1960 urging the government to protect the Cuban revolution.

In Peru, the Castroists were able to entice a section of the APRA away from Haya de la Torre. An APRA *rebelde* was founded which later changed its name to MIR (Movement of the Revolutionary Left). They won the support of the majority of the students at San Marcos University which up till then had been a bulwark of APRISMO. Together with the communists they infiltrated into the Popular Action Party of Belaúnde Terry, the future president, and could count on the active sympathy not only of the tiny socialist party but also of two new movements: the *National Liberation Front* of General César Pando, a known fellow-traveller, and the *Social Progressive Movement,* presided over by Alberto Ruiz, yet another pro-communist who was to run for President. While the communists were able to establish their control over some sections of the trade union movement, peasant-leagues arose in distant parts of the country and at their rallies there were shouts of "Viva Castro!" All these movements were united against the APRA, now accused of being pro-*Yanqui* and in collusion with the oligarchy. Because the army regarded APRA as its traditional enemy, leftist, including Castroist and pro-communist ideas, influenced a part of the officer corps, which up to then had always been considered a prop of the ruling classes.

In Ecuador on the other hand Fidelism managed to make capital out of the fact that a Latin American mediation commission (with the blessing of the United States) had decided in favor of Peru in a frontier dispute. President Velasco Ibarra made anti-imperialist speeches and strongly opposed any intervention in Cuban affairs. But for many people he did not go far enough. Among his left-wing critics were Vice-President Arosemena and the Minister of the Interior, Araujo Hidalgo, who left the government to become one of the leaders of Fidelism in Ecuador. When Vice President Arosemena returned from his visit to Russia in the summer of 1961 the masses welcomed him with shouts of *"Cuba sí! Yanqui no!"* and "long live Castro." In the autumn of 1961, a political crisis took place and there were strikes and street fighting; the armed forces split, Velasco Ibarra fled and Arosemena took his place. The causes of the upheaval were mainly domestic but the problem of their attitude towards the Cuban revolution played a part in Ecuador, just as it did in Brazil.

In Colombia the Castroists exploited the conflict within the Liberal Party. The pact between the Liberals and the Conservatives, which had led to the fall of Rojas Pinilla's dictatorship and the restoration of democracy, laid down that for the next sixteen years there would only be two parties, Liberals and Conservatives, which would hold the Presidency in turn. This arrangement prevented any other party from getting into power but resulted in bitter internecine struggles within the two legal parties. A left-wing movement developed in the Liberal Party which, although led by millionaire López Michelsen, was strongly influenced by Castroism and Communism. In addition there were other openly pro-Castro organizations, for example, the Gaitanists, and regional parties like the *Movimiento Popular Revolucionario* in Medellín.

The situation was the same in other countries. Fidelism had become a mass movement and the more it was attacked by the United States the stronger its influence grew. The Cuban revolution became the leading opponent of imperialism, and anti-imperialism is the deepest political sentiment in Latin America. Even before Castro's victory Eudocio Ravines rightly wrote, "One can discuss the existence or non-existence of imperialism, but what one cannot deny is the existence of a militant anti-imperialism directed against the U.S.A. which determines the policy pursued, without exception, by all Latin American countries."

30

FIDEL CASTRO

SECOND DECLARATION
OF HAVANA

*The interests of Cuban Premier Fidel Castro in
the rest of Latin America was evident early in his
first months in office. On frequent occasions during
1959 and then in 1960, he spoke with enthusiasm
for revolutionary change in other Latin lands. There
was evidence in some of his speeches that he saw the
rest of Latin America using the Cuban example. By
February 1962 when Castro issued his Second Declaration of Havana, he was clearly articulating a
call for change, reform, and revolution throughout
the hemisphere.*

*Still, he was not prepared to go on record as ex-
porting his revolution. He rejected such accusations
on this point, which were beginning to develop. "Revolutions are not exported," he said, "they are made
by the peoples." During this period, Cuban radio and
other propaganda organs were denying foreign
charges that Cuba was training young people from
other Latin lands in revolutionary tactics. Yet such
training was going on and Castro later talked about
it.*

*But the language of this declaration is restrained.
Its approach is Marxist-Leninist, but the emphasis is
on Latin America and its relations with the United
States. The declaration marked a significant turning
point in Cuban policy toward the rest of the hemisphere and, while parts of the speech were directed*

at internal issues, it has come to be more and more studied for its importance in the foreign field.

What is Cuba's history but that of Latin America? What is the history of Latin America but the history of Asia, ~rica, and Oceania? And what is the history of all these ~les but the history of the cruelest exploitation of the ld by imperialism?

~t the end of the last century and the beginning of the ~sent, a handful of economically developed nations had ~vided the world among themselves, subjecting two thirds of humanity to their economic and political domination. Humanity was forced to work for the dominating classes of the group of nations which had a developed capitalist economy.

The historic circumstances which permitted certain European countries and the United States of North America to attain a high industrial development level put them in a position which enabled them to subject and exploit the rest of the world.

What motives lay behind this expansion of the industrial powers? Were they moral, "civilizing" reasons, as they claimed? No. Their motives were economic.

The discovery of America sent the European conquerors across the seas to occupy and to exploit the lands and peoples of other continents; the lust for riches was the basic motivation for their conduct. America's discovery took place in the search for shorter ways to the Orient, whose products Europe valued highly.

A new social class, the merchants and the producers of articles manufactured for commerce, arose from the feudal society of lords and serfs in the latter part of the Middle Ages.

The lust for gold promoted the efforts of the new class. The lust for profit was the incentive of their behavior throughout its history. As industry and trade developed, the social influence of the new class grew. The new productive forces maturing in the midst of the feudal society increasingly clashed with feudalism and its serfdom, its laws, its institutions, its philosophy, its morals, its art, and its political ideology. . . .

Since the end of the Second World War, the Latin American nations are becoming pauperized constantly. The value of their capita income falls. The dreadful percentages of child death rate do not decrease, the number of illiterates grows higher, the peoples lack employment, land, adequate housing, schools, hospitals, communication systems and the means of subsistence. On the other hand, North American investments exceed 10 billion dollars. Latin America, moreover, supplies cheap raw materials and pays high prices for manufactured articles. Like the first Spanish conquerors, who exchanged mirrors and trinkets with the Indians for silver and gold, so the United States trades with Latin America. To hold on to this torrent of wealth, to take greater possession of America's resources and to exploit its long-suffering peoples: this is what is hidden behind the military pacts, the military missions and Washington's diplomatic lobbying. . . .

As to the accusation that Cuba wishes to export its revolution, we reply: Revolutions are not exported; they are made by the peoples.

What Cuba can give and has already given to the peoples is its example.

And what does the Cuban Revolution teach: that revolution is possible, that the peoples can make it, that in today's world there is no force strong enough to impede the peoples' liberation movements.

Our victory would never have been possible if the revolution itself had not been inexorably destined to arise from the conditions which existed in our economic-social reality, a reality which pertains even to a greater degree in a goodly number of Latin American countries.

It happens inevitably that in those countries where Yankee monopolist control is strongest, where exploitation by the reigning few is most unrestrained and where the conditions of the masses of workers and peasants are most unbearable, the political power becomes more vicious, states of siege become habitual, all expression of mass discontent is suppressed by force, and the democratic channels are closed off, thereby revealing more plainly than ever the kind of brutal dictatorship assumed by the dominating classes. That is when the peoples' revolutionary breakthrough becomes inevitable.

And while it is true that in America's underdeveloped countries the working class is in general relatively small, there is a social class which because of the sub-human conditions under which it lives constitutes a potential force which—led by the workers and the revolutionary intellectuals—has a decisive importance in the struggle for national liberation: the peasantry.

In our countries two circumstances are joined: underdeveloped industry and an agrarian regime of a feudal character. That is why no matter how hard the living conditions of the workers are, the rural population lives under even more horrible conditions of oppression and exploitation. But, with few exceptions, it also constitutes the absolute majority, sometimes more than 70 percent of Latin American populations. . . .

Wherever roads are closed to the peoples, where repression of workers and peasants is fierce, where the domination of Yankee monopolies is strongest, the first and most important lesson is to understand that it is neither just nor correct to divert the peoples with the vain and fanciful illusion that the dominant classes can be uprooted by legal means which do not and will not exist. The ruling classes are entrenched in all positions of state power. They monopolize the teaching field. They dominate all means of mass communication. They have infinite financial resources. Theirs is a power which the monopolies and the ruling few will defend by blood and fire with the strength of their police and their armies.

31

FIDEL CASTRO

WAVES OF THE FUTURE

✳

The first meeting of the Cuba-sponsored Organización Latino Americana de Solidaridad (OLAS), held in Havana in August 1967 produced a good deal of debate and fierce disagreement over the course that Communists and other leftists should follow in carrying out change and reform in Latin America. In the end, the Cuban-sponsored resolution calling for the vigorous pursuit of revolutionary activity in the hemisphere won out.

Fidel Castro outlines his own views on revolution in a speech to the concluding session of the conference. His remarks, widely reprinted throughout Latin America, begin with a long discussion of a number of hemisphere issues, including an attack on the United States for "imperialist designs" on Latin America. Then, he turns to the OLAS meeting itself.

We sincerely believe that we would not be fulfilling our duty if we did not express here that the OLAS Conference has been a victory of revolutionary ideas, though not a victory without struggle.

In OLAS, a latent ideological struggle has been reflected. Should we conceal it? No. What is gained by concealing it? Did OLAS intend to crush anyone, to harm anyone? No. That is not a revolutionary method, that does not agree with the conscience of revolutionaries. Let's be clear about this—*true* revolutionaries!

And we believe it is necessary that revolutionary ideas prevail. If revolutionary ideas should be defeated, the revolution in Latin America would be lost or would be indefinitely delayed. Ideas can hasten a process—or they can considerably delay it. And we believe that this triumph of revolutionary ideas among the masses—not all the masses, but a sufficiently vast part of them—is absolutely necessary. This does not mean that action must wait for the triumph of ideas—and this is one of the essential points of the matter. There are those who believe that it is necessary for ideas to triumph among the masses before initiating action, and there are others who understand that action is one of the most efficient instruments for bringing about the triumph of ideas among the masses.

Whoever stops to wait for ideas to triumph among the majority of the masses before initiating revolutionary action will never be a revolutionary. For, what is the difference between such a revolutionary and a latifundium owner, a wealthy bourgeois? Nothing!

Humanity will, of course, change; human society will, of course, continue to develop—in spite of human beings and the errors of human beings. But that is not a revolutionary attitude.

If that had been our way of thinking, we would never have initiated a revolutionary process. It was enough for the ideas to take root in a sufficient number of men for revolutionary action to be initiated, and through this action the masses started to acquire these ideas; the masses acquired that consciousness.

It is obvious that in Latin America there are already in many places a number of men who are convinced of such ideas, and have started revolutionary action. And what distinguishes the true revolutionary from the false revolutionary is precisely this: one acts to move the masses, the other waits for the masses to have a conscience already before starting to act.

And there is a series of principles that one should not

expect to be accepted without an argument, but which are essential truths, accepted by the majority, but with reservations on the part of a few. This useless discussion about the means and ways of struggle, whether it should be peaceful or nonpeaceful, armed or unarmed, the essence of this discussion—which we call useless because it is like the argument between two deaf and dumb people—because it is that which distinguishes those who want to promote the revolution and those who do not want to promote it, those who want to curb it and those who want to promote it, is useless. Let no one be fooled

Different words have been used: the road is the only one, it is not the only one, it is exclusive, it is not. And the conference has been very clear in this respect. It does not say *only* one road, although that might be said: it says a fundamental road, and the other forms of struggle must be subordinated to it, and in the long run, it is the only road. To use the word *only*, even though the sense of the word is understood and even if it were true, might lead to errors about the imminence of the struggle.

That is why we understand that the declaration [Second Declaration of Havana], by calling it the fundamental road, the road that must be taken in the long run, is the correct formulation. If we wish to express our way of thinking, and that of our party and our people, let no one harbor any illusions about seizing power by peaceful means in any country in this continent; let no one harbor any illusions. Anyone trying to tell such a thing to the masses will be completely deceiving them.

This does not mean that one has to go out and grab a rifle and start fighting tomorrow, anywhere. That is not the question. It is a question of ideological conflict between those who want to make revolution and those who do not want to make it. It is the conflict between those who want to make it and those who want to curb it. Because, essentially, anybody can realize if it is possible, or if conditions are ripe, to take up arms or not.

No one can be so sectarian, so dogmatic, as to say that one has to go out and grab a rifle tomorrow, anywhere. And we ourselves do not doubt that there are some countries in which this task is not an immediate task, but we are convinced that it will be their task in the long run.

There are some who have put forward even more radical theses than those of Cuba: that we Cubans believe that in such and such a country there are no conditions for armed struggle, but they claim that it is not so. But the funny thing is that it has been claimed in some cases by representatives who are not quite in favor of the theses for armed struggle. We will not be angered by this. We prefer them to make mistakes trying to make revolution without the right conditions than to have them make the mistake of never making revolution. I hope no one will make a mistake! But nobody who really wants to fight will ever have differences with us, and those who do not want to fight ever, will always have differences with us.

.   .   .

The importance of the guerrilla, the vanguard role of the guerrilla. Much could be said about the guerrilla, but it is not possible to do so in a meeting like this. But guerrilla experiences in this continent have taught us many things—among them the terrible mistake, the absurd concept that the guerrilla movement could be directed from the cities.

That is the reason for the thesis that political and military commands must be united.

This is the reason for our conviction that it is not only a stupidity but also a crime to want to direct the guerrillas from the city. And we have had the opportunity to appreciate the consequences of this absurdity many times. And it is necessary that these ideas be overcome, and this is why we consider the resolution of this conference of great importance.

The guerrilla is bound to be the nucleus of the revolutionary movement. This does not mean that the guerrilla movement can rise without any previous work; it does not mean that the guerrilla movement is something that can exist without political direction. No! We do not deny the role of the leading organizations, we do not deny the role of the political organizations. The guerrilla is organized by a political movement, by a political organization. What we believe incompatible with correct ideas of guerrilla struggle is the idea of directing the guerrilla from the cities. And in the conditions of our continent it will be very difficult to suppress the role of the guerrilla.

There are some who ask themselves if it is possible in any country of Latin America to achieve power without armed struggle. And, of course, theoretically, hypothetically, when a great part of the continent has been liberated, there is nothing surprising if under those conditions a revolution succeeds without opposition—but this would be an exception. However, this does not mean that the revolution is going to succeed in any country without a struggle. The blood of the revolutionaries of a specific country may not be shed, but their victory will only be possible thanks to the efforts, the sacrifices, and the blood of the revolutionaries of a whole continent.

It would therefore be false to say that they had a revolution there without a struggle. That will always be a lie. And I believe that it is not correct for any revolutionary to wait with arms crossed until all the other peoples struggle and create the conditions for victory for him without struggle. That will never be an attribute of revolutionaries.

.   .   .

The revolutionary, in pursuit of his ideal and revolutionary aims, uses various methods. The essence of the question is whether the masses will be led to believe that the revolutionary movement, that socialism, can take over power without a struggle, that it can take over power peacefully. And that is a lie! And those who assert anywhere in Latin America that they will take over power peacefully will be deceiving the masses.

. . . Really, the only thing that we can say is that it is an honor to our revolution that our enemies think so much about it; likewise, it must be an honor for all Latin American revolutionaries that imperialism has given so much attention to the problem of OLAS. . . . And the OLAS Conference has been held—a true representation of a genuine revolutionary movement, whose ideas are solid because they are based on reality. OLAS is the interpreter of tomorrow's history, interpreter of the future, because OLAS is a wave of the future, symbol of the revolutionary waves sweeping a continent of 250 million. This continent is pregnant with revolution. Sooner or later, it will be born. Its birth may be more or less complicated, but it is inevitable.

We do not have the slightest doubt. There will be victories, there will be reverses, there will be advances, there will be retreats: but the arrival of a new era, the victory of the peoples in the face of injustice, in the face of exploitation, in the face of oligarchy, in the face of imperialism, whatever the mistakes that man makes, whatever the mistaken ideas that may be obstacles on the road, they are unavoidable.

We have spoken to you with complete and absolute frankness; we know that the true revolutionaries will always be in solidarity with Cuba; we know that no true revolutionary, that no true Communist on this continent, nor among our people, will ever let himself be induced to take those positions which would lead him to an alliance with imperialism, which would make him go hand in hand with the imperialist masters against the Cuban Revolution and against the Latin American revolution.

We do not condemn anyone a priori, we do not close the doors to anyone, we do not attack anyone en masse, in a block; we express our ideas, we defend our ideas, we debate these ideas. And we have absolute confidence in the revolutionaries, in the true revolutionaries, in the true Communists.

Those will not fail the revolution, the same as our revolution will never fail the revolutionary movement of Latin America.

We don't know what awaits us, what vicissitudes, what dangers, what struggles. But we are prepared, and every day we try to prepare ourselves better, and every day we will be better and better prepared.

But one thing we can say: we are calm, we feel safe, this little island will always be a revolutionary wall of granite, and against it all conspiracies, all intrigues, and all aggressions will be smashed. And high upon this wall there will fly forever a banner with the legend *Patria o Muerte ¡Venceremos!*

32

JOHN GERASSI

A NEW INTERNATIONAL
IS BORN

John Gerassi, a friendly advocate of the Castro revolution, was in Havana during the Cuban-sponsored Organización Latino Americana de Solidaridad (OLAS) meeting. He saw the session as launching a new International, the fifth in chronology. To Gerassi, the new organization was designed, at least in part, to counteract the influence of the Organization of American States, which has long been viewed in Latin America as United States dominated.

OLAS's role was to encourage revolution in Latin America, or as Gerassi terms it, "the systematization and continentalization of Cuba's own revolution."

To most American reporters present, what was fascinating about the Organization of Latin American Solidarity (OLAS) conference, which took place in Havana during the first ten days of August, 1967, were its various sideshows. Some were disturbing, as when Stokely Carmichael, the main attraction besides Fidel himself, quipped that "America is going to fall and I only hope to live long

Reprinted from John Gerassi, "Havana: A New International Is Born," *Monthly Review*, 19, 5 (October 1967), 22ff., by permission of Monthly Review Press. Copyright © 1967 by Monthly Review, Inc.

enough to see it." Some were curious, as when leaders of Latin American Communist parties huddled in corners of the Havana Libre (ex-Hilton) Hotel's spacious, marble-floored corridors ironing out a common strategy like conspirators in an old-time Preminger movie. And some were enchanting, as when the huge triple-decked outdoor stage of the plush Tropicana night club suddenly came alive with multicolored waterfalls and luscious mulatto girls as naked as Latin Quarter chorus cuties. But what was truly dramatic during OLAS went almost unnoticed: the birth of a new International.

In launching the new, Fifth International, Fidel was risking a great deal—and he knew it. On the one hand, he could expect the United States-dominated Organization of American States (OAS) to find in it justification for an armed assault on Cuba. On the other, he could conceive that Russia's anger might be transformed into material retaliation, which would deprive Cuba of the oil it needs to keep running and the raw materials it requires to develop. Indeed, many Cubans were already talking of a "double blockade," and only partly in jest. But to be true to himself and to the Cuban Revolution, Fidel had to do what he did—and most Cubans, fully aware of the possible consequences, jubilantly and enthusiastically approved.

In essence, the new International was simply the systematization and continentalization of Cuba's own revolution—armed struggle through guerrilla forces which gradually gain the support of the peasant masses. As such, OLAS's task was to spell out the economic, political, cultural, and military reasons why armed struggle is necessary and to establish the machinery by which guerrillas in any one country of Latin America can count on the active support of those in any other. Thus, OLAS would officially have to reject Russia's "peaceful coexistence" policy; more, it would have to explain why such a policy necessarily leads to a betrayal of the poor and the exploited peoples of the Americas. Finally, OLAS would have to commit itself, more or less openly, to an outright interventionist position.

It is true, and perhaps Fidel was banking on it, that Russia could not afford, propagandistically, to punish Cuba for its revolutionary fervor, especially when most radicals and left-wingers already criticize Russia's lukewarm support of Vietnam. Indeed, during OLAS, one revolutionary, Comandante Francisco Prada, third in command of Venezuela's FALN (Armed Forces of National Liberation), publicly lamented the fact that Vietnam was "tragically alone."

Besides, Cubans have been silently convinced ever since the 1962 missile crisis that Russia was capable of abandoning them in a showdown with the United States. They might have harbored a false sense of security after Kennedy was reported to have made his no-invasion promise. But Vietnam changed all that. With America's increasing aggressiveness in that hapless country the Cuban leaders realized that Kennedy's promise was not worth very much—in fact, the State Department has since denied that there was such a promise. Thus they are certain that once the United States settles the Vietnam war one way or another, it will go after Cuba. On August 10, at the close of OLAS, Fidel explicitly stated that this was his conviction. He read a *Daily News* editorial which said (in retranslation), "Let's stick a memo in Uncle Sam's hat to trample Castro under foot with all necessary force to destroy his Communist regime, as soon as we win the war in Vietnam."

Though he scoffed that "If the danger posed to this country depends on a United States victory in Vietnam, we will all die of old age," Fidel made it clear that it was in Cuba's national interest, as well as in the interest of all revolutionaries in the small countries of the underdeveloped world, to create as many Vietnams as possible.

Sometime in 1965, Che Guevara, who had long thought

this to be the case, disappeared from Cuba to help organize the revolutionary movements of Latin America. To do so, he needed a fresh approach and a fresher commitment. The Communist parties of Latin America by and large accept Russia's coexistence policy. Like Russia, they claim that by playing the game of legality, entering elections, organizing the working class, etc., they will eventually be brought to power without bloodshed.

Che disagreed. He realized that the United States and its oligarchic partners in Latin America occasionally tolerated Communist legality only because it was ineffective and unproductive. Che knew that in every country of Latin America the "national bourgeoisie," which Karl Marx once expected would lead the first revolutionary assault on imperialism, was completely tied materially to American corporate interests. Furthermore, Che, who never underestimated his enemy, saw that American imperialism was not static but dynamic, that it could generate enough mobility within the cities to create a sense of progress in the urban masses strong enough to neutralize the traditional proletariat as a revolutionary force. Instead, said Che, it had to be the peasants who would make up the revolutionary force, and it is with them that the revolutionary vanguard must work. And since the peasants were neither organized nor controlled by the Communist parties, these parties could not be considered a revolutionary vanguard. The young French philosopher Régis Debray, picking up these thoughts and adding them to Che's book on *Guerrilla Warfare,* then constructed the basis for a new concept of revolution through the building up of small guerrilla bands in remote areas, where peasants are totally outside society and where advanced military technology loses its advantage. The role of the traditional Communist Party in these operations was discounted.

Naturally, Communist leaders were not very enthusiastic over these developments. At a meeting in Prague in May, 1967, they denounced the forthcoming OLAS meeting as divisionistic, and supported the Venezuelan Communist Party which had already been denounced by Fidel himself.

The Venezuelan case is the key to understanding the whole new process of revolution in the Americas. Back in 1961 it was mainly the Communists—the traditional, Moscow-line party, with relative strength in the cities—that launched the country's first armed struggle through the creation of the FALN. The orders, the money, the arms, and the food came from the city as the Party continued to lead the armed operations from its Central Committee headquarters. For a while, as the result of armed uprisings by leftists and Communists within the armed forces, it looked as if the armed struggle was rapidly gaining strength. But, as Presidents Betancourt and then Leoni came down hard on the Party, jailing the leaders and declaring their activities illegal, the FALN suffered greatly. It was then that the CP decided to abandon the armed struggle and return to legality. It ordered its field commanders to give themselves up.

Douglas Bravo, a member of the Central Committee of the Communist Party and commander-in-chief of the FALN, refused. He was trounced out of the Party and was denounced as an adventurer. His men were then cut off from funds and material and, it is said, were even betrayed. "The right-wing leadership of the Communist Party behaved like a spurned mistress—denouncing, lying, trying its best to isolate its former lover," Comandante Ellias Manuit, one of Venezuela's chief guerrilla fighters who was also kicked out of the CP, told me recently. To Manuit, Bravo, Prada, and the other fighters, this was an outright betrayal. Fidel thought so too. He said: "Maybe some day the Venezuelan people will ask them [the Communist leaders] about the millions of dollars they collected throughout the world on behalf of the guerrilla movement which they abandoned; whose members they left without shoes, clothes, food, and even the bare necessities; and which they have accused and attacked without scruples of any kind." And

Prada, who was chairman of the Venezuelan delegation to OLAS, told me, "For the sake of their own legal standing, they have abandoned every one of their principles, betrayed their comrades, and are in effect now in partnership with the repressive forces against the people."

What it all comes down to [is] this: If you are a revolutionary, you must fight; if you do not fight, you are not a revolutionary. And that was OLAS's motto, derived from the Second Declaration of Havana: "The duty of every revolutionary is to make the revolution."

V

Unanswered Questions

*

33

ROBIN CHAPMAN

THE FIRST TEN YEARS

*Ten years after Fidel Castro came to power, there
was general agreement that in such areas as health
and education—as well as cutting back on unemployment—the Castro government had made important
advances. But the economy, in general, was lagging.
It was far from the Utopia that the visionary supporters of the regime claimed. The economy, moreover, showed little likelihood of major improvement
in the early 1970s.*

The respected Bank of London and South America Review, *in which this article was printed, was
one of the first publications to come up with a ten-
year assessment. While accepting the general thesis
about the performance of the economy in the first
ten years, the publication concludes that, in the agricultural field, the potential for improvement is large
and that, "if this potential is successfully exploited,
there are excellent long-term prospects for economic
progress."*

The Revolutionary Government celebrated its tenth anniversary in office on 1st January 1969. Throughout this
period Cuba has experienced grave economic problems,
mainly because of incoherent and inconsistent economic
planning and its failure to overcome an almost total de-

Reprinted from Robin Chapman, "The First Ten Years: Problems
and Achievements," *Bank of London and South America Review*,
31, 30 (June 1969), 361–364, by permission of the publisher.

pendence on sugar. Development has been hindered by the difficulties in maintaining the infrastructure and industrial base that have resulted from the stringent U.S. trade embargo, by the economic dependence on the U.S.S.R., and by the limited success in finding trading partners other than the communist countries, to provide convertible foreign exchange. Moreover, the failure of the attempt to achieve rapid industrialization between 1960 and 1963 was a major setback; since 1964 the Government has been concentrating mainly on agricultural development and on restoring sugar production to pre-1959 levels. The Prime Minister, Dr. Fidel Castro, announced on 2nd January that a long-term plan for agricultural development was to be followed, and implied that industrialization plans were to be postponed indefinitely. The level of economic activity has been extremely low in recent years and such industrial development as now exists is concentrated on the food-processing industries; there is little domestic output of consumer goods and most of these are rationed.

Policies and Problems

The Government is trying to establish a pure form of communist society that would render the use of money unnecessary. All privately-owned businesses were expropriated in March 1968, with the exception of a small part of the agricultural sector; urban transport and entertainment facilities are free; and barter transactions are becoming customary, especially in country areas. The Government is concentrating on the development of rural communities and is curtailing the further expansion of cities. There has been a large-scale mobilization of labor to help harvest the sugar and other food crops; consequently unemployment, which amounted to 30 per cent of the labor force in 1958, has been practically eradicated. Economic policy-making is dominated by Dr. Castro, who makes all major decisions; projects are undertaken as if they were military adventures, often without adequate preparation.

Great emphasis has been placed on the diversification of agriculture and a large-scale mechanization program is under way. Extensive areas have been sown to citrus fruits, tobacco, rice and coffee; battery poultry farming has been introduced, and improvements to cattle herds are being brought about by higher-quality breeding. So far many of the Government's efforts to increase farm production have not been successful; for example, the planting of 90m. coffee trees around Havana produced poor yields and a previous campaign to increase livestock production by artificial insemination failed. It has been estimated in the U.S.A. that Cuba's production of foodstuffs per head in 1968 was 25-30 per cent below that of the late 1950s.

The most pressing economic problems in the past two years have been the severe drought in the eastern provinces and the growing shortage of petroleum products. The drought, which is reported to be the worst in Cuban history, has had disastrous effects on the sugar crop, and has made the official target of 10m. tons in 1970 virtually unattainable, although it is still officially adhered to. The 1969 sugar crop is estimated at only about 4.9m. tons, compared with 5.5m. tons in 1968; in fact sugar production has never again achieved the record figure of 6.8m. tons reached in 1961. When announcing the low 1969 crop late in May Dr. Castro stated that additional difficulties had been caused by the low productivity of labor, government disorganization, breakdowns of equipment and a shortage of spare parts. At the same time he announced that steps were to be taken to remedy this year's defects and that the harvesting of the 1970 crop was to be brought forward to July 1969, immediately after the completion of the 1969 crop, in an attempt to meet the target and to fulfill current export commitments. Prospects for achieving the target depend on the successful use for the first time of locally manufactured mechanical harvesters (delays, however, have apparently arisen in their production), and on the successful completion of a modernization program for the mills.

The severe oil shortage is aggravating existing difficulties in agricultural production, especially by slowing down the mechanization program. Cuba relies on Eastern Europe for 98 per cent of its crude oil supplies, as local production of petroleum amounted to only 2,200 barrels a day in 1967. The U.S.S.R. has reduced shipments in recent years; as a result, severe controls were imposed in January 1968 on local consumption and sugar mills were instructed to use alternative fuels. Soviet technicians have made repeated attempts to try to find new petroleum deposits but with little result; exploration activities are now to be concentrated off shore.

The Government began a long-term investment program in 1967 to try to overcome its mounting economic difficulties; public investment in 1968 was estimated at 31 per cent of the gross domestic product, compared with 27 per cent in 1967. Important infrastructure projects have been completed or are being carried out; these include a hydroelectric plant at El Mate and dams and irrigation works on the River Cauto. A program has begun for the training of more agricultural technicians and teachers, to replace those who have emigrated to the U.S.A. Great emphasis is being placed on education and some 16 per cent of total budget expenditure was devoted to it in 1967; it is claimed that illiteracy has been reduced from some 26 per cent in 1958 to 2 per cent at present.

Foreign Relations

Since 1960 Cuba has grown increasingly dependent on the U.S.S.R. for economic and financial aid, which has been estimated at the equivalent of over u.s.$450m. a year, including arms deliveries. Cuba's present debt on capital account is unofficially estimated at about u.s.$2md. The general principles of Soviet assistance are based on the agreement signed in January 1964, under which the U.S.S.R. is to purchase 24m. tons of Cuban sugar by 1970, valued at the equivalent of u.s.$3.2md.; the rate of delivery is regulated by the expected rise in Cuban sugar production. The U.S.S.R. remains Cuba's principal trading partner, to the extent of about half of Cuba's exports and imports. The two countries have signed annual trade and aid agreements since 1960; in recent years Cuba has been dissatisfied with Soviet supplies of machinery and equipment and has cast doubts on its value.

Cuban-Soviet relations were particularly acrimonious between 1965 and mid-1968. A dispute arose during this period as a result of Soviet policy towards Latin America, which was directed towards establishing diplomatic and commercial ties with existing governments, whereas Cuba was concentrating on their subversion by fomenting guerrilla revolts. The dispute was especially evident in the negotiations over the 1968 trade agreement; Cuba was seeking a three-year agreement but had to be satisfied with the normal annual arrangement. Relations have improved since August 1968, when Dr. Castro expressed support for the invasion of Czechoslovakia. In addition, the U.S.S.R. approves of the apparent decision of the Cuban Government to concentrate on solving its internal economic problems; there have been no more Cuban-supported guerrilla revolts since the Bolivian fiasco in October 1967. A pointer to the restored relationship was the visit in January 1969 to Havana by the Soviet Vice-President, Mr. Novikov; a technical assistance agreement was signed during his stay.

The U.S.S.R. is likely to continue bearing the heavy economic cost of supporting the Cuban Revolution, in view of Cuba's great nuisance value *vis-à-vis* the U.S.A., especially regarding the latter's dealings with other Latin American countries. The Soviet Government also realizes that any erosion of the Cuban Government's position would be a serious blow to Soviet prestige. Despite Cuba's economic dependence, it retains considerable freedom of action and so far has refused to commit itself in regard to the Soviet conflict with China.

Cuba remains keenly aware of its economic and diplomatic isolation and has intensified its search for alternative export markets; trade with Western European countries, particularly Spain, France and the United Kingdom, is being developed. The Government is hoping to increase sales of sugar in the world market (four-fifths of production is at present directed to Eastern Europe) but its quota under the new International Sugar Agreement, signed late in 1968, was not substantially increased. A severe shortage of foreign exchange persists, though payment for essential imports is nearly always made promptly. Recent U.S. press reports indicated that Cuba wished to improve relations with the U.S.A. and there is certainly a form of cooperation in managing the flow of Cuban refugees; it is unlikely, however, that there will be any real *rapprochement* in the near future.

Conclusion

In the past ten years, the Cuban Government has virtually abolished unemployment, improved health and educational facilities, and brought about a drastic redistribution of income. On the other hand, the country's average standard of living has progressively fallen, and attempts to develop other export industries have failed. In addition, economic policy has been based on idealism and experimentation; there has been little evidence of systematic planning and the sustained execution of projects.

There would appear to be no chance of a general economic improvement in the short-term. However, the decision to concentrate on long-term agricultural development is probably in Cuba's best interests; the country has great agricultural potential and a small population with a low rate of increase; it is expected only to double in the next half century. If this potential is successfully exploited, there are excellent long-term prospects for economic progress.

34

HUGH THOMAS

A SUMMING UP AT 10

Hugh Thomas, the British historian whose article on the Cuban revolution and its origins begins these selections, took a backward glance at the first ten years of the revolution in a two-part series for The Times *of London in 1969. He concluded that the revolution was still experimenting and that there were serious limitations on the sort of social revolution envisioned by Fidel Castro.*

Following several visits to Cuba in the 1960s, Professor Thomas concludes that there "has been a full-blooded social revolution in Cuba," but he expresses doubts about the government's shortcomings, including one that is much debated: Castro's personal leadership.

Castro has been in power in Cuba for 10 years now, but it is still not possible to make any general assessment of his regime. Everything in Cuba remains experimental, the economy remains at best on a knife-edge, there is no constitution and no real certainty about the future of Cuban society. All decisions depend more and more on Castro personally and his continuing apparent popularity makes it rather easy for him to change course almost at will.

Perhaps a profit and loss account of the activities of the

Reprinted from "Cuba's Ten-Year Revolution Still Experimenting" and "The Limitations of Cuba's Social Revolution," *The Times* of London (February 17, 18, 1969), by permission of *The Times*.

Cuban revolutionary government could effectively be made: on the one side more education, free health, milk for children, a sense of community, and much encouragement for the arts; on the other the absence of liberty, intolerance towards the not inconsiderable group of middle-aged middle-class people, the persistent atmosphere of crisis and tension, the tragedies in hundreds of families divided by politics, and the strident propaganda. But such an account would not really get very far, for several reasons.

Some of Castro's most remarkable achievements have been destructive. Thus he has destroyed the terrible corruption which characterized not simply the Batista regime but also the democratic regimes before Batista and even the earlier colonial administration. He has destroyed all North American influence in Cuba, even if some cultural manifestations, such as baseball, are too deeply rooted to be extracted. He has destroyed private enterprise completely and is now busy destroying the city as such.

In place of these things, of course, there has been the revolution, an extraordinary creation certainly, the product of Castro's oratory, energy, and his restless and intolerant intellect, aided earlier by Guevara's unbending clarity of purpose. Yet though the revolution seems to be a work of art of Castro's (and frankly, like a work of art, admired or hated for subjective reasons, rather really than for any material benefit or disadvantage it may have brought), its character has been influenced, perhaps decisively, by the institutions or the attitudes which it has sought so resolutely to destroy.

What, then, is one really to make of the sudden turn taken by Castro and the Cuban leadership in 1960–1961 towards identification with the Soviet bloc? To carry out this extraordinary switch from the proclaimed "liberal" aims of the revolution, however one views it, required remarkable audacity and willpower on Castro's part. Was this change the consequence of long-concealed Marxist politics on the part of the leadership, or did the malevolence or folly of the Eisenhower Administration force Castro into totalitarian policies against his better nature? Both interpretations now seem curiously outdated.

Ten years after Castro's entry into Havana, his ears ringing with the cheers of the white middle-class more than the workers, and of the Church at least as much as of the Communist Party, it seems evident that the long period of economic, cultural and political dominance of Cuba by the United States drove Castro to take the most extreme course that he could, perhaps in defiance of Cuba's immediate economic needs or deserts and probably in defiance of the desires of both the Cuban Communist Party and the Soviet Union. At this point economies and strategy took over: if Cuba was to break with the United States commercially, only the Soviet Union could buy the huge quantity of Cuban sugar previously taken by the United States: if Cuba were to break with the United States politically, and specifically to challenge her, denounce her, and accuse her in the most intemperate language of the most barbarous crimes, only the Soviet Union could provide her with the arms needed to defend herself.

Similarly, the puritanism, particularly of the present stage of the Cuban revolution but implicit throughout, is —however much outsiders may dislike or even fear it— explicable only in terms of the wild debauch suffered for generations by Cuba in general and Havana in particular. Just as a major assault could be launched on Castro's economic policies on the grounds that it is inherently absurd to have a major trading partner so far away as Russia, so doubtless a defense could be made, in terms of the foreign exchange that they brought in, especially during the 1950s, of the brothels and casinos for which Havana was famous. But of course the economic considerations are not the critical ones.

This is also true of the destruction of the last vestiges

of private enterprise last March during the so-called revolutionary offensive (now, apart from the private farmers, there is no private commerce of any sort in Cuba: even the barrow boys and newspaper stalls have vanished). It is impossible to believe that this makes much sense economically. On the other hand, the small shopkeepers, the barmen and the small businessmen of Havana were clearly not only a center of disaffection but because of their past were closely identified either with the United States or more notably with the Spaniards; and one of the main reasons for the failure of the Cuban Republic between independence in 1902 and the Castro revolution in 1959 was the continuance of economic power in the hands of Spaniards who were reluctant or unable to take part in politics.

The revolution has also been a Latin American experience par excellence rather than a Caribbean one. In so far as Castroism has intellectual forebears, they are to be found in the Mexican or Guatemalan revolutions, perhaps the Peronist revolution in Argentina, and also perhaps in the revolutionary traditions of Spain, Spanish anarchism and the Spanish Civil War. The fact is though that Cuba, with its economic concentration upon sugar (to which it has now returned after an abortive effort at industrialization), its substantial Negro minority, its continuing dependence on world market prices, its lack of an indigenous Indian population, and its sub-tropical and agreeable climate, is in all respects a Caribbean country. It is, therefore, ironical, though for the Caribbean entirely appropriate, that contact with the rest of the Antilles, by sea or air, by cultural exchange or even by propaganda voice, is nil. It is much harder to get from Cuba to another Caribbean island today than it was before 1492.

Thus too the complete alignment which the Cuban leaders suggest that their country has or should have with the rest of the underdeveloped world and their suggestion that Cuba is the model for the rest of Latin America, is also a work of art, a combination of brilliant gestures rather than a philosophy based on economic or even political realities. The increased Cuban emphasis on agriculture does make some sense in a fertile island, but affords no worthwhile message for countries such as Mexico, Peru or Bolivia, whose soil one cannot see supporting any more people. Then the Cubans, with their relatively low rate of reproduction, have no need of a population policy—unlike most other Latin American countries. Even the suggestion that armed struggle, *à la* Sierra Maestra, is the way to social reform in South America is an attitude which, even if it leads many brave men in the Andes to their death in the next few years, is somewhat unrelated to reality.

In the past Cuba was more an underprivileged suburb of North America, a part of the old world in decay, than an outlying spur of the under-privileged world of the future. Further, Castro's skilful manipulation between 1956 and 1959 of the liberal press, particularly the North American press, and what might be called his political management of his guerrilla war, and which played a great part in his victory, is simply not a possibility for the rest of Latin America. Indeed there are occasions when Castro's revolution, in its protest against the sordid and corrupt capitalist politics in Cuba, seems more of a challenge to the advanced countries than to the underdeveloped ones: a signal for revolutionary Florida more than for Bolivia. For Castro and his friends did not smash a poor, sleepy, backward ex-Spanish colony: they were faced with a very rich country where the wealth was unequally distributed, where riches more than anything else had ruined the hope of democratic politics, where there was a sophisticated tradition of gangsterism comparable with Chicago, and where the key element in the destruction of the "liberals" was less the poverty of the countryside than the number of television sets available for Castro to use.

. . .

Cuba is a potentially wonderful country, of beauty and fertility. The Cubans are marvellous people, gay, long-suffering and suffused with love of country. Castro, now in power for 10 years, is an outstanding man, whose good faith it would be foolish to question. He rules Cuba like an eccentric and inventive autocrat, still depending on his great gifts of oratory for what is undoubtedly a close contact with the masses. His regime excites fascination all over the world, but especially among the Latin American youth who appreciate what a remarkable achievement it is to keep going so long in the teeth of such hostility from the United States. Nevertheless, the central question about the Castro regime remains that of political liberty.

Of course there has been a full-blooded social revolution in Cuba such as has not occurred anywhere else in Latin America; the old bourgeoisie has been destroyed and is now in exile or lingers in crumbling houses. The working class have been set economically and socially free as never before. They have free access to nursery schools for their children after their forty-fifth day, they have free health and education up to university level. Every type of sport is organized for them free, telephones in the cities are free, cinemas are free, buses in the towns may soon be free, and perhaps in the long run all the necessities of life will be provided free. Castro's speeches over the last year suggest that he envisages a future in which the new man, conscious of his duty to society, will be able to go from cradle to grave without the filthy taint of money.

It is just possible that these things will be achieved. For while Cuba is rich in agricultural potential the population density is low and the rate of reproduction is also low by Latin American standards—it will probably only double in the next 50 years. Furthermore the charm, and perhaps also the fecklessness and the unpunctuality, of the Cubans prevents Cuban communism from gathering to itself all the characteristics of communism in east Europe or Russia. But for all this the question of the political structure seems paramount.

For in spite of Castro's continuing attraction for many, and in spite of the frequent more or less interesting experiments which characterize his regime, its efficiency, decency and happiness are limited by the nature of the system or lack of system. Many theoretical descriptions of the nature of each stage in the revolution's process are given. But in practice all decisions in Cuba have been taken by Castro, and in spite of much support for many of the things he has done the Cuban government is personal rule carried to an extreme degree.

The shortcomings of this are many. The political concept most talked about at the moment is that of the new man, the man living free from the tyranny of money and the philosophy of the "full shop window." Regardless of whether the Cubans are so utterly different from other people that they will actually like this indefinitely, one wonders whether this is a final statement of Castro's political philosophy, towards which he has been working for a long time, or whether it is really a skilful theoretical justification for the fact that there are no goods in the shop windows. It is hard to say. It is also hard to be sure that within a year or so this policy will not be formally shelved by Castro as a mistake, and some quite different line pursued with equal enthusiasm.

Another question relates to the tremendous effort being placed on sugar production, and in particular the vaunted goal of 10 million tons of sugar. In 1959–62 many people would have refused to entertain the possibility that in 10 years' time, instead of a sustained effort to diversify agricultural production, the revolutionary government would be pursuing the far from revolutionary notion of a major sugar drive. Probably, with their new and advantageous international sugar agreement, the Cubans will sell 10 million tons of sugar in 1970, if they produce it. But whether they could always do so in a world where so many new countries produce sugar is more than doubtful. It is also doubtful whether Cuba should continue to tie up so much capital, effort and technical knowledge in sugar production. The trouble with the regime at the moment is that with no national forum for discussion, and with a controlled and appallingly dull press, there is no means by which doubts about these matters can be effectively aired.

There is then the whole question of the regime's relations with Russia. Was it, as would seem likely, Russian pressure that determined Castro's support of the Russian invasion of Czechoslovakia? Or was it because Castro was ideologically out of sympathy with several trends in eastern European countries generally?

In his speech giving support to Russia over Czechoslovakia, Castro expressed horror at the thought that voluntary work in some eastern European countries meant overtime with extra pay. Yet if it was really ideological doubts rather than Russian pressure which dictated Castro's stand, why did the Cuban press at first give such unusual publicity to the whole Czechoslovak experience?

What about Cuba's financial relations with the Soviet Union? No figures have been published, but an informed guess is that the Cuban debt on capital account runs to $2,000m., with current account costs to the Soviet Union running at the rate of over $300m. a year. What is to be done about these terrible debts which, with arms being given free, apparently relate only to civil expenditure? Are the Cubans going to have to export all their fresh fruit, beef, and fish for a generation to pay the Russian price? Frankly, it looks like it. The fact that the Cubans are easy-going and, in a far from disagreeable climate, seem able to put up with anything does not affect the contention that in a country whose Government puts itself forward as playing an exemplary role for the rest of the underdeveloped world these matters should be made clear. It is understood, for instance, that Guevara went wrong by suggesting that there should be no such sordid things as debts and loans between socialist countries, only gifts— is that true or not?

Another point where the personal rule of Castro is important relates to the situation in Havana. The present policy of the regime is to build up agriculture and rural communities in order to try to escape the further expansion of cities. Looking at the all-consuming megalopolis with its nightmarish shanty towns, at Mexico City, Lima, or at other Latin American capitals, it is impossible not to feel some sympathy for this approach. But is this an excuse for the Cuban Government's present neglect of Havana, one of the most handsome cities of the new world, and the slow decline of parts of it into slum? Is it correct or even wise to build village communities while denying the citizen of Havana a bag of cement to repair his house?

Other questions relate to justice. On the whole minor offences seem to be judged with reasonable equity, political offences are not. The trial of Aníbal Escalante and the "microfaction" last year, with (as in other major political trials of the regime) the lengthy personal appearance of Castro in the role of witness-cum-prosecutor, was highly distasteful. There is also an unknown number of political prisoners, perhaps 15,000, perhaps more, of whom perhaps half are in the process of "rehabilitation" (agricultural work and Marxism-Leninism). It is believed that the hard cases are still in tough jails: and it would be interesting, to put it mildly, to have some news of the whereabouts and state of health of such people as David Salvador, Hubert Matos, or Alberto Muller, and other prominent or minor opponents of the regime in its early days, who presumably linger forgotten in some disagreeable and overcrowded cell.

Of course, there is a state of semi-war between Cuba and the United States, which partly explains the continued incarceration of such men, but nevertheless these are not things which can be brushed aside by talking with an ever greater emphasis of such achievements of the regime as the magnificent and humane lunatic asylum, the great growth in primary education, the improved health, or the rationalization of the sugar industry.

Finally, considering how uneasily the Cubans take to the bureaucracy of this ambitious state socialism, it is difficult to believe that a free press would not unearth some scandals within the administration. One of these may exist in respect of the proposed coffee drive. Coffee has been planted in the sun and on the flat, on the assumption that it will do well there, in contrast to the old coffee plants which required mountainous and very shady conditions. No one really knows what will be the future of these plants. But even in the event of this being a Cuban ground nuts scandal, in present circumstances could one count on the details coming to light? A coffee director might be dismissed, a national confession might be made by Castro, then the Cubans would be asked to sail off enthusiastically on another adventure. The fact that a majority, in their mesmeric fascination with Castro, would probably accept such a volte face does not mean that this situation is fundamentally stable.

The social revolution over which Castro has presided has brought material benefits to many. But the continuing absence of political liberty and predictability severely limits their worth, their survival, and their integrity.

35

EDWARD GONZALEZ

THE LIMITS OF CHARISMA

*As the assessments of Fidel Castro's first ten years
in power began coming in, a pattern gradually
emerged. Many of these analyses laid particular stress
on Castro's unique style of leadership and his charisma, but questioned whether they were valid for
the future. There were signs also that Castro himself
had begun pondering the direction of the revolution
and his own role in it.*

*Edward Gonzalez, a professor of political science
at the University of California, wrote the article
from which the following excerpt is taken after visits
to Cuba in 1967 and 1968.*

For more than a decade since his rise to power, Fidel
Castro's charisma and radical style of leadership have
functioned as the linchpin of the Cuban Revolution. As
the supreme *caudillo* in Cuban politics, he has had the
final word in both ideological and policy determinations
of the regime, and he has asserted unifying authority over
factional tendencies. More important, his personal appeal
has been essential in mobilizing Cuban society and stimulating popular support. In a system that has not yet developed institutions truly responsive to popular demands,
Castro has provided the personal link between the regime

Reprinted from Edward Gonzalez, "Castro: The Limits of Charisma," *Problems of Communism*, XIX, 4 (July–August 1970), 12–
13, 17–24, by permission of the publisher.

and the masses, thereby imbuing the Cuban revolutionary process with a dynamic, populist character.

At the same time, the regime's very dependence on the personality and personal authority of its *Lider maximo* has tended to impede the institutionalization of the revolutionary process, creating tension between the need for his dominant charismatic authority and the need for a more ordered system of governance. To grasp the import of this fact, it may be helpful to analyze the Cuban experience of the past decade in terms of two broad phases. In the first phase—embracing several critical stages of development in the years 1959–66—Castro strove to consolidate and expand his power, to transfc ... ms political revolution into a radical social revolution, and to build a socialist-communist system. In the international sphere, he developed ties with the Soviet bloc, defeated the U.S.-sponsored invasion of Cuban exiles at the Bay of Pigs, survived the 1962 missile crisis, and militantly encouraged armed revolution elsewhere in the hemisphere. In this whole period—when it was necessary to break prerevolutionary patterns of internal and external dominance, and when there existed favorable conditions for doing so—Castro's charisma and radical political style were both successful and relevant to his aims.

After 1966, however, the course of the Cuban regime began to shift emphatically toward concentration on domestic economic development. . . .

On the foreign front, four developments after 1965 increased Cuba's isolation and lessened her external leverage. First, seeing the futility of armed struggle, the Soviets and Latin American Communists moved to disassociate themselves from the insurgent guerrilla movements on the continent in order to work with established Latin American governments. Between 1965 and 1968 the Soviets pushed for the normalization of diplomatic and trade relations with anti-Castro governments in Chile, Brazil, Colombia and Venezuela, even though the latter two were targets of guerrilla activity. Castro considered Moscow's moves a blatant betrayal of revolutionary internationalism and a sacrifice of Cuba's interests. In an address of August 10, 1967, to the first conference of the Latin American Solidarity Organization (OLAS), Fidel acidly declared that ". . . if internationalism exists, if solidarity is a word worthy of respect, the least that we can expect of any state of the socialist camp is that it refrain from giving any financial or technical aid to those regimes." The scuttling of the Fidelista insurgent forces by local Communist parties similarly incensed Havana. Nowhere was this more apparent than in Venezuela. There, the Venezuelan Communist Party (PCV) took steps to disengage itself from the guerrilla forces from April 1965 onward, leading eventually to Castro's violent denunciation of, and open break with, the PCV on March 13, 1967.

The second development disturbing to Havana was the course of the war in Vietnam, which increased Castro's doubts about the genuineness of the Soviet commitment to Communist solidarity. Moscow had not deterred "imperialist aggression" nor actively responded to the U.S. bombing of a bona fide Communist state, as called for by the Cuban leadership. Together with the Soviet failure to assist the Arab states in the 1967 Arab-Israeli war and the Kosygin-Johnson talks at Glassboro, the Vietnam war reinforced the fears of the Cuban regime that Moscow was capable of sacrificing its allies.

The third reversal underscoring Cuba's vulnerability was the clear demise of the Fidelista insurgent forces in Venezuela, Peru and Colombia after mid-1965. The moribund continental revolution confronted Havana with the prospect of losing not only its supportive movement in the hemisphere, but also its principal source of international leverage. To arrest this development, the Cubans attempted to reconstitute and transform the revolutionary movement. First, they provided support for a new guerrilla *foco*, established in Bolivia by Ernesto Che Guevara in late

1966, with a force that included seven former members of the Central Committee of the Communist Party of Cuba. Next, Havana injected new content into the doctrine of guerrilla war through the publication in early 1967 of Régis Debray's book, *Revolution in the Revolution*. The Cubans' final step was to provide the continental revolution with an institutional base by convening the aforementioned conference of the Latin American Solidarity Organization in August 1967. Attended by some 160 Latin American delegates in Havana, the OLAS conference broke decisively with Moscow's line on peaceful revolution and established a permanent Executive Committee to promote armed revolutionary struggle.

The final and most traumatic setback for Havana was Guevara's capture and execution in October 1967, ending the Bolivian guerrilla *foco*. The Bolivian fiasco signaled the bankruptcy of Fidel's policy of continental revolution. With Che dead, Havana was left with a bureaucratic appendage in OLAS, but without much hope of attracting new revolutionaries. Without a viable revolutionary movement in the hemisphere, the Castro regime was deprived of its principal external resource in dealing with Moscow —at a time when Cuban-Soviet relations had become increasingly strained. Indeed, Soviet retaliation against Havana's insubordination was not long in coming. On January 2, 1968, Castro announced the immediate rationing of gasoline because of the "limited" possibility of the Soviet Union meeting Cuba's growing fuel consumption needs. Fidel thus needed to find new counters to Soviet pressures, and to restructure Cuba's relationship with Moscow and the hemisphere, just when domestic problems were becoming more pressing.

Following Guevara's death, Havana's attention was redirected inward toward the revitalization of revolutionary élan and the waging of the development struggle. Castro's speeches throughout 1968 and 1969 were virtually devoid of references to the continental revolution, concentrating instead on domestic political and economic issues. While the themes of Che's guerrilla struggle and sacrifice and the war in Vietnam were sounded, they were used mainly for inspirational purposes in mobilizing the populace toward greater productive efforts. Havana's reorientation was highlighted in the 1968 centennial celebration of Cuba's quest for independence, with Castro's revolution portrayed as an integral part of "One Hundred Years of Struggle" from 1868 to 1968. Having focused inwards, the regime sought to regain revolutionary momentum through (a) a return to ideological militancy, (b) new emphasis on the commitment to a 10-million-ton sugar harvest, and (c) militarization of the Castroite Revolution.

The regime's new phase of ideological fervor began with a "revolutionary offensive" launched in March 1968. Puritanical in intent, it aimed at accelerating the construction of "real communism" by eradicating capitalism and residual bourgeois vices from Cuban society. In his aforementioned speech of March 13, 1968, Castro stressed that revolution would not be an "easy road" gilded by Soviet assistance, and called upon the Cuban people to display "everyday heroism" by accepting necessary deprivations. Declaring that there could be no "accommodation" with capitalism in the new society, he announced that the remaining private non-agrarian sector was to be abolished immediately because of profiteering and blackmarket activities by "anti-social" elements. In short, "capitalism," "parasitism," and the "exploitation of man" were to be "dug out by the roots" in creating Cuba's Communist society.

By the end of March, 55,600 small, privately-owned retail, service and manufacturing establishments were nationalized, giving Cuba the distinction of having the highest ratio of state to private ownership of any Communist country in the world. The immediate effect of this measure, however, was to aggravate discontent, partly as a result of new bottlenecks in the distribution of goods and services previously supplied by the private sector.

Nevertheless, the renewed emphasis upon ideological militancy continued. In the fall of 1968, the Ministry of the Revolutionary Armed Forces (MINFAR) spearheaded a drive against "bourgeois" intellectuals and antirevolutionary literature, insisting that there must be no "ideological softening" in the revolutionary movement. At the end of March 1969, a "National Forum on Internal Order" was convened to examine the problem of "antisocial behavior." Attended by representatives of the party, MINFAR, the Ministry of Interior, and various mass organizations, the forum discussed measures to rekindle revolutionary zeal in the populace and to cope with such problems as the rising rate of juvenile delinquency and crimes against property.

In the meantime, Castro had launched an effort to mobilize popular attention and energy by making a national crusade out of the commitment to produce 10 million tons of sugar by 1970. This enormous goal had first been announced in the fall of 1964 as the final target in a five-year production plan for 1965–70. From 1965 to 1967, it got little mention in official pronouncements and propaganda—partly, no doubt, because sugar production failed to meet the planned levels, and also because the regime's major interest of the moment was the continental revolution. Very shortly after the Bolivian fiasco, however, Fidel suddenly began to emphasize the 1970 sugar target in terms that made its achievement both a matter of national honor and a test of Castroism itself.

.   .   .

Standing in the way of this maximum goal were such "objective" conditions as the limited production capacity of the sugar mills, the unpredictability of weather conditions, the inadequacies in transportation facilities, and the low productivity of the non-professional cane-cutting force. One way Fidel sought to overcome these obstacles was to rely on "subjectivism," or the "Sierra Maestra complex." In the same manner that his small guerrilla force had defeated Batista's army, the work force, by its revolutionary will, determination and effort, would collectively triumph over all obstacles standing in the way of bringing in the harvest. Mobilizing several hundred thousand volunteers, Castro made the harvest a "historic battle," a test of character for the Cuban people.

Castro did not depend on "subjectivism" alone, however; soon after the all-out harvesting effort was announced, the regime took steps leading to the increasing militarization of the economy. Beginning in 1968, the Revolutionary Armed Forces (FAR) became a developmental weapon funneling supervisory personnel and manpower into the economy and organizing part of the labor force along paramilitary lines. These steps helped compensate for the dearth of competent civilian managers and technicians in the field by supplying army officers with command and organizational skills, as well as relatively high levels of technical competence. The army also helped to overcome organizational deficiencies in the party which, to use Castro's term, had impeded the waging of "simultaneous battles" on several economic fronts. In addition, the militarization of the labor force was aimed at inculcating the work discipline necessary for realizing production targets.

Beginning in 1968, therefore, army officers could be found in crucial positions at the provincial and regional levels of the sugar industry. The two most important sugar-producing provinces of Oriente and Camagüey were under army command, while junior officers assumed management of the most important sugar *centrales,* especially those undergoing conversion into super-mills. The provincial command posts reportedly were linked in turn with headquarters in Havana. In addition, the labor force was increasingly organized along military lines in the form of columns, battalions and brigades—including a 40,000-man Centennial Youth Column in Camagüey, in which youths served to fulfill their military obligation. Finally, the army's mechanized "Che Guevara" Brigade was directly employed in clearing away scrub lands for agricultural development.

The growing reliance on the FAR as a developmental weapon and organizational model continued throughout 1969 in preparation for the 1970 harvest. In March 1969 Castro stressed the use of the army in solving production problems in Camagüey province. In October Armando Hart, party Organization Secretary, extolled the example of the army in agricultural work, stressing that the production rate of the FAR labor brigades exceeded that of other agricultural workers. In November Fidel fully acknowledged the increasing significance of the FAR. He announced that between 80,000 and 100,000 armed forces personnel would be mobilized for the 1970 harvest. Referring to the need for "discipline and good work habits" in the labor force, he called upon the FAR to provide the necessary direction:

> The armed forces represent . . . the institution with the most experience in organization; they are the ones with the most discipline. They must contribute that spirit of organization and discipline . . . as well as their experience.

In Castro's bid to regain revolutionary momentum, the 10-million ton target provided Cuban society with an all-consuming goal, while the militarization of the revolution became the organizational means for attaining that objective. The future of the militarized model, in turn, depended upon the success of the 1970 harvest.

Well before the harvest was in, it was clear from Havana's own reports that the Cubans would not manage to reach their 10-million-ton target, but that they would succeed in producing a new record harvest of 8.5 million tons. On balance, this performance represents a setback for Castro (of which more shortly). But the position of the FAR and the attractiveness of the militarized model may have been enhanced, since they appear to have been decisive in setting the new record of production. As will be seen, such a development could hold crucial significance for the future of the Cuban Revolution.

The recovery of domestic revolutionary momentum was paralleled by bold efforts on Castro's part to exact a firmer Soviet commitment to Havana. Deprived of his hemispheric leverage following Che's death, Fidel severely strained Cuba's relationship with Moscow throughout most of 1968 in an effort to force a new understanding with the Soviets. This phase of political maneuvering, which was characterized by mutual retaliations, came to an end with Fidel's speech on the Soviet bloc invasion of Czechoslovakia in August 1968. Thereafter, a new compromise emerged which has since produced closer bonds between the two countries, but which also has left Cuba precariously dependent upon Moscow.

.   .   .

The recent Cuban-Soviet reconciliation marks a significant departure from Castro's earlier political approach to Moscow. To be sure, the accommodation was reached only after hard bargaining; but in contrast to the past, it was an extraneous factor—the Czech crisis—that gave Fidel the singular opportunity to press for a trade-off. Otherwise Castro would have had little to bargain with. His stance on armed struggle has lost a good deal of its significance since the collapse of the revolutionary movement on the Latin American continent. Moreover, Moscow's position has been strengthened by the Cuban economy's continuing need for maximum Soviet assistance, and particularly by the fact that the 1964 trade pact is due to lapse at the end of 1970. Hence, Cuba has been placed in a position of critical dependency, leaving Fidel with little room to maneuver. One way remains for Castro to regain leverage, and that is to explore new alternatives for Cuba in her policy vis-à-vis the Western hemisphere.

The recent developments in Cuba's domestic and foreign policies pose critical issues which affect the character and direction of the Cuban Revolution. Internally, the issue is whether charisma, radicalism and the resultant popular basis of the Revolution can be reconciled with the organizational imperatives of sustained economic development. Externally, the issue is whether Cuba can overcome her hemispheric isolation and reduce her dependency upon the Soviet Union by coming to terms with Latin American governments.

Fidel's charisma and revolutionary style appear to have become less relevant to the new development process. The commitment to the 10-million-ton harvest was the product of Fidel's radicalism, reflecting his personal decision-making authority and his emphasis on subjectivism as the motive force. But his revolutionary style probably did no more than supply the necessary inspirational force for the 1970 harvest. It was the new reliance on the armed forces as a developmental force, and on the militarized model of production, that evidently provided the needed institutional support and organization for the collective effort. At issue, therefore, is whether the regime can reconcile the functions and prerogatives of charismatic leadership with the institutional structures and orderly processes which are needed to promote rapid economic growth.

While it should help to resolve immediate production problems, the militarized revolutionary model seems incompatible with the Cuban Revolution's earlier voluntarism and populism. Such a model involves a regimented command system directed from above. It would thus close off the possibilities of building responsive institutions that could provide for effective popular participation in influencing national policies.

The choice before the regime is whether to push on with its accelerated developmental program under the militarized model or some other command system, or to opt for a more responsive system at the expense of some of its more radical goals. Ironically, however, even if the militarized path is chosen, Castro's presence and personal ties with the masses may be needed to make the new revolutionary order more palatable.

On the international front, Havana needs to overcome its isolation within the hemisphere both to gain a greater sense of security and to reduce dependency on the Soviets. Here, however, the regime may face a dilemma in choosing between Cuba's diplomatic and revolutionary interests. This is clearly illustrated by the Peruvian case. On the one hand, Castro has indicated that he is encouraged by recent Peruvian developments, and he may even be looking to the anti-Communist Peruvian military regime as a potential anchor in realigning right-wing and left-wing nationalism in Latin America. On the other hand, any move by Cuba toward the establishment of relations with Peru (or any other country) would require that Havana associate itself with governments confronting insurgent groups and urban terrorists. In turn, this could cut Fidel off from whatever remains of the revolutionary Left, leaving him open to the charge of having abandoned the revolutionary struggle. Nevertheless, if assertive nationalistic tendencies continue to develop among non-Fidelista groups in Peru and elsewhere in Latin America, Havana may decide to forsake its revolutionary objectives in favor of Cuba's diplomatic interests. Such a step would signal a new direction for the Cuban Revolution.

The 1970 harvest ended with a record production of 8.526 million tons. Nonetheless all indications are that it represents a major personal defeat for Castro, reflecting adversely on his credibility and radical style of leadership. Consequently, it may signify a watershed in Cuba's internal development in the same way that Guevara's death proved a turning point in Fidel's efforts to revolutionize the hemisphere.

In speeches of May 19 and 20, and most recently of July 26, Castro acknowledged personal as well as collective "responsibility" for the harvest "setback" and "defeat." In the latter speech he also revealed a number of other reversals in the economy and gave a gloomy forecast of the continued hardship and supreme effort that lie ahead in Cuba's drive for economic development. Overall, he called for the strengthening of the Communist Party apparatus and mass organizations in an apparent effort to arrest demoralization in the populace, reverse the trend toward a slackening of work, and control dissenting elements within his regime. He further indicated that administrative reforms would be adopted to improve the coordination of economic activities and to remove party personnel from management functions at the plant level.

These and other steps suggest that Castro is under pressure from technocratic and reformist elements in Cuba. Supported by the Soviet Union, and bolstered by Fidel's defeat in the sugar harvest, they may be pressing for greater influence in the formulation of economic policies under a less personalized decision-making system.

36

K. S. KAROL

WHERE CASTRO WENT
WRONG

*K. S. Karol, a Polish-born socialist, living in Paris
and contributing regularly to English and French
periodicals, visited Cuba often during the 1960s. Basically sympathetic to the ideas of the Cuban revolution, his commentaries nevertheless grew increasingly
critical of the revolution's performance in the economic field and blamed Castro for some of the
economic failures.*

Publication of his book, Guerrillas in Power, *on
the Cuban revolution in 1970 attracted considerable
attention first in France and then in the English-
speaking world. The book includes many of his criticisms of the revolution, but judging from the reviews
of the book many of the reviewers missed Karol's
basic sympathies with the revolution. These sympathies are evident in the following article, which appeared in the English weekly, the* New Statesman.

"You in Europe tend to underestimate the role of the
great figures of history," said Armando Hart, a leading
member of the Cuban government, as we talked one day
in Havana. His aim was to convince me that without Fidel
Castro there would have been no revolution in Cuba, that

Reprinted from K. S. Karol, "Where Castro Went Wrong," *New
Statesman* (August 7, 1970), by permission of the publisher.

this little island would never have been able to resist American pressure or stand up to its unlikely ally Russia. It is hardly surprising that all his old comrades in arms have such unstinted admiration and devotion for Fidel. But this hero worship, however historically deserved, expresses itself all too often in plain docility. There is no question of their ever contradicting Fidel and even less of engaging in a political trial of strength to challenge any of his decisions. . . .

But it isn't only at the summit of the Cuban pyramid that political life is reduced to its most *simpliste* expression. In his direct dialogue with the rank and file, Fidel Castro never dreamed of developing institutions which would allow the workers to express themselves, or give them a say in the management of their affairs. There is no hypocrisy on this subject in Havana. There, foreign visitors are never subjected to boring Soviet-type lectures on the superiority of the "socialist" electoral system compared with that of the "formal democracies." In Cuba no one is elected nor does anyone pretend otherwise. There is no Supreme Soviet, even for appearances' sake, and the Cuban Communist Party has not yet deemed it necessary to summon its first national congress. All decrees of state and party are provisional, handed down from above, on the order of Castro and his close collaborators.

For years the enemies of the Cuban revolution have accused Fidel of having concentrated all power in his own hands to satisfy his appetite for power. I believe, on the contrary, that the present situation results from the whole process of government gradually sliding into Castro's control and that he has been more the victim than the beneficiary of this development. For twelve years this indefatigable man has subjected himself to a punishing routine in order to tackle alone an incredible burden of problems, both great and small, and to arouse the productive enthusiasm of his countrymen. Unfortunately, I got the impression that his own output was disproportionately small in relation to his efforts because the task that he had set himself was beyond the capacity of one man.

During a long stay in Cuba in 1968 I tried to discuss with Castro himself the problem of the lack of an institutional framework in Cuba and its consequences. It was at a farewell dinner at an experimental farm some 50 miles south of the capital, and we had started off on the various contemporary problems. Once more Fidel explained to me that the target harvest of 10 million tons of sugar set for 1970 would be reached and that its benefits would be not only economic but political. I had no technical arguments with which to oppose him although I already sensed that the grandiose sugar plan, involving the drainage of all manpower into one sector, might well unbalance the whole economy. However, this is not what I would like to discuss first. When the occasion occurred, I raised the question of Cuba's institutional vacuum and the excessive *dirigisme* of a machine appointed from above. Fidel isn't one of those leaders who allow interviewers to express themselves at length the better to deal with them. He immediately grasped the import of my question and cried, polemically: *"Aha! no hay instituciones, no hay instituciones!* True, but listen . . ."

He rose and began a long defense of the past and present of the Cuban revolution: "Do you know how many real revolutionaries there were in Cuba at the moment of revolution? Well, there wasn't even one percent, note that —not even one percent! We ourselves, the vanguard who had organized the guerrillas, what did we know about real revolution? And what means had we to bring it about? Well, I'll tell you: the people wanted the revolution because they hoped it would bring them higher wages and enough for all, immediately. We ourselves didn't really know the potentialities of the country and we had no powerful political organization at our disposal. We had to learn everything and create everything practically from scratch. But we learned very quickly that this country was small, poor and underdeveloped, that it was in no position to fulfill the aspirations of our people quickly. In these circumstances were we to allow those who were better educated, more articulate and better organized than the others to profit from a proletarian democracy and grab the biggest slice of the national cake? Or was it better to explain to the people that, in order to have goods to distribute, we had to produce them collectively, and that we had to organize society in terms of the needs of the poorest and not those of the most eloquent? . . ."

He told me that he detested the fig leaves devised by the European socialist countries to hide their "democratic nakedness." He didn't believe in the Soviet kind of elections, with a governmental single list receiving 99.999 percent of the vote. His idea was rather to continue the dialogue direct with the rank and file, to inspire the workers to create wealth together and to develop a socialist awareness from the great economic battle so that they might make a transitional leap forward to a new society in which there would be no money, no selfishness, no unhealthy competition. After this "leap," the people themselves would know how to work out the institutions which suited them best. And to show that his idea was far from utopian, he quoted to me the figures of Cuba's enormous agricultural potential—its capacity to support not the present 8 million population but 60 million at least. His optimism was a trifle contagious. His arguments about the progress to be made and the prospect of imminent transformation made one think that perhaps he was right, that all would sort itself out soon to the satisfaction of all and to the greater good of the Cuban socialist democracy.

I would not be quite truthful if I said that he completely convinced me, since the figures drawn from Cuban official sources made it plain that the situation was not exactly bright; and some experience of life in Havana enabled me to assess the dreadful drawbacks of rationing and the poverty which has existed in Cuba since 1961. But it was read-

ing Castro's speech of 26 July last that brought back to me
the memory of our conversation at the experimental farm.
For Castro had not made one of those sorties in the Nasser
manner just to strengthen his support among the people.
He spoke of his failure with the same sincerity with which
he had told me two years ago of the imminence of his victory. He had really believed that this "decisive effort" which
he had demanded from his country would enable him not
only to gather a record sugar harvest but also to win back
confidence. But somewhere his plan went wrong and, having concentrated all responsibility in his own hands, he
blames no one but himself.

However, sometimes good comes out of ill. Checking
the balance sheet of this depressing harvest, Fidel came to
the conclusion that the present one-man system must no
longer continue. He spoke of the need to reinforce the
rank-and-file organizations and to build a national government machine with real power at both provincial and
local levels. He has sworn that this administrative framework must be separated from the party because the latter
must not be charged with day-to-day administration. In
short, even if he hasn't said very precisely how he will set
about carrying out his new program, he has for the first
time shown a real interest in democratic socialism for
Cuba. Some have even concluded that he is going to give
up the administrative tasks which until now have tied him
down in order to concentrate more on the building up of
the party and the creation of new organs of government.

"We are paying dearly for our ignorance," he cried to
the deeply moved crowd. However, I don't believe that it
was the lack of technical know-how in the sugar industry
that landed Fidel Castro where he is. If his program has
failed it is because he overestimated the role that he
should and could play in a post-revolutionary society. All
the evidence about Fidel reveals a certain aristocratic
mind, the sense of duty of a member of the elite who
believed that he knew that he must determine the aims and

lead the masses to a happier future. Now he seems to realize that the Cuban workers are not simply demanding that the plans of their well-intentioned leaders be carried out—that they want to work out their own plans and see these put into effect. If this is so, Fidel Castro's new awareness can still be salutary for the future of the Cuban revolution. Whatever the present difficulties—and they are enormous—it is too early to talk of his defeat.

37

RENÉ DUMONT

THE ECONOMIC GAMBLE

*Among European critics of Fidel Castro's economic
planning, few have been as outspoken as René Dumont, the French socialist and agricultural specialist,
who during the 1960s frequently served as an adviser
to the Cuban government. In Dumont's view, the
Cuban effort in 1970 to produce 10 million tons of
sugar was a rash gamble, doomed to failure almost
from the start.*

*In the following passage, Dumont argues that many
of the Cuban revolution's economic projects in the
late 1960s were too grandiose and produced only
modest results. He also criticizes what he, along with
other observers in France, regards as a growing trend
toward militarization in Cuba.*

*Like K. S. Karol, Dumont has strong sympathy
for the ideals of the Cuban revolution. They both are
part of an increasingly large group of French and
other European analysts who have been less favorably received in Cuba in recent years, largely because of the criticism they have for the revolution.
However, Dumont and Karol do disagree on some
points. For instance, Dumont favors closer ties with
the Soviet Union for Cuba, while Karol argues the
other way.*

Reprinted from René Dumont, *Cuba: Socialism and Development*,
pp. 221–228, 231–232, by permission of Grove Press, Inc., and
Georges Borchardt, Inc. Translated by Helen R. Lane. Copyright ©
1970 by Grove Press, Inc.

In the spring of 1969, the year of decisive effort, the whole country bustled about trying to reach the goal of ten million tons of sugar, which Castro keeps reminding his compatriots is a "matter of honor," that must be held to come hell or high water. Sugar was planted everywhere, in some places after hastily clearing land. The amount of effort put into irrigation has been enormous: 340,000 hectares of cane fields will be irrigated in 1970, as against 80,000 in 1965; but the question was whether the enormous amount of cane thus obtained, even if it did not reach the goal that had been fixed, could be harvested. In February and March 1969, Cuban newspapers emphasized how difficult it would be to finish harvesting the cane in the province of Camagüey even with the enormous amount of work contributed by volunteers from Havana. Despite the re-establishment of "sugar secrecy," which forbade the publication of the figures, the expected 1969 harvest was often estimated to be closer to 6 than to 7 million tons.

Cuba is very proud of its mechanical loaders and harvesting combines, but there are still a limited number of them, and they do not seem to work properly under any and all conditions. Plans are now being made to harvest cane only once every two years, though there is little mention of the large loss in sugar that such a technique would represent by comparison with the traditional harvest once a year: in the second year the growth of the cane is substantially reduced. In the face of probable difficulties in finding sufficient foreign outlets at a profitable price, there is much talk of sugar chemistry, of paper made out of bagasse, wax, medicine. But the stem of the cane must not be squeezed too tightly if a good quality of paper is to be made of it, and this leads to losses of sugar. And the cost of transporting the large amounts of necessary bagasse to one place, as must be done for a modern paper factory, may very well be prohibitive . . .

Fidel Castro often mentions cane as a very important source of cattle feed in the future. In 1960 I pointed out to him how profitable it would be to use the tops of the leafy stalks as forage. With irrigation these "white tips," as they are called in the Antilles, will stay greener and keep more of their protein. But when Fidel speaks of putting millions of tons of molasses to use, he forgets to supply economic statistics to support his proposal. As he wishes—rightly—to develop greater milk production, he must first see that his Frisian cows or those that are a cross between Zebu and Frisian cattle, have a great many proteins. Molasses has no protein at all and the added urea cannot supply more than a very small amount of the necessary nitrogen. It would be better to develop Pangola grass (abundantly treated with fertilizer rich in nitrogen and irrigated), bersim clover, or alfalfa if they prove successful, for these do not need to go through a factory. The sugar plan is going to absorb investments of more than a billion dollars, to the detriment of expenditures that more careful study would surely have proved to be more profitable. An economy cannot be run like a guerrilla operation, with reactions where sentiment plays an important role.

Castro has of course paid a great deal of serious attention to agricultural and economic problems. He has learned a great deal in this area, but he still has a great deal to learn, and always will have—a fact that in large measure he is unwilling to recognize. He therefore decides things a bit too quickly, and his entourage does not always have the chance—or the courage—to point out his weaknesses to him, though Che Guevara was not at all afraid to do so. It is said that he was soon put in his place by British researchers when he visited a station for research in animal genetics and tried to teach them their job. They spoke of going back home, and he backed off.

Fidel's visit to the Niña Bonita cattle center, shown on television and described in the newspaper *Granma* on January 31, 1969, was proof of his predilection for techniques that appear to be most up-to-date, without their ever having been proved profitable economically. This broadcast was doubtless a good popularization of the problems involved in cattle raising and animal genetics, but as it did not show the slightest interest in production costs, it caused the directors of *granjas* watching the program to continue to underestimate the importance of such a concern, which nonetheless is essential.

Ten million tons of sugar is not the Cubans' only ambitious goal. They are cautiously making a move in the direction of agricultural diversification again; this time there is less of a shortage of personnel and less of a lack of administrative personnel than in 1960–1961 when, as we have seen, such a move was a failure. Fidel still launches giant projects to dry up the lowlands along Cuba's coasts, without making economic studies of the problem a first priority. Raising the production of the rice, beans, and tubercules or *viandas* which constitute Cuba's basic foods to a satisfactory level is much more pressing. Certainly the poor are better fed than they were before the Revolution, when they were rationed by the lack of money that resulted from unemployment and low wages, but Cuba nonetheless could do better.

To announce, however, as Castro did, a cumulative improvement in agricultural production of fifteen per cent per year in geometric progression during the next twelve years does not seem like *responsible behavior*. One can certainly propose higher goals than those hoped for, in the hope of getting people to work harder. But these goals must not be exaggerated, for they risk causing bitter disappointments. A goal of 700,000 tons of citrus fruit has been announced for 1975 and 4,600,000 tons in 1980, on 300,000 hectares, the greater part of which are just now being planted. But the 1968 production is around 160,000 tons, as against 98,000 in 1962.

This would all be very well if the planting was done under the very best of conditions; but this does not always seem to be the case, due in particular to *excessive haste*. The volunteer workers (though not all of them) often demonstrate their good will, but they are not competent generally. And if such quantities of citrus fruits were grown, to whom would they be sold, and at what price? Canning the juice makes citrus fruit lose much of its value, and the competition from the United States' dumping it on the market may be very difficult to meet.

On January 24, 1969, *Granma* said: "Ninety-four hectares were planted in cacao in 1968, and the goal for 1969 is to plant 1,340 hectares of it in the Victoria de Girón area . . . In the near future Matanzas will have 8,000 hectares of cacao trees . . . Individual palm shelters had to be resorted to, for the plants had become too large to stay in seed-beds; the need to transplant them was urgent. But the Angola peas that were to furnish them the necessary shade were not planted in time."

Quotations of this sort, showing the difficulties of realizing inordinate goals, could be multiplied. The directors of the *granjas* continue to worry more about fulfilling plans in terms of the number of hectares they put under cultivation than about the quality of the work and the yields per hectare. Thus *Granma* on February 14, 1969, said: "The plan for the growing of pineapples at Ciego de Avila looks forward to having 40,000 hectares in full production in 1973. The present area under cultivation is around 1,200 hectares." I saw these pineapples being planted in 1960, and pointed out at the time that there was too much space between the plants and suggested that it was a good idea to plant them in double rows close together so as to have the high density indispensable for high yields. In photographs that have appeared recently (are they really recent?) I noticed that they were still planted in single rows too far apart.

The yields per hectare were 10 tons of fruit in 1968; it was then hoped that the yield would be 11 tons in 1969 and 20 to 23 tons in 1970, for "the use of better techniques of cultivation promises magnificent results." Let us wait until this doubling of the yield really comes about:

I can still see in my mind's eye the semi-abandonment that I saw in 1963; it was pitiful. Cuba continues to promise sensational results "in the near future," without worrying about the many times it has had to go back on promises made in the past.

In poorer soil, on the tertiary sands east of Abidjan, African growers belonging to SALCI are currently getting 65 tons of fruit per hectare. With competition so fierce on the market for canned pineapple, even yields of 23 tons will hardly be competitive.

The Cuban effort is nonetheless very important; the rate of investment is probably around 30 percent of the gross product, and would seem to be beginning to bear fruit. Production is increasing, but much more slowly than promised. Milk production could increase very rapidly if the cows were much better fed than the first piebald Canadian cows of 1963; this is less costly than acclimatizing them and makes this acclimation easier. But when Fidel announced: *"At the end of 1970 the production of milk is going to be four times higher than at the end of 1968"* he was imitating the Chinese leaders of February 1959. These latter announced that their compatriots would be much better fed if only a third of the land that had been plowed were put under cultivation. This is not the best way to get people to take you seriously.

The milk production of a large herd of cattle has not quadrupled in two years anywhere in the world; this fact ought to make for prudence. IR-8 rice will permit rapid progress provided that it is better cared for, and its successor IR-5 should have been tried sooner. But to announce that the yield has gone in one year from fourteen to eighteen quintals per hectare, thanks in particular to seeding by plane, as if such progress were a great success, is to neglect calling to mind the fact that this yield is not yet back to the 1959 level.

There is one crop—coffee—that has a political side to it, showing that Cuba has not given up "attacking" the

South American economy at its most sensitive point. Cuba is planting millions of coffee trees with all its might, *Cattura* in the plains, which represents a certain progress from the technical point of view. It is very probable, however, that its technical proficiency has not become the equal of that on avant-garde Brazilian farms, where the coffee trees are planted very close together, are kept in production only a few years, and yield up to twelve tons of dry coffee beans per hectare.

Cuba has announced a goal of 920,000 quintals of coffee for 1970, that is to say 92,000 tons (if the goal is measured in metric quintals; the statement does not specify). But in November 1967, the international coffee agreement reduced Cuba's export quota from 12,000 to 3,000 tons, for it had not taken advantage of its right to export during preceding years. No doubt Cuba hopes to find a market in the socialist countries. The U.S.S.R., however, has a political and economic interest in keeping up trade with South American coffee producers, for coffee is almost their only source of exchange currency. If consumption of coffee in the U.S.S.R. came close to that in the United States (the latter drinks *almost half* the commercial coffee in the world), there would be few difficulties. But the majority of Russians prefer tea and the amount of hard currency the Soviet Union has available is still limited.

Here again, Cuban economic policy cannot be carried out effectively if it relies on its own forces alone; this country must, willy nilly, take Soviet interests into account. From this point of view, it is easier to understand Castro's speech of August 23, 1968, on the Czechoslovakian affair. Apparently Castro took sides with the Soviet Union and approved its armed intervention in Prague. But he did so grudgingly, and continues to keep his distance, in particular through an attack on the Novotny regime, and hence of the after-effects of Stalinism, which was even harsher than his accusations against Dubcek.

.   .   .

The Army, a crucible where vast efforts are being made to forge the new man, totally dedicated to his Revolution, is called upon in straits such as these. The Army has always helped in agricultural production, especially in the sugar-cane harvest, but also in the construction of schools and houses for workers, roads and canals, etc., but its role in production was not made an official policy until 1968. Recruits must henceforth devote more of their time to work in the fields and thus receive a theoretical and practical agricultural education, which is certain to contribute to the modernization of rural areas and the popularization of the latest technical developments.

Newspapers often talk about the exploits of the Che Guevara Brigade, which has a total enrollment of about 5,000 men, grouped in 36 platoons, each of which has 20 bulldozers or heavy tractors at its disposal. It has cleared tens of thousands of hectares of land, often covered with marabou, that eventually will become sugar plantations, intensive pastures, and rice paddies. It also participates in the construction of dams and irrigation canals. It seems to be thoroughly aware of errors made previously, for it carefully maintains its equipment, takes care itself of the technical education of its cadres, and works according to a list of priorities established by those in charge of the development of agriculture and cattle-raising.

It proclaims its total disinterest in material stimulants, and it is interesting to note that the whole brigade—officers and men, engineers and cooks—all receive the same salary of 160 *pesos* per month, plus food, lodging, and medical care. Gutelman stresses, however, the fact that agricultural workers on State farms earn no more than 90 to 120 *pesos;* the soldier in this brigade thus has a big advantage, even though his officer has none at all.

Battalions of civilians have been formed on this military model, for instance, the women's brigades of tractor drivers of the green belt around Havana or the province of Oriente. Government offices, nationalized companies, and so forth, furnish workers for the harvesting of care and coffee beans and caring for the crops; they are organized on the same principles. Civil defense, finally, is working along the same lines to organize production in case of war. Cuba is already on a war footing. *"The militarization of organization,* where the interest of the group, the principle of authority, and above all the social consciousness of the group predominates, constitutes *the logical alternative to organization based on individual interest,"* Gutelman concludes.

This alternative in no way appears to us to be the only one imaginable. We always hesitate to entrust the building of socialism to military men, and many other solutions are possible. The drama of Cuba is the fact that despite certain hesitant appearances of liberalization, the discussion of basic political principles is almost impossible except from within the party, and even then this is possible for only a minority of the leaders. Building a society that has rejected the profit motive is a magnificent endeavor. But the militarization of an authoritarian brand of socialism is in no way the only solution possible. It does not allow the full flowering of man, which demands that he be trusted more, that he be given more initiative and more responsibilities, and this is not very military.

38

A. R. M. RITTER

A CANADIAN VIEW

Fidel Castro's effort to create "a new man" is frequently a major item in his speeches and it is a prime topic for the propaganda writers in Havana. Just how much success Castro has had in molding Cubans of various generations into the new man is a debatable point. A. R. M. Ritter, a professor of economics at Carleton University in Ottawa, Canada, takes something of a dim view of the whole issue after visits to Cuba in 1968 and 1969. Not all observers agree with the Canadian professor, but his view is fairly widespread.

According to Premier Fidel Castro, the high warrior-priest of the Cuban state religion, the major task of his revolution is "essentially the task of forming the New man."

The Cuban new man is not unlike the Soviet new man in Russia during the Nineteen Thirties. . . .

It is impossible to estimate how successful the Cuban regime has been so far in creating the new man. I can only judge on the basis of Cuban friends I have made and persons I have met more or less by chance.

Certainly one meets students who are fine products of the educational system. I have also met older people, brought up before 1959, who are deeply committed to the

Reprinted from A. R. M. Ritter, "Castro's New Man Falling Short of the Ideal," *The Globe and Mail* (September 12, 1969), p. 7, by permission of the publisher.

ideals of the regime and who try to live up to the model of the new man.

But I have met fine people everywhere and with the strangest ideologies, or none at all, who try to live good and productive lives. I have also met Cubans, now disenchanted with the regime, who still try to live up to basic human ideals of altruism and brotherhood.

At the same time, in the dealings I have had with ministries or bureaucrats in Havana, I have experienced a great gap between what is promised and what is delivered. Indeed, to get officials to do anything, their promise is usually not enough and you must get on their backs if you expect results. But then, bureaucrats may be quite similar everywhere.

The absence of student unrest and the much commented-upon commitment of youth to the revolution and Castro cannot be taken as evidence of success in recreating human nature. Those who are not considered integrated into the system are not permitted to enter the universities. Thus, those who want an education must act as if they were integrated. But the official ideology does have great credibility and the system does seem virtuous in view of the experience under Batista, the Bay of Pigs, the embargo, Vietnam and the Dominican invasion. The system probably elicits support from a majority of students.

The prospects for achieving a close approximation of the new man, however, are not good. First of all, it is not possible to have a system permanently at the revolutionary fervor pitch of a guerrilla-band. And a system in which people work for the heroism and joy of working and receive income according to their needs must wait until material abundance prevails or until Cuba becomes a nation of ascetics. Material abundance is generations away by the standards of the advanced countries in 1969.

The old bourgeois consumption habits will not die off automatically or be purged given the closeness of the

United States, the memories of near-affluence—though only for the few—before 1959, the presence of relatively rich tourists and foreign technicians, and the emergence of a new ruling caste, possessing many of the old bourgeois consumption privileges.

In the second place, the more advanced Communist countries have not yet been able to recreate man successfully. Interestingly, after 50 years of trying to create a new Soviet man, for example, the Russians in Cuba are reputedly the major suppliers on the black market.

In the third and most important place, the new caste which is emerging threatens merely to transform the channels through which the old bourgeois egoism, selfishness and opportunism can be expressed, and to co-opt the new men into the new caste and the system for materialistic gains.

In view of the experiences of the East European countries and Russia, perhaps it is not surprising that the new Cuban elite is appropriating for itself various economic privileges denied to the average Cuban. The emerging inequities, however, are still small in comparison with those under President Batista.

The economic privileges of the new caste make a sham of the equalitarianism of the official ideology. Castro preaches hard work, sacrifice for the future, altruism and non-bourgeois consumption attitudes. But at the same time the elite makes less material sacrifice and lives not unlike the old bourgeoisie.

Castro proclaims that the 56,000 small businessmen had to be eliminated, for they were privileged exploiters. But so far nothing has been said of the privileges of the new caste.

Those outside the elite who are aware of these privileges are understandably somewhat demoralized and cynical.

Though, theoretically, exploitation of the workers when the proletariat is dictating is supposed to be impossible, the exploitive nature of the distribution of economic privileges is not lost to many Cubans.

The success of this year of decisive endeavor and the future path of Cuban political economy depends upon whether the mobilized masses work efficiently and vigorously. Can Castro's cajoling and new promises counteract creeping cynicism?

The members of the new caste itself are probably unaware that there may by something irregular and hypocritical in their privileged status. And the chances are that the new caste will continue to grow into a new socialist middle and upper class, co-opting the capable and the ambitious. But Castro's actions have proven to be most unpredictable.

39

LEE LOCKWOOD

A NEW PHASE

American photojournalist Lee Lockwood accepts some of the criticisms of the Cuban revolution made by such commentators as K. S. Karol and René Dumont. But he is much more sanguine than they about the future of the revolution as the following excerpt from his book-length photographic and journalistic interview with Fidel Castro illustrates. Lockwood's view suggests something of Castro's immense staying power and serves as a reminder that the Cuban leader cannot be underestimated.

Since the death of Guevara, there has been in Cuba a decided shift in the focus of national attention away from international issues and toward more domestic concerns—as expressed by Castro's determination to make Cuba economically self-sufficient by 1970 through agriculture. The burden of possibility for this achievement lies squarely on the shoulders of the Cuban people; the government, in calling on its citizens for ever more hard work and sacrifice, is invoking the spirit of Che Guevara. The "revolutionary offensive" announced by Castro early this year is at once a memorial to Che and a rededication of the Cuban people to the sacrificial and rigor-enduring spirit of the Sierra Maestra (in principle, at least, not unlike the cultural rev-

Reprinted from Lee Lockwood, *Castro's Cuba, Cuba's Fidel,* pp. 356–358, by permission of the author and The Macmillan Company. Copyright © 1967 by Lee Lockwood.

olution in China). Individuals are asked to purge them
selves of "egoistic" concerns about their material welfare
and join in the great agricultural battle for economic sur
vival. In line with the revolutionary offensive, bars and
night clubs have been closed down, and all remaining small
businesses have been nationalized, thus bringing to near
completion the socialization of the Cuban economy.

On the whole, although as Castro himself noted there
has been a tangible increase in "inquietude and uncer
tainty" within the country, Cubans of all classes have
responded to the Spartan demands with patience and dedi
cation. This seems remarkable, since Cubans have experi
enced little more than sacrifice and hardship for ten years
However as the "older generation," those who made the
Revolution, are beginning to show signs of wear, it is the
youth who are carrying that revolution forward. Their
energy is kinetic, and their enthusiasm for the task is noth
ing short of exalted.

As 1968, "the year of the heroic guerrilla," draws to a
close and the Revolution prepares to celebrate its first dec
ade of power, what are its perspectives for the future
Castro's internal support, though somewhat diminished
during the last three years (if one can measure such things
without conducting polls or holding elections) is still strong
Although shortages continue and the sugar crop is well
below expectations, Cuba's long-run economic prospect
appear healthy as agriculture becomes more diversified and
better organized.

Politically, however, Cuba today is more isolated than
at any other time since 1959. With the exception of Can
ada and Mexico, she is treated as an untouchable by all the
nations of her own hemisphere. (Whatever desires the
former may have for increased ties with Cuba are easily
held in check by the U.S.) The American economic block
ade continues, with great (though far from total) effective
ness. Cuba still relies on the Soviet Union, ten thousand
miles away, for economic survival and military protection

While it is not likely that the U.S.S.R. would willingly withdraw her support from the only Socialist nation in the Western Hemisphere, if Castro, as a matter of principle, persists in his virulent ideological attacks on Moscow, he may eventually succeed in forcing a rupture that Russia's leaders do not desire.

Those of Castro's enemies who long have characterized him as a base opportunist who "turned" Communist and took Cuba into the Socialist camp for reasons of expediency rather than conviction must now be sorely puzzled by the fact that Fidel has chosen precisely that moment in history when he is irreconcilably alienated from the United States and hardly on speaking terms with China, to embark Cuba upon an ideological collision course with the Soviet Union. Obviously, it would be much more in Castro's material interests to cooperate with the Soviets than to attack them. Moreover, the Soviets would be willing to accept ideological disagreement as long as it were kept on the level of intra-party conversation and debate; what they cannot accept is that Castro has determinedly transformed what ought (in their eyes) to be a private discussion into a public polemic.

In fact, one of the most exciting attributes of the Cuban Revolution is the fact that the very combination of uncompromising idealism and unfaltering courage which characterized Castro's first attack on the Moncada Barracks in 1953, which sustained his guerrilla war in the mountains, and which brought him to victory in 1959 are still dominant today, after ten years in power. Although his programs have undergone significant transformations, his ideals, the ideals of his Revolution, have not. Despite formidable temptations and pressures from both within the society and from abroad, the Cuban Revolution has consistently, throughout a decade of adversity, refused to sacrifice principle to expediency. Today, Cuba, with all her imperfections, represents the only attempt in the entire world to test the proposition that it is possible to construct a society and to conduct foreign relations by placing ethical values first and practical considerations—up to and including survival—second. Undoubtedly this is why Cuba's Revolution continues to appeal to so many outsiders of all classes, cultures and ideologies, especially to young people in search of values everywhere.

In spite of the fact that the Cuban example has not been successfully emulated in the ten years since Castro took power, in spite of the chilling setback to Che Guevara's effort in Bolivia, Castro and his followers remain dedicated to the spread of the revolutionary movement by means of armed struggle throughout the colonialized world. To achieve this end they must contend not only with the implacable resistance of American imperialism but also with the intransigent opposition of the Soviet Union and of most of the Communist parties of the third world, over whom Russia holds sway. Today, Fidel Castro stands like an angry prophet nearly alone in a venal world that is weary of violence and would rather live in compromise than die for an ideal. Ten years after coming down from the mountains, Fidel seeks to make Cuba the Sierra Maestra of the globe and the Cuban Revolution its guerrilla *foco:* "the small motor which gets the big motor started." Once again, Castro is leading a guerrilla war against impossible odds, isolated, but with conviction firm, striving to strike the spark that will ignite the world into another, grander, ultimate revolution. The process does not end, it merely enters a new phase.

CHRONOLOGY

1959:

Jan. 1 Batista flees, Castro assumes control

Jan. 3 Castro named commander in chief of army

Jan. 7 U. S. recognizes Castro government

Jan. 8 Castro arrives in Havana after triumphal march from East

Apr. 15 Castro visits Washington, meets Vice President Nixon

May 17 Agrarian reform law promulgated

July 17 Urrutia out as president, Dorticós named

Oct. 17 Raúl Castro named minister of armed forces

1960:

Jan. 11 U. S. protests "illegal" seizure of American property

Jan. 19 Castro accuses U. S. of intervention

Jan. 20 U. S. withdraws Ambassador Philip Bonsal

Feb. 13 Soviet Union and Cuba sign economic pact

Mar. 5   75 killed as French munitions ship blows up in Havana harbor; U. S. blamed

July 6   U. S. cuts sugar quota to 760,000 tons

July 23 China and Cuba sign economic pact

Aug. 28 Cuba walks out of Organization of American States

Oct. 20 U. S. embargos exports to Cuba

Dec. 2   U. S. authorizes first funds ($1 million) for Cuban refugees

1961:

Jan. 3   U. S. severs diplomatic relations with Cuba

Apr. 17 Bay of Pigs invasion, crushed Apr. 20

May 1   Castro declares Cuba a "socialist nation"

July 24 Eastern Airlines plane skyjacked, first such incident

Sept. 10 Cuba deports 136 Roman Catholic priests

Dec. 2   Castro delivers his "I am a Marxist" speech

1962:

Jan. 3   U. S. calls Cuba threat to hemisphere

Jan. 10 Cuba signs trade pact with Soviet Union, calling for $700 million in trade in 1962

Jan. 31 Organization of American States excludes Castro government

Oct. 22 President Kennedy discloses crisis over Soviet missiles in Cuba

Nov. 2 Missiles "dismantled," returned to Soviet Union

1963:

Mar. 21 Castro chides Soviet Premier Khrushchev over his actions in missile crisis

Mar. 29 U. S. bars exile raids on Cuba

Apr. 27 Castro visits Soviet Union

June 5 Organization of American States says Cuba being "converted into a Soviet military camp"

Dec. 3 Organization of American States votes to look into Venezuelan charges that Cuba is shipping arms to hemisphere

1964:

Jan. 7 British Leyland Motor Company sells Cuba 450 buses, challenging U. S. blockade of island

Feb. 18 U. S. curtails military aid to Britain and France for trading with Cuba

Mar. 6 Cuba cuts off water to U. S. Guantánamo naval base

Apr. 19 Castro charges U. S. using U-2 flights to conduct aerial surveillance; U. S. admits flights April 20, calling them "necessary"

June 29 Juana Castro, Castro's sister, defects, charging him with betraying Cuba to "Russian imperialism"

1965:

June 7   Castro hails 1965 sugar harvest which tops 6
           million tons

Sept. 25   Castro announces Cubans can leave island,
           first time since missile crisis

Oct. 7–   Thousands of Cubans leave island in small
     18   boats

Nov. 6   Cuba and U. S. agree to start airlift of exiles
           starting Dec. 1

1966:

Feb. 6   Castro attacks China for reneging on rice ex-
           port deal

1967:

July 31   Cuba opens Organization of Latin American
           Solidarity meeting, calling for "violent revolu-
           tion" throughout Latin America

Oct. 8   Castro friend and longtime associate Ernesto
           Che Guevara killed in Bolivia trying to export
           "violent revolution"

Nov. 6   Cuba snubs Soviet Union, orders ambassador
           to skip Kremlin ceremony honoring 50th an-
           niversary of Soviet revolution

1968:

Jan. 2   Cuba rations gas in new austerity program

Feb. 3   Aníbal Escalante, pro-Soviet Cuban official,

sentenced to 15 years for giving "false information to Russian officials"

1969:

Jan. 1   Cuba says more than 500,000 have gone into exile since Castro came to power

July 5   U. S. says aerial skyjacking reaches "crescendo"; urges Cuba help in stopping incidents

Oct. 10   Cuba rejects U. S. plan to bring skyjacking before United Nations

1970:

June 15   Cuba ends sugar harvest after producing 8.5 million tons, a record, but 1.5 million tons short of goal

July 26   Castro tells Cuban people troubles plague economy and warns hard times ahead

Nov. 12   New Chilean government of Salvador Allende recognizes Cuba, breaking Organization of American States ban on relations

1971:

Aug. 6   Cuba suspends refugee airlift, then permits resumption August 16, after permitting 240,000 Cubans to leave for U. S.

Nov. 5   19 Cuban sugar technicians, who flew to New Orleans unannounced and without visas, return to Havana

Nov. 8   Castro arrives in Chile for four-week visit

1972:

June 21   Cuba announces 1972 sugar production at 4 million tons, a new low

June 22   Peru launches effort in Organization of American States to get sanctions lifted from Castro government; effort fails

Nov. 11   Castro announces reorganization of government, installing nine-member supercabinet dealing mainly with economic matters

1973:

Feb. 15   Cuba and U. S. sign five-year "memorandum of understanding" to curb hijacking of aircraft and ships between two nations

May 25   Argentina recognizes Castro government

Sept. 12 Chile breaks relations with Cuba

Sept. 21 Castro in Algiers defends Soviet Union at nonaligned nations meeting; incurs sharp rebukes from some fellow speakers

1974:

Jan. 12   Cuban ambassador in Mexico City suggests few obstacles to Cuba–U. S. rapprochement remain

Apr. 19   U. S. facing *fait accompli,* grants permission to U. S. automakers to allow their Argentine subsidiaries to sell cars and trucks to Cuba

June 30   Cuba holds elections for municipal assemblies in Matanzas province—first balloting in 15 years

SUGGESTIONS FOR

ADDITIONAL READING

The materials selected for this volume represent a wide variety of sources. Castro's revolution is without doubt one of the best documented events in modern times. The bibliography grows rapidly and now, fifteen years after Castro came to power, there is a third generation of literature on the revolution being published in books and magazines.

The first generation sought to view the revolution as the unique phenomenon that it is. But these accounts were, in many respects, exploratory; some were clearly personal in their approach by newsmen and others who witnessed the revolution as it began to take shape. A second generation was deeply involved with the nitty-gritty of Castro's decision to embrace Communism and of the events of the early 1960s as Cuba moved away from its traditional ties with the Western Hemisphere bloc and into the Soviet bloc. Finally, the third generation is involved in viewing Cuba in a somewhat sophisticated fashion, looking at developments on the island in a more dispassionate way than was evident in many of the writings of the first two periods. This is not to suggest that earlier accounts generally lacked such wisdom; many displayed it. But time has a way of permitting better perspective, and this is what is clearly at work in the writing of today.

In any effort to get at the most significant writing about the revolution, there is no better place to start than with the words of Fidel Castro himself. The Cuban leader's speeches, averaging more than two hours apiece and coming with frequency, are unquestionably the most important political documents of the revolution. They regularly appear in the weekly English language edition of *Granma,* the official organ of the Cuban

Communist Party and Havana's one morning newspaper. They are also reprinted in a variety of publications issued in English by the Cuban government for propaganda distribution in the United States. Martin Kenner and James Petras edited a collection of his speeches titled *Fidel Castro Speaks* (New York: Grove, 1970). It has usefulness, but is limited to only sixteen speeches and omits such important Castro talks as the one of August 1968, supporting the Soviet invasion of Czechoslovakia. Lee Lockwood's *Castro's Cuba, Cuba's Fidel* (New York: Macmillan, 1967), mentioned in the text, is a compilation and distillation of several interviews he had with Castro in 1965, interviews which touch on virtually every important subject in Cuba. A number of important Castro speeches are reprinted in abridged form in W. Raymond Duncan and James Nelson Goodsell, eds., *The Quest for Change in Latin America: Sources for a Twentieth Century Analysis* (New York: Oxford, 1970).

One of the problems faced by all compilers of Castro's speeches and writings is the tremendous bulk of useful material for inclusion. Rolando Bonachea and Nelson P. Valdes have partially solved this by projecting a three-volume compilation of important Castro speeches and written material. The first volume, *Revolutionary Struggle: The Selected Works of Fidel Castro* (Cambridge, Mass.: M.I.T. Press, 1971), recognizes, however, that a process of winnowing out is necessary. Moreover, since Castro goes on talking and making news in the process, all these compilations, even the more detailed ones, are dated almost before they are issued.

There are several biographies of Castro that deserve mention. Herbert L. Matthews, *Fidel Castro* (New York: Simon & Schuster, 1969) and Enrique Meneses, *Fidel Castro* (London: Faber and Faber, 1968) are probably the best, but both include a good deal of personal experience in Cuba as newspapermen. Mr. Matthews, whose career with the *New York Times* included a noted trip into the Sierra Maestra to interview Castro, attempts to justify that controversial journalistic visit when it hardly needs justifying. Compare these more recent biographies with an earlier one, rushed into print when Castro came to power, by Jules Dubois. Titled also *Fidel Castro* (Indianapolis: Bobbs-Merrill, 1959), its author is the late Chicago *Tribune* correspondent in Latin America. Despite the values of these books, Fidel Castro still waits a true biographer.

Hugh Thomas' massive study of Cuba's history, *Cuba: The Pursuit of Freedom* (New York: Harper & Row, 1971), is probably the single most important book in English on the subject. Fully half of it deals with the period before Castro going back to the mid-1700s and is useful in setting the tone for the Castro revolution. His explanation of the revolution deserves careful reading.

So does Jaime Suchlicki's *Cuba: From Columbus to Castro* (New York: Scribner's, 1974), a well-researched, but concise history that goes beyond mere description and looks at significant trends in Cuban history during the past 500 years, providing trenchant analyses of these trends.

Also useful is R. Hart Phillips' *Cuba: Island of Paradox* (McDowell, Obolensky, 1959), although now a trifle dated. Mrs. Phillips was the *New York Times* correspondent in Havana in the years before Castro came to power. Much of what she writes has an intimate ring to it. While Mrs. Phillips was generally unimpressed with Castro, her *New York Times* colleague, Herbert L. Matthews, mentioned previously, was favorably inclined to the Cuban leader as his *The Cuban Story* (New York: Braziller, 1961) shows.

Two interesting accounts of the early years of Castro's rule are *My Fourteen Months with Castro* by Rufo López-Fresquet (New York: World, 1966) and *Cuba: Castroism and Communism, 1959–1966* by Andrés Suárez (Cambridge, Mass.: M.I.T. Press, 1967). López-Fresquet was Castro's first minister of the treasury, while Suárez was assistant minister. They both were early Castro supporters, but fell out with him over the movement toward Marxism.

The early Castro years saw the appearance of several books and many articles by Theodore Draper. Two of the most important books are *Castro's Revolution: Myths and Realities* (New York: Praeger, 1962) and *Castroism: Theory and Practice* (New York: Praeger, 1965). Some of Draper's views are now considered obsolete, but in the early 1960s his views on the direction of Castro's revolution were widely accepted. Draper, for example, argued that Castroism was in part a myth and that this might well prove its Achilles' heel.

As time went on, other views of the revolution began to appear. Some of these are collected in Rolando E. Bonachea and Nelson P. Valdes' useful *Cuba in Revolution* (Garden City, N.Y.: Doubleday, 1972), a collection of articles by such scholars as Richard Fagen (on Castro's charismatic leadership), Carmelo Mesa-Lago (on the economic significance of unpaid labor, which also appears in this volume), and Michel Gutelman (on socialism in agriculture).

Mesa-Lago's own *Revolutionary Change in Cuba* (Pittsburgh: University of Pittsburgh Press, 1971) is a similar collection. It includes a very useful analogy between Stalinist and Fidelista political models by Irving Louis Horowitz. There is also a section on society with articles on education, church-state relations, and the literary scene. This title includes a variety of Mesa-Lago's own writings on Cuban economics under Castro.

Yet another collection is Jaime Suchlicki's *Cuba, Castro and Revolution* (Coral Gables, Fla.: University of Miami Press, 1972), containing a group of essays on various internal and external aspects of the revolution by ten specialists. One of the most interesting is that of W. Raymond Duncan on Cuban nationalism and citizenship under Castro.

Also on the issue of nationalism, attention should be directed to Ramón Eduardo Ruiz's *Cuba: The Making of a Revolution* (Amherst: University of Massachusetts Press, 1968), an interesting, but controversial look at anti-Americanism and its impact on Cuban leaders of the revolution.

Edward Boorstein's *The Economic Transformation of Cuba* (New York: Monthly Review Press, 1968) is a good starting point for a study of the Cuban economy during the Castro years. A United States Marxist, Boorstein worked for Castro during the early 1960s. He is obviously in favor of the changes brought about by Castro, but he is not uncritical of the Cuban performance during the early years of the revolution.

On the issue of socialism, as practiced by Castro, there is a growing shelf of literature. Leo Huberman and Paul M. Sweezy in *Socialism in Cuba* (New York: Monthly Review Press, 1969) were among the first to look at the issue. Bertram Silverman in 1971 edited a whole volume of articles on the controversy of moral versus material incentives (*Man and Socialism in Cuba* published by Atheneum). Many of the selections were first published in European journals and books in the early 1960s, but they appear here for the first time in English. There are included a number of articles by Ernesto Che Guevara.

Guevara's views on a range of issues are contained in *Venceramos! The Speeches and Writings of Che Guevara*, edited by John Gerassi (New York: Macmillan, 1968). The literature on Guevara is extensive. It becomes more so each year. Recent editions of his Bolivian diaries contain ample bibliographies.

Two European authors, René Dumont and K. S. Karol, stirred a good deal of controversy in the early 1970s with their articles and books that were sharply critical of Castro and his revolution. Dumont's *Is Cuba Socialist?* (New York: Viking, 1974) and Karol's *Guerrillas in Power* (New York: Hill & Wang, 1970) were first issued in French following extensive visits to Cuba by the two authors. Dumont, a distinguished economist and sympathizer with Castro's Cuba, charged that mismanagement and militarization were causing serious problems for the island, while Karol, also a sympathizer with a pro-Chinese bias, argued that Castro's dependence upon the Soviet Union was responsible for much of the island's economic breakdown.

United States–Cuban relations have generated more heat than light over the years. But there are some useful articles and books now in print. *Cuba and the United States,* edited by John Plank (Washington, D.C.: Brookings Institution, 1967), although dated, remains a significant contribution to the subject. Articles included deal with pre-Castro times as well as the contemporary period and many look toward the future.

More recently, Edward Gonzalez prepared a short, but perceptive analysis of U. S.–Cuban relations, including some specific policy suggestions for an eventual rapproachement between the two nations. Titled *Partners in Deadlock: The United States and Castro, 1959–1972* (Southern California Arms Control and Foreign Policy Seminar, 1972), it also examines the origins of Cuban nationalism.

Robert D. Crassweller's *Cuba and the U.S.: The Tangled Relationship* (Foreign Policy Association, 1971) is a similar analysis, which particularly emphasizes Castro's impact on the nature and course of the revolution and on relations with the U. S.

No subject in relations between Washington and Havana has stirred as much interest as the Bay of Pigs invasion. Haynes Johnson's *The Bay of Pigs* (New York: Norton, 1964) is a good starting point. Karl S. Meyer and Tad Szulc's *The Cuban Invasion* (New York: Praeger, 1962), a selection from which is included in this book, asks a number of moral questions about the incident. Some of these questions are also treated in

Robert F. Kennedy's *Thirteen Days* (New York: Norton, 1969), which deals with the subsequent missile crisis. Ronald Steel in an article in the *New York Review of Books* (October 10, 1972) reviewed five other titles on the missile crisis and his piece is a good beginning for a look at that crisis.

Books by one-time United States ambassadors to Cuba are numerous. Earl E. T. Smith, who was in Cuba just before Castro came to power, wrote of his experiences and his dislike of Castro in *The Fourth Floor: An Account of the Castro Communist Revolution* (New York: Random House, 1962). He is extremely critical of State Department policy makers— lodged on the department's fourth floor, hence his title—who did not in his opinion do all they could to prevent Castro's rise. A more dispassionate look is contained in *Cuba, Castro and the United States,* by Philip W. Bonsal (Pittsburgh: University of Pittsburgh Press, 1971). Bonsal was ambassador to Cuba for twenty months after Castro came to power. He is obviously not enamored with the revolution, but he has a fairly high opinion of some of Castro's efforts. Moreover, he is not entirely complimentary to the United States and its role in Cuba in the early days of the revolution.

One of the most fascinating aspects of the revolution has been the mass migration of Cubans to the United States, Spain, Mexico, Venezuela, and elsewhere in the years since 1959. This story is still to be told adequately. But several preliminary discussions of the issue are available. Of these, the best is Richard R. Fagen, Richard A. Brody, and Thomas J. Cleary, *Cubans in Exile* (Stanford, Calif.: Stanford University Press, 1968). Its subtitle, *Disaffection and the Revolution,* suggests the theme.

This bibliography merely suggests some of the books that are available. No mention is made of the steady stream of articles, theses, and other writings. Yet many of these are rich in detail, analysis, and speculation. The University of Pittsburgh's Center for Latin American Studies publishes twice yearly a *Cuban Studies Newsletter* listing many of these articles. This very useful publication in recent issues has carried an annotated bibliography of Castro's major works from January 1959 through December 1970 and a bibliography of Cuban belleslettres under the revolution.

A variety of university libraries are gathering growing collections of Cuban source material. The University of Miami's

Center for Research on Caribbean Studies and Yale University's Antilles Program are but two of these. A Center for Cuban Studies has been organized in New York City and while its work is hampered by lack of funds, it does have valuable material in its collections.

A good deal of useful current information is published in *The New York Times, The Christian Science Monitor, The Washington Post,* and *The Miami Herald.* But for the most part, the United States press does not provide a fruitful source of information; newspapers in other lands—France, Spain, England —generally do much better, although the reporting is often prorevolution and somewhat biased.

United Nations publications are another source, but scholars have generally found Cuban statistics in these publications unreliable and dated. This is one of the problems in doing research on Cuba. The state of official Cuban economic records is somewhat less than desirable, a situation that Castro himself has frequently noted.

Nevertheless, the growing body of literature on the Cuban revolution is impressive. The preceding list in this brief bibliographic essay represents only a very limited sampling of what is available in English, to say nothing of what is in print in other languages. Moreover, judging by the steady flow of material, this list would need to be updated within months of publication to keep it current. Still, many of the preceding titles will stand the test of time.

A Note on the Type

The text of this book was set on the Linotype in a face called TIMES ROMAN, designed by Stanley Morison for The Times (London), and first introduced by that newspaper in 1932.

Among typographers and designers of the twentieth century, Stanley Morison has been a strong forming influence, as typographical advisor to the English Monotype Corporation, as a director of two distinguished English publishing houses, and as a writer of sensibility, erudition, and keen practical sense.

Composed, printed,
and bound by
The Colonial Press Inc.,
Clinton, Mass.

BORZOI BOOKS ON LATIN AMERICA

Under the General Editorship of John Womack,
Harvard University

Also available in a hardbound edition

THE EXPULSION OF THE JESUITS FROM
LATIN AMERICA
Edited by Magnus Mörner

A DOCUMENTARY HISTORY OF BRAZIL*
Edited by E. Bradford Burns

BACKGROUND TO REVOLUTION *
THE DEVELOPMENT OF MODERN CUBA
Edited by Robert Freeman Smith

IS THE MEXICAN REVOLUTION DEAD? *
Edited by Stanley R. Ross

FOREIGN INVESTMENT IN LATIN AMERICA*
Edited by Marvin Bernstein

WHY PERON CAME TO POWER *
Edited by Joseph R. Barager

MARXISM IN LATIN AMERICA*
Edited by Luis E. Aguilar

A CENTURY OF BRAZILIAN HISTORY SINCE 1865 *
Edited by Richard Graham

REVOLUTION IN MEXICO:
YEARS OF UPHEAVAL, 1910–1940 *
Edited by James W. Wilkie *and* Albert L. Michaels

THE LIBERATOR, SIMÓN BOLÍVAR *
MAN AND IMAGE
Edited by David Bushnell

THE INDIAN BACKGROUND
OF LATIN AMERICAN HISTORY *
THE MAYA, AZTEC, INCA, AND THEIR PREDECESSORS
Edited by Robert Wauchope

INTERVENTION IN LATIN AMERICA*
Edited by C. Neale Ronning

FROM RECONQUEST TO EMPIRE *
THE IBERIAN BACKGROUND TO LATIN AMERICAN HISTORY
Edited by H. B. Johnson, Jr.

NATIONALISM IN LATIN AMERICA*
Edited by Samuel L. Baily

Also available in a hardbound edition

THE ROMAN CATHOLIC CHURCH
IN COLONIAL LATIN AMERICA
Edited by Richard E. Greenleaf

THE BLACK LEGEND *
ANTI-SPANISH ATTITUDES IN THE OLD WORLD AND THE NEW
Edited by Charles Gibson

BARTOLOMÉ DE LAS CASAS *
A SELECTION OF HIS WRITINGS
Translated and edited by George Sanderlin

POLITICAL ESSAY ON THE KINGDOM
OF NEW SPAIN (ABRIDGED) *
By Alexander von Humboldt
(*With an Introduction by Mary Maples Dunn*)

COLONIAL TRAVELERS IN LATIN AMERICA
Edited by Irving A. Leonard

THE ROMAN CATHOLIC CHURCH
IN MODERN LATIN AMERICA
Edited by Karl M. Schmitt

Also available in a hardbound edition